Desktop Management with Novell ZENworks

Desktop Management with Novell ZENworks

Gerald Foster

O'REILLY®

Beijing · Cambridge · Farnham · Köln · Paris · Sebastopol · Taipei · Tokyo

Desktop Management with Novell ZENworks
by Gerald Foster

Published by O'Reilly & Associates, Inc., 101 Morris Street, Sebastopol, CA 95472.

Editor: Robert Denn

Production Editor: Maureen Dempsey

Cover Designer: Hanna Dyer

Printing History:

April 2000: First Edition.

Library of Congress CIP data can be found at *http://www.oreilly.com/catalog/zenworks/*.

ISBN: 1-56592-711-7
[M]

Table of Contents

Preface ..... *ix*

1. ***Introduction*** *1*
   - The Network Operating System 2
   - The Desktop Operating System 4
   - Operating System Configuration and Rollout 4
   - ZENworks Components 7
   - A Final Word 9

2. ***The ZENworks Installation*** *10*
   - The ZENworks Product 10
   - NDS Considerations 13
   - Installation 21
   - Installing Software Metering 31
   - The NWADMIN Program 31
   - A Final Word 33

3. ***The NetWare Clients and Related Components*** *35*
   - Client Configuration 35
   - The Windows NT/2000 Client 53
   - The Windows 95/98 Client 60
   - The Windows 3.x Client 67
   - The Workstation Manager 68
   - The Help Requester 72
   - A Final Word 73

4. *ZENworks Policy Packages* 74
NDS Considerations 75
Creating Policy Packages 76
Adding Actions 78
The Policy Scheduler 79
Windows NT Dynamic Local User 80
The Helpdesk Policy 82
The Desktop Preferences Policy 83
The NT User Printer Policy 85
About User and Computer System Policies 85
Windows 95/98 and NT User System Policy Packages 88
Windows NT and 95/98 Computer System Policies 103
Windows 3.x Computer System Policy 116
Client Configuration Policy 116
Computer Printer Policy 117
RAS Configuration Policy 118
Remote Management Policies 119
Restrict Login Policy 121
Search Policy 121
Extensible Policies 123
Workstation Import Policy 124
Workstation Inventory Policy 125
A Final Word 128

5. *Workstation Objects and Inventory* 129
NDS Considerations 129
Workstation Objects 131
The Inventory Server and Database Server 139
Workstation Inventory 141
Software Inventory 145
Reporting 148
A Final Word 157

6. *The Novell Application Launcher* 159
NAL Overview 160
How the Application Launcher Works 160
NDS Considerations 162
The Application Install Process 163
The NAL User Interface 163

The snAppShot Tool *166*
Application Objects *172*
Making Applications Work *219*
Launcher Configuration *221*
Application Folders *226*
A Final Word *227*

7. *Application Metering* *229*
Preparing the Server *230*
Creating a Metered Certificate *231*
Linking the Certificate with an Application *236*
A Final Word *237*

8. *Remote Management* *238*
Remote Management Prerequisites *238*
How Remote Management Works *239*
Remote Ping *241*
Remote Control *242*
Remote View *242*
Remote File Transfer *243*
Remote Execute *244*
Remote Chat *244*
Remote Diagnostics *245*
A Final Word *247*

A. *The Future of ZENworks* *249*

B. *Integrating Other Authentication Systems* *251*

C. *Other Sources of Information* *253*

Index *257*

Preface

Why Should You Use ZENworks?

In every IT department there is some component that isn't managed as well as it could be. In some organizations this problem is more prevalent than in others. This unmanaged component might not be a great and vital part of what you do; but if it does involve a part of your workstation service, you should be concerned. Workstations consume a very large amount of the work performed by IT departments and represent an area that should be thoroughly thought out and controlled in a way that is acceptable to the users.

I spent some years working with Windows NT workstations and servers, and when I started looking at NetWare and Windows NT workstations, ZENworks was the clear way forward. After spending some time with the product, I was struck by its power and sophistication. I had not seen anything resembling it in a career stretching back almost 20 years. I was hooked. As with all sophisticated products, ZENworks is complicated. Novell has done a good job in reducing the complications, but you have to understand exactly what it is doing and why, or you cannot make full use of this worthwhile product.

Who This Book Is For

IT departments have to evaluate and make decisions fast; is the product going to do the job? If not, get rid of it quick and look at something else. When I started looking at ZENworks, it was a new product; there were no books on the subject. This book is for all of you who need a quick but in-depth technical review of the product, with my experiences thrown in. The book will also help those who are using it, but have not looked at all of the product yet—how to move through the phases of implementation. This book isn't just for NetWare administrators—if you use another Network Operating System then you will probably think very hard about using Novell Directory Services (NDS) after reading this book.

If you have NetWare and want to use PCs in that environment, then ZENworks is what you should be using. If you are not using NetWare but need workstation management, then you should consider NetWare and ZENworks as a solution. The users will probably be unconcerned with which choice you make, provided they get the applications they need, on the platform they like.

Organization of This Book

Chapter 1, *Introduction*
: This Chapter discusses workstations and network operating systems and how to choose them. I introduce ZENworks and discuss how it helps to resolve issues about managing problems of Total Cost of Ownership.

Chapter 2, *The ZENworks Installation*
: The installation of ZENworks is not straightforward. It is easy to do, but you need to know how it should be done. This chapter introduces the NDS and discusses the issues around where objects should be placed for greatest performance.

Chapter 3, *The NetWare Clients and Related Components*
: The NetWare client is not really a part of ZENworks, but it is an essential part of the system and some components of it are specifically for ZENworks. This chapter discusses how each of the clients works and how to configure them.

Chapter 4, *ZENworks Policy Packages*
: ZENworks policies are a big and important part of the product. This chapter discusses every part of the policy packages and the effects they will have on your workstations.

Chapter 5, *Workstation Objects and Inventory*
: This chapter discusses what workstation objects are for, how to create them, and what effects they have on your NDS. I also discuss the inventory system, how it works, and how to configure it.

Chapter 6, *The Novell Application Launcher*
: The Novell Application Launcher helps you to deliver applications in a managed way to your workstations. It is a big part of ZENworks and one of the most useful. This component will greatly assist you in managing your applications, but it is a big and complicated component itself.

Chapter 7, *Application Metering*
: This chapter discusses how you can manage the legal part of your applications, including how to ensure that you are not exceeding the number of licenses you have purchased for your network.

Chapter 8, *Remote Management*
: The remote control function can save you a great deal of work. It allows you to remotely manage workstations without having to visit them. This useful utility requires a great deal of configuration. This chapter discussed the remote control tools and how they can be configured in you organization.

Appendix A, *The Future of ZENworks*
: This appendix describes ZENworks and ZENworks for Servers.

Appendix B, *Integrating Other Authentication Systems*
: This appendix describes NDS for other systems.

Appendix C, *Other Sources of Information*
: This appendix lists other sources of ZENworks information.

Conventions Used in This Book

The following typographical conventions are used in this book:

`Constant width`
: is used to indicate command-line computer output and code examples.

`Constant width italic`
: is used to indicate variables in examples and in registry keys.

Italic
: is used to introduce new terms and to indicate URLs, variables or user-defined files and directories, commands, file extensions, filenames, directory or folder names, and UNC pathnames.

This is a note tip. The owl indicates a note or tip relating to the nearby text.

This is a note warning. The turkey indicates a warning, something that you should pay close attention to.

How to Contact Us

We have tested and verified the information in this book to the best of our ability, but you may find that features have changed (or even that we have made mistakes!). Please let us know about any errors you find, as well as your suggestions for future editions, by writing to:

O'Reilly & Associates, Inc.
101 Morris Street
Sebastopol, CA 95472
(800) 998-9938 (in the United States or Canada)
(707) 829-0515 (international/local)
(707) 829-0104 (fax)

You can also send us messages electronically. To be put on the mailing list or request a catalog, send email to:

info@oreilly.com

To ask technical questions or comment on the book, send email to:

bookquestions@oreilly.com

We have a web site for the book, where we'll list examples, errata, and any plans for future editions. You can access this page at:

http://www.oreilly.com/catalog/zenworks

For more information about this book and others, see the O'Reilly web site:

http://www.oreilly.com

Acknowledgments

I would first like to thank my editor Robert Denn who helped me through the production of this book and also his support staff who assisted me when I needed help.

I must also thank my wife Wendy who not only put up with my horribly unsociable hours whilst I was writing all these pages, but also for her editorial skills. Wendy, armed with a red pen, can take one of my "finished" chapters and add more red characters than the black ones. My two children Katie and Ian are also due—it is also they who put up with me whilst I lived and dreamed ZENworks during the writing of this book.

I also thank my technical reviewers Mathew M. Lavey, Ashley J. Meggitt, Adrian Asher, and Terry F. Hall. My thanks to you who took the time to read, digest, and constructively comment.

Last but not least I would like to thank my family, colleagues, and friends who supported me through the whole process.

1

Introduction

Novell's Zero Effort Networking (ZENworks) is a suite of software specifically designed to help manage Windows Desktop systems and user applications. The product is wholly reliant on NetWare 4.11 or greater servers as a back engine, where Novell Directory Services (NDS) is the heart of the system. The NDS is a hierarchical database storing such information as NetWare servers and users as objects in a tree structure. During the course of this book, I shall discuss the different components of ZENworks and explain how the new objects created by ZENworks affect the structure and performance of the NDS. I will also cover each of the special ZENworks objects in detail, outlining what they are for, how they work, and where the pitfalls lie.

ZENworks is designed to help you solve the complex problems surrounding Total Cost of Ownership (TCO). It includes mechanisms for managing desktops, users, workstations, and applications along with tools to assist the IT support staff in the remote diagnostics of workstations and assistance to users. The components of ZENworks are integrated as part of the NDS used to manage the clients as shown in Figure 1-1.

Each of the components shown form a part of the product, where the configuration data is stored in the NDS. The components can be modified by IT support staff, where changes can affect the workstations or users. This means that you are able to manage your workstations and users from a single point without having to make personal visits to them. ZENworks gives the ability to make great strides in solving the problems of TCO, allowing you to govern your IT service in a strategic way. It is very useful to begin the process of strategic IT service delivery with a clear plan for the delivery of your IT service.

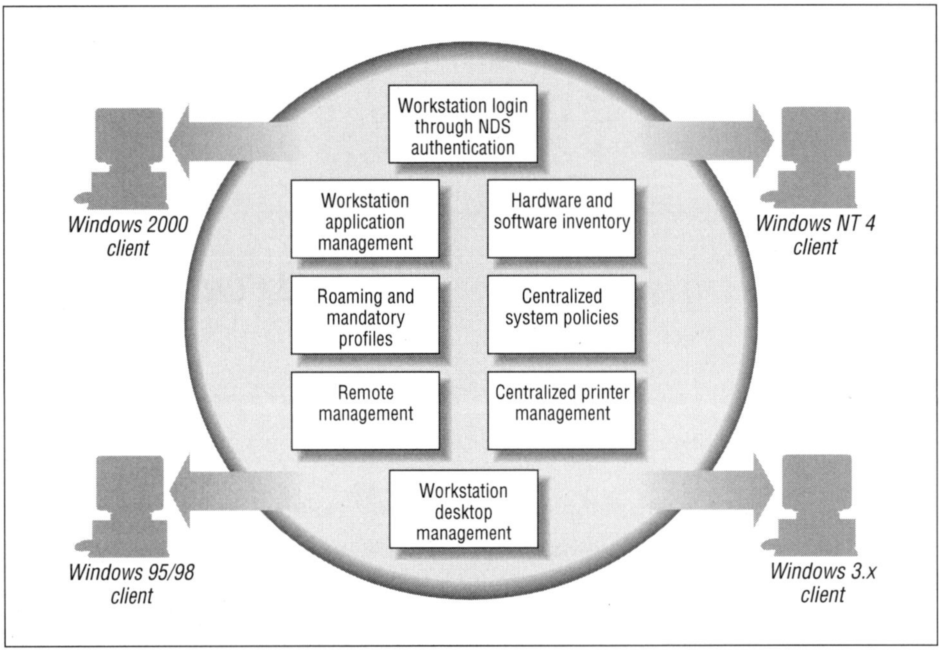

Figure 1-1. Novell ZENworks

The Network Operating System

One of the important decisions you need to make is the choice of network operating system for the fileserver. This can be a difficult choice and it largely depends upon your requirements. Your choice needs to address following issues:

Existing infrastructure
: If you have an existing system and client software that relies on it, the cost of replacing that system may be worthy of consideration in your decision. If you already have a NetWare network, it may not require a huge change to upgrade it to support your current requirements.

Existing expertise
: There is a cost associated in retraining staff who are already expert in the use of certain systems. In many cases the experience gained from years of system management can not be covered by training courses.

Specialized software required on the fileserver
: If your requirements dictate that a fileserver should be running a particular application and the application runs only on a particular server, this may influence your choice of fileserver operating system.

Number of users

If you have a very large number of users, it is important to ensure that the fileserver's authentication system is able to support that number of users and any foreseeable future growth. NetWare has clear advantages over some competitors in this area; the number of users in your organization is unlikely to challenge the capacity of NetWare (provided your NDS is correctly designed).

Desktop management system

A desktop management system can give you huge savings in potential extra staff. If you decide that the choice of desktop management system will form a part of your decision-making, that choice may affect which fileserver you eventually choose. The choice of ZENworks for desktop management will require you to be running a NetWare fileserver.

Requirements for workstations

If your workstations require special functionality on the fileserver, this may also affect your decision. For instance, if you have a lot of Apple Macintoshes that need to communicate with the fileserver, the network protocols available on the fileserver may affect your choice. Most network operating systems can support a wide range of workstation types.

Geographical organizational structure

A geographically diverse organization creates challenges for how workstations, users, and file services can be integrated across the network. If your organization requires a high level of integration, you should prepare a plan for how this could be achieved for each fileserver type being considered. NetWare is very well suited to such organizations, but again the NDS design should be carefully considered, along with fileserver location.

The future

What is the future of the selection of systems you have in mind? What would happen if the vendor ceased to exist? For most major players in the market, this is not an issue. The market is very competitive both in terms of cost and technical functionality. It would be prudent to take a careful look at some of the small, new companies whose life expectancy may be short, even if their technical offering is very good. NetWare has been a major player in the market for many years and, with their leading-edge technology in directory services, will continue to be for some time.

Cost of hardware and software

Last, but certainly not least, is the cost consideration. Within reason, it is best not to allow cost to bear too much on fileserver choice. There is usually insufficient difference between any number of systems to force you to make a decision based on cost alone. The issue of requirements and the solution to TCO are much more important and potentially costly than differences between fileservers.

Don't allow cost to rule the roost when it comes to choosing infrastructure components. If one choice cost $100,000, another $15,000, and another $10,000, you may well eliminate the high-end choice, simply on the basis of cost. The other two are essentially the same and should be treated as such. The difference in functionality could be worth a great deal more.

The Desktop Operating System

Similar to the fileserver choice, the desktop operating system is also driven by requirements. In this case though, the requirements are usually mostly application driven. The list of applications that you have derived from planning exercises must be supported by the operating system upon which you run them. You could argue that this case is clear cut, but there are caveats. If you have an application that is an extreme case because it will only run under DOS or Windows 3.1, don't treat its requirements as the lowest common denominator. If a particular application must have Windows 3.1 because it simply will not run on a 32-bit platform, don't be tempted to accept Windows 3.1 and downgrade all other applications to run on it. If some applications cause you problems, they themselves must be reconsidered. When you are making this important decision, legacy applications must be phased out where possible. If the company that wrote the software hasn't kept it up to date, it may not survive anyway.

Given the amount of work involved in redesigning the desktop operating system, the fileserver, and any other infrastructure, you are hardly likely to decide to roll out Windows 3.1. Indeed there is an argument for delivering the highest level of operating system possible if it can be achieved. In the world of Microsoft operating systems this will be Windows NT or Windows 2000. The reason for this choice is clear: its multitasking is good, and it is robust and secure. If there are technical problems with this choice, Windows 95/98 is an adequate replacement for it.

Operating System Configuration and Rollout

Operating system configuration is easy. If you don't need a component get rid of it, and if you need a component add it in. Wait a minute, though: which ones do you or don't you need? The actual work of operating system configuration usually isn't a problem; you may have some problems with it, but for the most part it is really about just doing it.

Use the concept of managing one workstation to allow you to ensure operating system consistency. There are several programs on the market which will allow you to save the contents of your hard disk to a file and replicate it to other workstations. This will give you a consistent image on all workstations. Even if there is a problem with your image, it will be a problem on all workstations and you are able to globally correct it. The moment you allow a workstation to diverge from the standard image, you will make the support of many workstations impossible.

A proper planning document will usually reveal some of the requirements, which will allow you to make a start. Some of the requirements you can deduce yourself. It is a good idea to make a list of which characteristics of the workstation are desirable and which are undesirable. With this at hand, begin to develop one workstation to achieve a perfect operating environment by working methodically through the list. It is helpful to save your "perfect operating system" by backing up your work at certain stages. This backup is frequently referred to as an "image." Making images can be time consuming, but worthwhile. If you make a mistake after two days of work, you can roll back to a previously saved image. There are various programs on the market to do this. The most popular is the GHOST program, although there are others.

Here is an example (and much simplified) plan for the development of the standard workstation to be used in the LNYP company. It is very important to write down exactly what you have done during the whole operation, so that you or others can refer to them later:

1. Install the operating system with as few components as possible.
2. Install only the network protocols that are required.
3. Save the image with a recognizable, sensible name, for instance: *LNYP001*.
4. Install and configure the NetWare client and other components (if you are using NetWare).
5. Log in and check that the system works.
6. Save the image.
7. Make a list of all the processes or services and devices on the system and find out what they do. Decide which ones you need and which you don't.
8. Save the image.
9. Make a list of all the different hardware types on all the workstations in your organization and add devices for them. This will include video drivers, audio drivers, mouse drivers, printer drivers, etc.

10. Save the image.
11. Apply any service packs and hot fixes. Tidy the desktop, clear the event viewer, empty the wastebasket, tidy any other flaky areas.
12. Save the image.

This will leave you with a basic operating system that you can roll out to your machines. You will obviously require some applications, so add them as well, but don't save them into the base operating system image. It is better to maintain a base operating system and roll any applications onto it as required. I use the Novell Application Launcher to add any needed applications, then save the image with a new name. For instance, if I had an image called *LNYP005*, I would add the applications and save the image as *LNYP005A*. Subsequent slightly different versions of the image can be saved as *LNYP005B*, etc. This permits me to always return to the base operating system whenever necessary. You can also use an environment variable such as *LNYP_DTVER=5* to differentiate it from other implementations if necessary.

Replicating your perfected system with its applications is frequently referred to as a *rollout*. To rollout your perfected image, you need to download the image to each workstation. There are usually device drivers that are inappropriate for the workstation, so you will need to switch those off and perhaps make some other slight modifications; remember to write down all you have done. It is probably a good idea to beta test your implementation to some users to get feedback about problems. It is difficult to make it perfect the first time around, so modify the base image, put the applications back, and roll out the next beta revision until you have a working, acceptable system for your users. It is also a good idea to introduce a training program for users so that the progression onto the new system is not as stressful. The introduction of any new system will be controversial, but it is clearly beneficial to limit this controversy as much as possible with an appropriate training program.

Having finished the beta program, it is time to do a full rollout. Perform the install on a workstation or group of workstations. Allow the user to log in to see if it works okay, and make sure they are happy. Leave them to it and go on to the next station and perform the same action. You will eventually get around the whole organization with your new desktop system. When a user has problems, which they eventually will, it is simply a matter of reinstalling the operating system by pulling down the image again, a task that will take just a few minutes. Some image replication programs allow you to download the image to more than one machine at a time using TCP/IP multicasting. The advantage here is that you are able to download the image to a group of machines simultaneously. This is clearly an advantage when you are rolling out to large clusters of workstations.

ZENworks Components

ZENworks consists of several major components that relate to the functions shown in Figure 1-1. These components will combine to provide a comprehensive system that will assist greatly in solving TCO problems faced by your organization. ZENworks components are discussed in the following sections.

NetWare Client

The NetWare client is not really a part of ZENworks, but it is provided because all the ZENworks components rely on it. The client provides authentication to the NetWare system and a high level of integration into the workstation architecture. There is a client for DOS, Windows 3.x, Windows 95/98, Windows NT, and Windows 2000. There is also a client for Macintosh available from *http://www.prosofteng.com.* It should be noted that none of the ZENworks components are available for either DOS or Macintosh.

When a workstation's configuration details are changed in an NDS object, the workstation must be able to read and obey the changes that have been dictated. The NetWare client contains agents that perform the changes to the workstation on your behalf. The NetWare client is discussed in Chapter 3, *The NetWare Clients and Related Components.*

Desktop Management

The user desktop is an important place. It must have sufficient functionality to allow the users to perform their work, but not much that they will venture into inappropriate areas. ZENworks manages the desktops through the use of policy packages, which control a variety of aspects of the user desktop. There are NetWare policy packages for Windows 3.x, Windows 95/98, and Windows NT/2000. There are some similarities between these packages and some differences also. The NetWare policy packages have the following functionality:

- NDS-authenticated access to Windows NT/2000
- Windows system and user extensible policies
- Remote Management configuration
- Desktop preferences including roaming or mandatory profiles
- Printer management

These policies form the heart of your desktop management, where all the configuration is held in NDS objects that are modified through a GUI interface. The ZENworks policy packages are discussed in Chapter 4, *ZENworks Policy Packages.*

Application Management

The application is, at heart, a potential troublemaker. It is frequently the application that starts to play up when users call the help desk and it frequently means a visit to the workstation and user to solve it. The Novell Application Launcher (NAL) allows you to repackage an application so that it is delivered in the way you wish, not the way the manufacturer thinks it should be. The application is dynamically made visible to the user's desktop and will install itself in the way you want. The user is also able to reinstall the application if required, which ultimately saves you the trouble of making a trip to the workstation and having to reinstall the software manually.

The Application Launcher is one of the most powerful features of ZENworks and one that is practically unrivaled by other desktop management packages. This topic is covered in detail in Chapter 6, *The Novell Application Launcher*.

You also need to ensure that you have an adequate number of licenses. The ZENworks Software Metering component allows you to specify how many licenses you have purchased and enforce these license terms. Chapter 7, *Application Metering*, explains this topic and how it can be implemented.

Desktop Maintenance

A Windows workstation is a dynamic place with many changes happening all the time. Some of these changes happen on their own and some occur deliberately. These manual actions include hardware changes and software changes. It is not always possible to keep track of all changes on the workstation and indeed some are not worth keeping track of at all, but hardware and software changes are worth the effort of tracking. This would normally mean performing a regular inventory of the workstation to ensure that the list of changes is up to date. This is a huge effort and usually the list is out of date before it can be completed. The ZENworks Inventory allows you to regularly check the hardware and software installed on all or some of your workstations and to produce reports. This topic is covered in detail in Chapter 5, *Workstation Objects and Inventory*.

In spite of all your effort, you will probably have problems with workstations, even if it is the user that is the problem. The ZENworks Remote Management utilities will allow you to connect to a workstation and perform a variety of functions on it, including sharing the screen, keyboard, and mouse with the user to demonstrate the desktop's capabilities. These utilities are covered in detail in Chapter 8, *Remote Management*.

A Final Word

Although the ZENworks suite of software allows you to perform management of your users, workstations, and applications without leaving the comfort of your office, this in itself can be dangerous. Don't lose touch with your users by locking yourself away and waving your ZENworks magic wand. There will always be problems as far as the users are concerned and they must be given the opportunity to voice them before the problem gets out of hand. Users have good long-term memory; they rarely remember the things you did right and always remember the things you did wrong. As long as you keep communicating with them and helping them, they will comply. If you complete the rollout and alienate the users, you will have won the battle but lost the war.

Working on a detailed plan is not only a great help to those performing the work, but to those who support it as well. Limit what you implement as much as possible; this will restrict the workstation's functionality, but that is unimportant provided it fulfills the organization's role.

The cost of workstations, software, fileservers, etc. is relatively unimportant in comparison to TCO. Although cost should be a consideration, it should not be a primary one. The desktop management system should be a primary consideration because it has the potential to handle most of your TCO problems. If you are installing or re-installing your desktop systems, a desktop management system should be on your shopping list. In Chapter 2, *The ZENworks Installation*, I discuss how to install ZENworks, and what it will affect. It is the obvious first step to take in making use of the product, but one that should not be rushed into.

2

The ZENworks Installation

Installing the software is the easy bit, right? Well, okay, that may be true in some cases, but in this case you must consider what you wish to install and where. It is worthwhile to think about the implication of the effect a large suite of software will have on your already existing infrastructure. Chapter 1, *Introduction*, discussed the structured development of your strategy and requirements. These requirements should be considered carefully before installing the software.

ZENworks is a powerful product, which will go a long way, if not all the way, towards the management of your PC desktops, but you will need to think carefully about how to place the objects in your NDS to maximize performance. ZENworks has two product packs, so you will also need to think about which components you wish to implement and therefore which pack to use. In this chapter, I review the ZENworks components and also the implications of their installation and placement in your NDS.

The ZENworks Product

The ZENworks product consists of a series of components that perform functions to assist with the management of Microsoft Windows PC (Intel only) systems. These PC systems or workstations will be installed as distributed desktops around your organization. The components consist of programs that run on the client workstation, and schema modifications to be made to the NetWare Directory Services (NDS). Most of the software is installed on the NetWare server and is launched from there when required, but some will need to be installed on the workstations.

The product comes in two basic packages, the Starter Pack and the Full Pack. The following sections will outline which components are in each pack and what their purposes are.

The Starter Pack

The Starter Pack is freely downloadable from Novell's web site, *http://www.novell.com*, and arrives as a self-extracting executable. This package consists of the following components:

NetWare Client
: ZENworks includes a client for Windows 3.x, Windows 95/98, and Windows NT/2000. This client provides a secure authentication mechanism to a NetWare server and device drivers to allow for comprehensive integration with the NetWare network and filesystem. This client is discussed in detail in Chapter 3, *The NetWare Clients and Related Components*. It is very unlikely that you will not use the client. Indeed, you will need to install it on at least one workstation, just to perform the server installation.

Workstation Manager
: The Workstation Manager is an agent installed on the workstation, which enables or disables features on the workstation on behalf of the user. The Workstation Manager functionality varies depending on which platform is being used and is discussed in detail in Chapter 3. If you do not install the Workstation Manager, then a lot of the functions, such as ZENworks policies, will not be enabled by the workstation. This is because it is the Workstation Manager that performs the work. If you wish to manage the workstation via the policy packages, then you will need the Workstation Manager running on the workstation.

NDS policy packages
: Policy packages are objects in the NDS where central management of the client workstation is controlled by defining settings that affect users or workstations. The policies are tied to the user and workstation objects in the NDS by associating the policy with a user or groups of users and workstations. The policy packages contain the configuration details for most of the ZENworks components, which are enabled by the Workstation Manager running on the client. The policies are discussed in Chapter 4, *ZENworks Policy Packages*.

Workstation objects
: Workstation objects are registered in the NDS by enabling a policy in the user policy package. If you wish to use computer policy packages or to associate an application with a workstation, then you will need to have workstation objects registered in the NDS. The workstation object is discussed in Chapter 5, *Workstation Objects and Inventory*.

Novell Application Launcher (NAL)
: The Novell Application Launcher is a large component of ZENworks. It consists of application objects that are stored in the NDS tree containing application execution and installation information. These objects are made available

to the user through a client component running on the workstation. The user is able to execute the software through the application object and if it isn't installed, the object will perform the installation for the user. Application management is a very big problem for most organizations. The Application Launcher is a very useful tool for managing end-user applications and their configuration. More details regarding NAL can be found in Chapter 6, *The Novell Application Launcher*.

The Full Pack

The Full Pack can be purchased from your NetWare retailer. This pack has all the Starter Pack components as well as lots of extra features, including:

Hardware Inventory
: Collecting and managing a hardware inventory is a tedious business if you have to visit each workstation and collect the information. The Hardware Inventory module runs on the workstation at scheduled times and collects the data for you, then stores it in a Sybase database installed on one of your servers. More details about the Hardware Inventory can be found in Chapter 5.

Software Inventory
: A software inventory has the same problems as a hardware inventory; the data is difficult to manage and tedious to collect. In addition, it can be, at best, a moving target! As soon as you have finished manually inventorying a PC, the user will install some other piece of software, making your database instantly outdated. The ZENworks Software Inventory will run at scheduled times, collect the information for you, and store it in the Sybase database that is also used for Hardware Inventory storage. Details about the Software Inventory can be found in Chapter 5.

Remote Management
: The Remote Management component allows the Helpdesk support staff to connect to a user's workstation and share the screen, keyboard, and mouse from their admin station. Remote Management allows support staff access to the user's workstation without leaving the Helpdesk unattended. To find out more, turn to Chapter 8, *Remote Management*.

Software Metering
: If you are licensed to use some of your software concurrently, you can ensure that the license terms are met using Software Metering. To use this software you will need to install the NetWare Licensing Service on the server and will have to launch the application through the NAL. More information about Software Metering can be found in Chapter 7, *Application Metering*.

Helpdesk

The Helpdesk program runs on the client workstation and is available to the user to report problems. The configuration for the program is held in a policy package object where it is read by the client program. The Help Requester sends email detailing the problem. The program is particularly useful when integrated into a helpdesk system, which can read trouble tickets via email. Details of the Helpdesk program can be found in Chapter 3.

Virus checking

The full product also comes with a license for Network Associates Virus Scan software. This software ensures that your workstations are protected from the menace of software viruses.

NDS Considerations

The NDS is the heart and soul of your network infrastructure and should be treated with care. The NDS is made up of containers and objects that are organized in a tree formation. The design of the NDS tree in your organization should be carefully considered, especially when installing a product like ZENworks, which can add a large number of objects to the tree. Your NDS tree will probably consist mostly of users and other objects such as servers, volumes, and print queues. ZENworks can add objects for every workstation and every application available in your organization. This is not a problem as such, as the NDS can easily hold a very large number of objects. Placement of these objects, especially in relation to other objects associated with them, needs careful consideration.

> Consider the placement of all of the ZENworks objects. The product will improve your desktop management, but improper placement of the objects themselves could cause performance degradation.

Background

The NDS is based on the X.500 standard developed by the Institute of Electrical and Electronic Engineers (IEEE). The standard defines a directory service (electronic telephone book) for the lookup of email addresses in an X.400 email service. This standard is the basis upon which the NDS is designed.

The directory service is a hierarchical database made up of objects. An *object* is a distinct entity that is stored in the NDS database. There are a variety of object types available, and each type has distinct properties. There are roughly two types of objects: a container object that contains other objects, and leaf objects that do not. The following list gives some examples of standard NDS object types:

Containers
: A container object is one that can contain other NDS objects including other container objects. The container object is used to form branches in the NDS tree.

Users
: A user object is a leaf object that contains details about the user, including his name, user ID, password, home directory, and a great deal more. Each user has a user object that describes him uniquely.

Groups
: A group object is a leaf object that can contain a list of other objects. The group object differs from the container object in that it contains a list of objects rather than the objects themselves.

Servers
: A server object is a leaf object that contains information about a NetWare server.

Printer
: A printer object is a leaf object that contains information about a particular printer.

Volumes
: A volume object is a leaf object that contains information about a NetWare volume, its size, and which server it is located on.

There are a wide number of objects available to build into your NDS tree. The containers are created to form a tree structure, the top of which is called the *root*. Objects are placed into the containers where they are permanently stored.

The directory can be divided into logical segments called *partitions*, which are stored on a server. In the simplest model, a single server will hold all partitions. The problem with having a single server is that if it should become unavailable for some reason (crash, hardware fault, reboot, etc.), then the NDS service disappears with it. The way to get around this problem is to have more than one server and replicate the partitions to the other server. That way, the NDS is still available should you need to shut down a single server, provided you have replicated all the important partitions. If a server that has the user objects stored on it is unavailable, a user can still log in to the NDS if her user object has been replicated to another server.

The ZENworks product contains 11 new object types that will need to be stored in the NDS. These new objects are:

- Windows NT user policy object (also used for Windows 2000)
- Windows 95/98 user policy object
- Windows 3.x user policy object
- Windows NT workstation policy object (also used for Windows 2000)
- Windows 95/98 workstation policy object
- Windows 3.x workstation policy object
- Container policy object
- Application object
- Application folder object
- Workstation object
- Workstation group

The placement of these objects is important, and to place them you will need to understand the NDS. There is a great deal that can be written on this subject, but I shall only touch on some of the important areas, so that you can form an opinion about where to place these important new objects on your own.

Tree Design

The design of your tree should be considered carefully. An improperly designed tree may give rise to performance problems, particularly if your organization has a Wide Area Network (WAN), which provides data communications between offices in different parts of the country or in different countries. Your tree will need to have a name, which should be carefully thought out, as it will not be possible to change it later without deleting the tree and starting again. Having given the tree a name, you will have to start to build the tree by creating top-level containers.

The NDS tree is organized by creating containers and sub-containers. These containers include the following types:

Country (C=)
: This container is always created at the highest level of the tree, just below the root. The Country container is not often used in the NDS, but is defined in the X.500 standard and is therefore compliance.

Locality (L=)
: This container is used as a sub-container under Country, Organization, or Organizational Unit. It may have a value of East, West, etc. In reality, the Locality container is rarely used.

Organization (O=)

This container is mandatory and must reside under either the Root or a Country container.

Organizational Unit (OU=)

This container is optional but very useful for subdividing containers, such as Organizations, into units such as departments. You will probably use Organizational Units for containing most of the objects in your tree.

Novell makes recommendations about how to design the NDS Tree:

Design the top of the tree based on Wide Area Network (WAN) infrastructure

If you have an organization with offices connected by a WAN, you should consider basing the top of your tree with this in mind. If you have the head office in London with other offices in New York and Paris, then these should form the top of your tree as shown in Figure 2-1. If you do not have a WAN, then the top of your tree can be based on Divisions or Departments.

Design the bottom of the tree based on the organization structure

This area of the tree will contain departmental containers with the users placed in them.

Do not use global groups or groups with users that span across WAN links

Groups should be used sparingly in the NDS. Groups that categorize users and span different containers and different parts of the tree are not a good idea. Groups of users across WAN links should also be avoided for WAN performance reasons. Where possible, use a container instead.

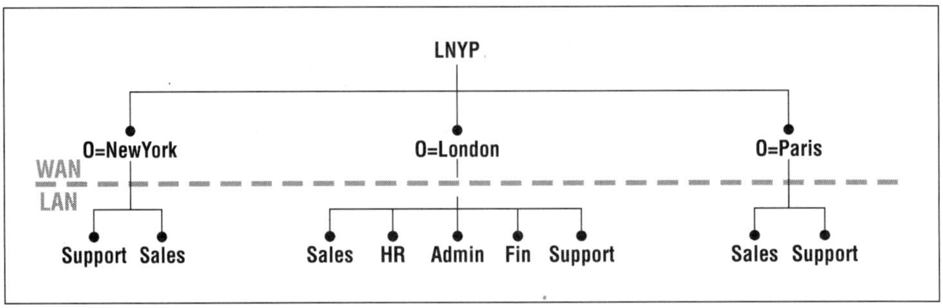

Figure 2-1. NDS tree design

The tree shown in Figure 2-1 shows how the LNYP company, which has offices in London, New York, and Paris, dictates the top-level design.

How to Partition the Tree

The partitioning the NDS tree is performed using the NDS Manager program and should also be considered carefully. Partitions are important because it is these that are replicated. The following recommendations are made by Novell to help you decide where the partitions or logical divisions should be made. Keep in mind that replication will affect the network, so the bandwidth must be considered, particularly on slow (WAN) links. Novell makes recommendations about partitioning and it is worthwhile to consider them carefully:

Partition the top of the tree based on WAN infrastructure
: Keep the partitions for each remote office on the local server at that office. Keeping in mind the replication, partition the tree to keep local users, servers, and other local objects together.

Do not create a partition that spans a WAN
: A partition, which contains offices, separated by a WAN is not recommended due to network performance.

Partition around the local servers in each geographical area
: If you have an office or more than one office (connected by a fast network) in a region, make that section of the tree a single partition. If your organization is located in a single area entirely connected by a Local Area Network (LAN), then partition by division, department, or top-level container.

Partition the bottom of the tree based on size
: The size in this case refers to a number of objects. The maximum number of objects recommended in this case is 1,000 to 1,500 per partition.

The LNYP tree is shown in Figure 2-2 and has been partitioned according to WAN infrastructure.

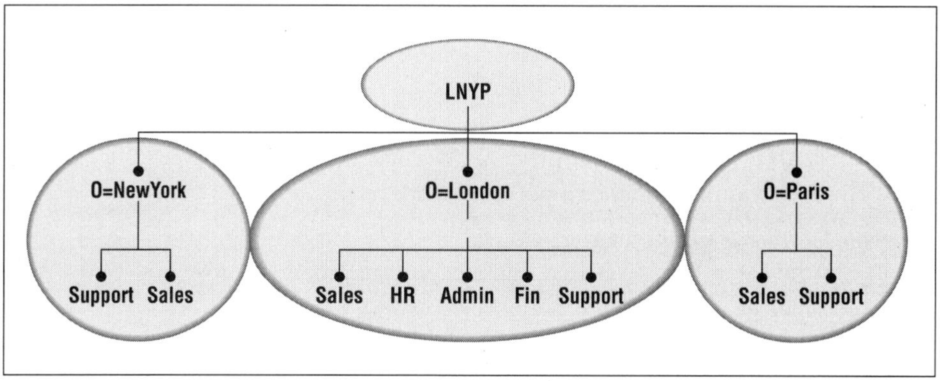

Figure 2-2. NDS partitioning

How to Replicate the Partitions

Replication is a term that refers to the copying of a partition to another server. One of the benefits of this is lookup time and another clear benefit is fault tolerance. If your NDS spans a WAN, proper replication prevents ZENworks objects from consuming WAN bandwidth needlessly. Each partition has a main replica called the *Master Replica*. There are four type of replicas, defined as follows:

Master Replica
: There can only be one Master Replica for any partition. This replica is created automatically when a partition is created. It is used to read and update NDS objects.

Read-Write Replica
: There is very little difference between the Read-Write Replica and the Master Replica. If you require a replica with read-write NDS object permissions, create it as Read-Write.

Read-Only Replica
: Read-Only Replicas are used to hold a copy of a Master Replica.

Subordinate Replica
: Subordinate Replicas are automatically placed on a server whose parent partition has a replica on the server, but a child partition is not on that server.

You will need to decide which server will hold the Master Replica and which will hold the Read-Write or Read-Only Replicas or Subordinate. There are guidelines from Novell about how to make replicas, which are as follows:

Maintain three replicas for fault tolerance
: This is the optimal number of replicas, but if the office is small, with fewer than three servers, two replicas will suffice. It is recommended that you not have more than ten replicas, because of the overhead imposed by the replication process.

Replicate locally (if possible)
: If it is possible, replicate the partition to servers on the same Local Area Network (LAN). The replication process does not necessarily require a lot of network bandwidth, but rather a good network response time.

Replicate to provide bindery service access
: If you have bindery services installed, you may need to replicate more than three times to support any bindery services.

Place the Master Replicas at main or central sites
: The location of Master Replicas should be considered for central sites where the replication cycle can be completed within 30 minutes.

Figure 2-3 shows the tree discussed previously with the arrows pointing toward the servers that hold the partition replicas. Note that the root partition is replicated to the three sites for resilience.

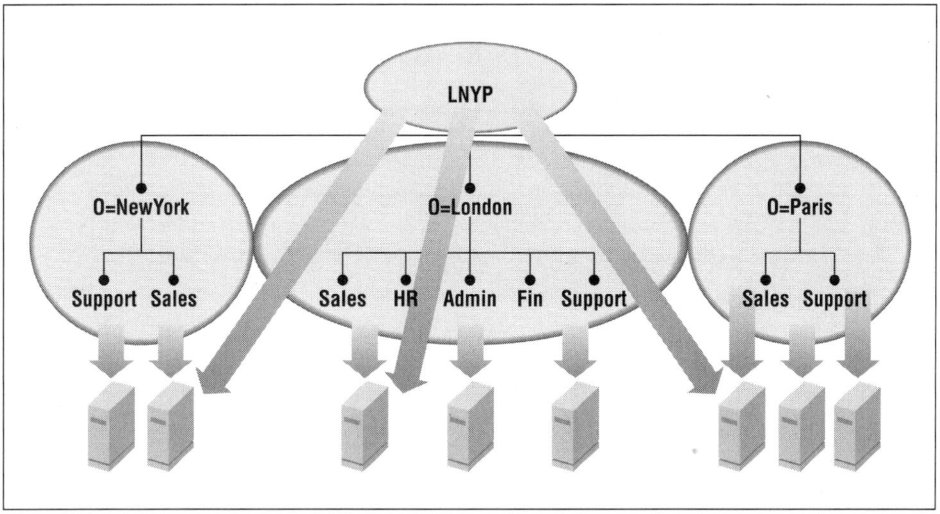

Figure 2-3. NDS replicas

The partitioning and replication of an NDS tree is performed using the NDS Manager (*NDSMGR32.EXE*) program, which is shown in Figure 2-4. This program will allow you to perform management and diagnostics of your NDS tree. The following functions can be performed by this program:

- Create partitions in your NDS tree
- Replicate partitions to other servers in the tree
- Perform an NDS repair of your tree
- Perform upgrades to the NDS software
- Print a partition list, replica ring, etc.
- Diagnose NDS problems

Where to Put the ZENworks Objects

ZENworks can potentially double the number of objects in your NDS. In order to accommodate these objects, you will need to plan where they should go. This does not mean redesigning your entire tree, but adding to it and placing the objects in sensible locations. The following new objects will be available after the installation:

Policy package objects

There are seven types of policy package objects, all of which are best placed near the object with which they are associated. The user policies should be close to user objects and workstation policies should be close to workstation objects. More detail about object location can be found in Chapter 4.

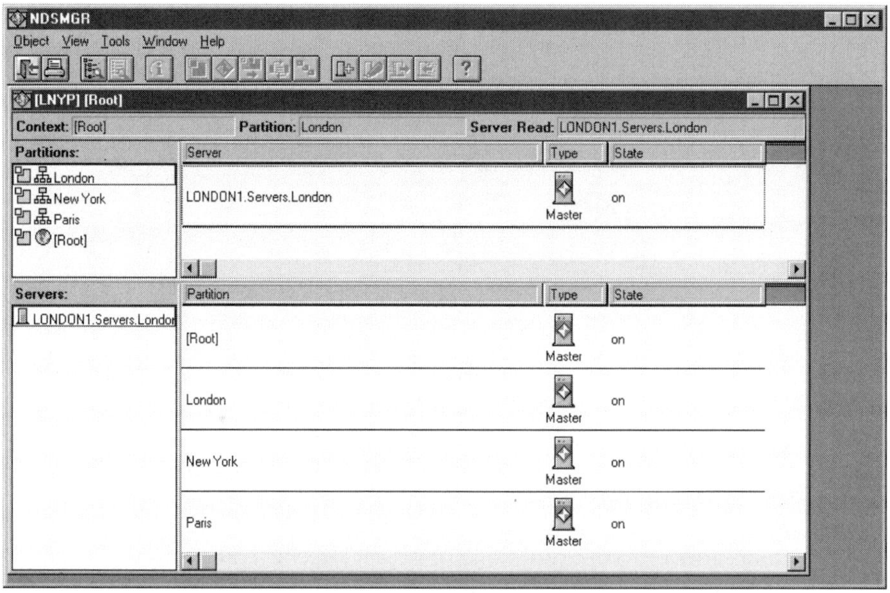

Figure 2-4. The NDS Manager

Application objects

When the user logs in and the NAL client starts up, it will search for all application objects associated with the user or workstation. It is a good idea to place these application objects close to the objects they are associated with and to limit the scope of the search using the NAL configuration page in the container. More details on this can be found in Chapter 6.

Application folder objects

These objects can be placed almost anywhere. The folder object is used by the system administrator as a convenient place to organize application objects. The application object stores the folder information as well, and it is from there that the user gets the information. Turn to Chapter 6 for more information about application folders.

Workstation objects

Most organizations have lots of users and lots of workstations. You have probably made considerations about where to put your users, but the location of workstation objects will also be important. If all of your users also have a workstation, then you will have to give as much consideration about the placement of workstation objects as you did user objects. More information on this subject is available in Chapter 5.

Workstation group objects

Workstation groups should be located close to the workstations, but should not be allowed to span a WAN link. If you need more information about workstation groups, this can be found in Chapter 5.

Installation

Now that you know what you want to install and where you want to put it, you can start the install. If you have downloaded the Starter Pack, you will need to unpack it and run *Winsetup*. Create a directory to store the self-extracting archive and execute it. You will find that it will extract into that directory with *Winsetup* at the top level. If you have purchased the Full Pack, insert the CD-ROM and run *Winsetup*. Before the installation to the server is done, you will need to install the client software on the PC, so you will have to do the workstation install first.

Installing the Workstation Software

The installation of the workstation software can be performed manually or automatically according to an install script. You will probably wish to perform the initial install manually to get a feel for how to configure it for other workstations. The workstation consists of the following components and characteristics:

The NetWare client

Allows the workstation to authenticate to the NDS and/or a Windows NT/2000 Domain

Uses network protocols IPX or TCP/IP to communicate to NDS and servers

Contains a GUI Windows map-drive function with all the features of the DOS map command

Contains GUI NetWare rights and Volume information functions

Can map NetWare print queues to local printer ports

Logs into or out of NetWare server and trees

Workstation Manager

Performs work on the workstation on behalf of the user

Schedules this work as and when instructed by the NDS policy

Creates a local account on Windows NT/2000 workstation to enable login

Computer printer

Sets up print queues and assigns drivers according to policy package configuration

Application Launcher Service

Performs the work of installation on behalf of the user (under Windows NT/2000, the user may not have rights to install files and Registry keys)

The software components available for each platform will vary, so I will look at each one separately, along with their minimum specification. Having determined that the minimum specification has been met for the platform you are installing to and which components should be installed, the process of installation can continue. You will need to decide how to set basic settings such as NDS tree name and default context. The workstation will need to be rebooted after the installation.

Windows NT and Windows 2000

For the installation on Windows NT/2000, you will need to be logged on as an Administrator. In addition, you will need the following minimum resources on the workstations:

- Windows NT 4.0 Workstation, Server, or Terminal Server Edition with Service Pack 3; Windows 2000 Professional, Server, or Advanced Server
- Intel 486 processor for Windows NT 4 or Pentium for Windows 2000; none of the client software will run on the Alpha platform
- 20 MB RAM
- 10 MB disk space
- VGA graphics
- Network card with connection to a NetWare Network

Windows NT/2000 will require at least the client to be installed, but the Workstation Manager will grant access to the workstation after authentication if you have installed a Windows NT user policy and enabled Dynamic Local User. In the case of Windows NT Terminal Server Edition or Windows 2000 Server, a user will be presented with the NetWare Login Dialog Box when he connects with a thin client, allowing access to the Terminal Server with NDS authentication. There are several options available during the install, as shown in Figure 2-5, which I will now explore.

The Windows NT/2000 installation has several options which you may wish to choose or to ignore. If you wish to simply authenticate to the NDS and have that authentication grant access to Windows NT/2000, just select the Client and the Workstation Manager, but don't forget to enable the Dynamic Local User policy in the Windows NT user policy package, which is discussed in Chapter 4. The following options are also available:

Novell Distributed Print Services (NDPS)

This option allows the NDPS agent to be installed on the workstation. This agent allows a print queue that is managed by the NDPS service on the server to follow the user or to stay with the workstation.

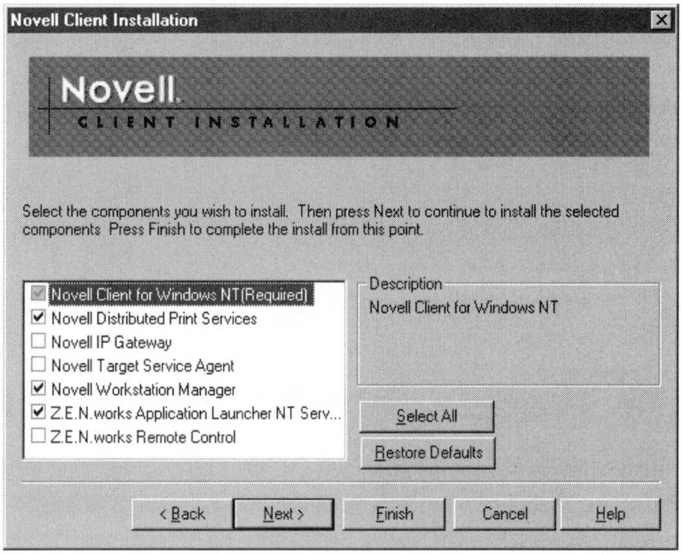

Figure 2-5. Windows NT installation options

Novell IP Gateway

If you wish to have some applications that require TCP/IP on the workstation, but do not wish to install the protocol, then this service will work for you in most cases. If you enable this component, an IP agent will be installed which will redirect any Windows Socket demand to a process running on the server. This server process performs the TCP/IP work on the workstation's behalf.

Novell Target Service Agent

The Target Service Agent is a process that runs on the workstation to respond to a backup request from a server.

Novell Workstation Manager

If you wish to use any policy objects to manage the user's desktop and to manage the workstation, you will need to install this component. The Workstation Manager runs on the Workstation with System privileges so that any work required to be done on the workstation can be performed without having to give the user extra privileges.

ZENworks Application Launcher NT Service

If you plan to use the Novell Application Launcher as part of your workstation management scheme, then this service will also need to be installed. When the application is installed on the workstation, there may well be components that need to be installed that exceed the user's privilege. Under Windows NT/2000, all work of this kind is passed over to the Application Launcher Service that is running with System privileges.

ZENworks Remote Management

If you plan to use Remote Management as part of your help service to users, the Remote Management Agent should be installed on each workstation.

Windows 95/98

To install the client components, you will need the following minimum resources on the workstation:

- Windows 95 with Service Pack 1 or Windows 98
- Intel 486 processor
- 16 MB RAM
- 14 MB disk space
- Network card with connection to a NetWare Network

To use the full ZENworks functionality under Windows 95/98, you will need at least the Client to be installed, but the Workstation Manager will enable extra functions to help secure the workstation via the policy packages, which are covered in detail in Chapter 4. There are several options available during the install, as shown in Figure 2-6, which I will discuss next.

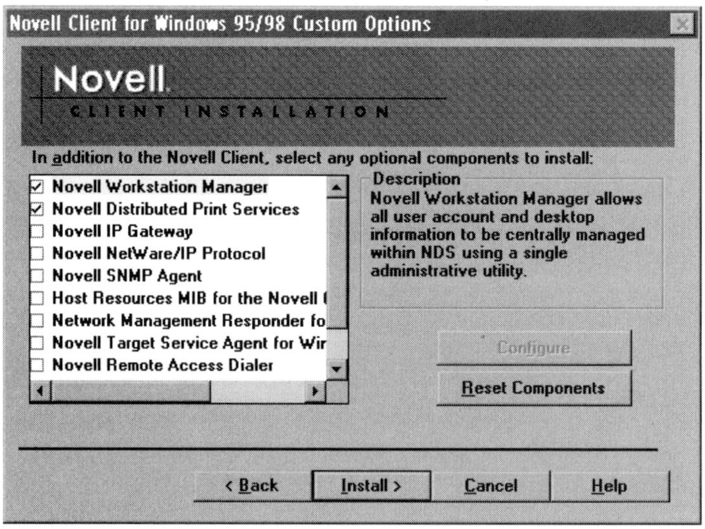

Figure 2-6. Windows 95/98 installation options

The Windows 95/98 installation will contain the components listed below. If you are unsure which components to select (this being the first time), you can check the Novell Workstation Manager, and the client will be installed automatically. It is probably best not to select them all, as you may find the results confusing. The following are the options:

Novell Workstation Manager
: This enables the workstation's user account and desktop to be centrally managed via the Windows 95/98 policy packages. These policy packages are discussed in Chapter 4.

Novell Distributed Print Services
: By enabling this option you will allow bi-directional communication between your workstation and a networked printer.

Novell IP Gateway
: If you use a Novell IP Gateway Server, then this component allows your applications on the workstation that use Windows Sockets to use the Gateway server to perform the TCP/IP work for you without having to install the TCP/IP protocol.

Novell SNMP Agent
: The Simple Network Management Protocol (SNMP) allows a SNMP management console to view the workstation as a manageable object. Each workstation will need to have a SNMP agent installed. This component enables a SNMP agent that can use IP or IPX transports.

Host Resources MIB for the Novell Client
: A Management Information Base (MIB) is used by the SNMP agent to perform work on the client and pass it back to the SMNP management console. This MIB returns inventory information about the workstation.

Network Management Responder (NMR) for the Novell Client
: In order to allow the Management console to collect information about the system, an agent needs to be present to collect and respond to these requests. The NMR provides information about the system to the Management console.

Novell Target Service Agent for Windows 95/98
: This is a backup agent that backs up a selected drive to a server.

Novell Remote Access Dialer
: This agent provides extended dialup networking to include NetWare IP.

Novell NDS Provider ADSI
: The Novell Active Directory Service Interface (ADSI) provides an interface to the NDS for NDS-aware applications.

Novell Remote Management Agent
: This installs the Remote Management client software on the workstation.

Windows 3.x

To install the client components you will need the following minimum resources on the workstation:

- Windows 3.x
- DOS version 5.0 or Novell DOS 7
- Intel 386 processor
- 8 MB RAM
- 15 MB disk space
- Network card with connection to a NetWare Network
- Memory Manger installed (such as *emm386.exe*)

There are several options available during the install, as shown in Figure 2-7, which I will discuss next.

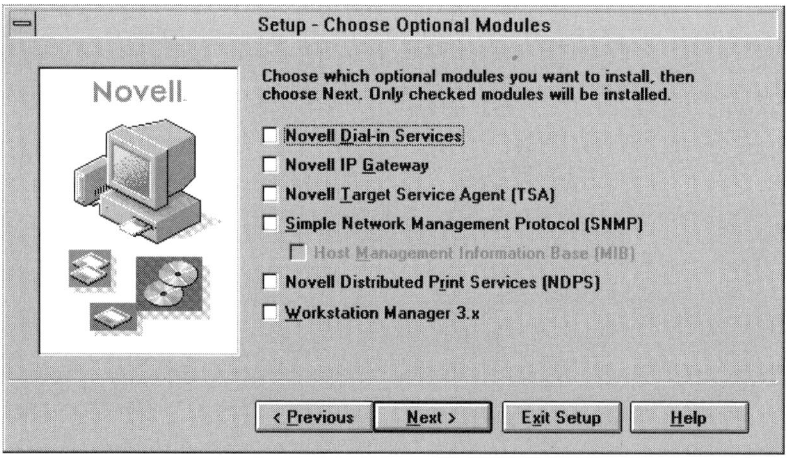

Figure 2-7. Windows 3.x installation options

The Windows 3.x installation will contain the components listed below. If you are unsure which components to select just check the Workstation Manager 3.x box and the client will be installed along with it. It is probably best not to just try them all, as you may get unexpected or confusing results. The following are the options:

Novell Dial-in Services
: This option installs the remote access dialer and should be selected if you wish to use NetWare services via a modem link.

Novell IP Gateway

The Novell IP gateway allows the workstation to communicate with a server running the Novell IP Gateway service. This service allows a workstation to use the Internet and other external IP services without having an IP address on the workstation.

Novell Target Service Agent (TSA)

By selecting this option, you will have support for the TSA installed on the workstation. This software allows the Storage Management Service (SMS) on the server to backup all or portions of the workstation.

Simple Network Management Protocol

This option will install the SNMP, which allows a management console to view the workstation as a manageable object. The agent can use IP or IPX transports.

Host Management Information Base (MIB)

A MIB is used by the SNMP agent to perform work on the client, and pass it back to the SNMP management console. This MIB returns inventory information about the workstation.

Novell Distributed Print Services (NDPS)

The NDPS allows a network of workstations to use networked printers.

Workstation Manager 3.x

By installing this option, you enable certain features of the workstation to be managed through a ZENworks workstation policy object. The policy objects are discussed in detail in Chapter 4.

Remote Management Agent

This agent allows the workstation to be controlled by an administrator.

Unattended Installations

After you have decided how to configure the client software, you may wish to prepare an installation that can proceed unattended. The Novell Client Installation Manager, *NCIMAN.EXE*, can be used to create configuration files, which can correctly configure the client during the install, as shown in Figure 2-8. The program creates a file called *unattend.txt* that is read by the setup program when the `/u` qualifier is added to the command line.

The unattended install may be very useful if you wish to upgrade the client automatically, by running the install during the login process, or at other times via an action in a policy package. You may also wish to provide a client to users whose machines are outside your control, requiring you to install the client software in a particular way.

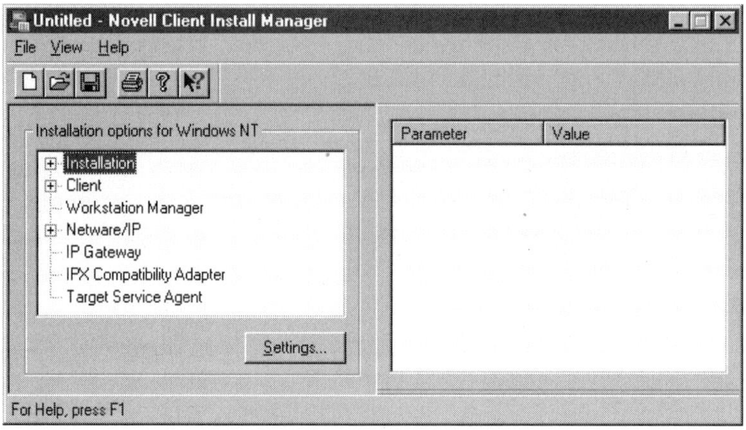

Figure 2-8. NetWare Client administrator

Installing the Server Software

The server installation is quite straightforward, but you will need to decide which machine it will be installed to before beginning. The install program initially offers to install to the servers to which you are authenticated. This is the same as the list of servers shown at the top level of Network Neighborhood. If you wish to install to another server, authenticate to it first to make it appear in the list. It is probably safer if you log out of any server you don't want the files to be installed to. The install will also make changes to the NDS schema, so make sure you are logged in to the correct tree with full Admin rights to the NDS and the server filesystems.

Make sure you are authenticated to all of the servers you wish to copy the files to before you perform the install. There is no way to authenticate to a server during the install process.

The server will need to have the following minimum resources:

- NetWare 4.11 with Support Pack 6 installed
- NDS Version 5.99a
- 64 MB RAM
- 200 MB disk space on the *sys* volume for a complete installation
- If you plan to install Software Metering, you will need to have Novell Licensing Services (NLS) installed and running on the server

The NDS will have its schema modified during the install to include support for the following object types:

- Windows NT user policy package object (also used for Windows 2000)
- Windows 95/98 user policy package object
- Windows 3.x user policy package object
- Windows NT computer policy package object (also used for Windows 2000)
- Windows 95/98 computer policy package object
- Windows 3.x computer policy package object
- Container policy package object
- Workstation object
- Workstation group object
- Application object
- Application folder object

These additional objects are not a problem in themselves, but they will serve to increase the number of objects in the NDS. It is therefore recommended that the *sys* volume have sufficient space for these extra objects. It is also important to realize that space will be required on the servers which hold replicas of the containers where you plan to store these objects.

Make sure you have a recent backup of your NDS. In the unlikely event that something goes wrong you will be thankful for it!

It is important that the NDS replica ring be fully synchronized before you start the install procedure. If one of your servers has been down for some time and it holds a replica of the NDS partition to which you are installing, then you must make sure that the replication is complete before you start. It is also recommended that no one be using the software installed on the *sys\public* volume.

It's finally time to do the install. Run the *winsetup* program either from the CD-ROM or from the self-extracted file, and select the Install ZENworks option. If you wish to install the Sybase database for the hardware and software inventory, the installation will do this for you, but you must decide on which server it should be installed. The server must also have the TCP/IP protocol installed and configured on it, as the data can only be transferred using this protocol. If you have not installed the TCP/IP protocol on the server yet, the install will still proceed, but you may get a warning from the installer. After the Welcome screen, you will need to agree to the license terms. In the next screen, select the Custom option and you will be presented with several following check boxes.

Application Management and Distribution

This will install the Novell Application Launcher software and object schema will be installed.

Workstation Maintenance (available only in the Full Pack)

This will install the Remote Management software.

Desktop Management

This will install software that supports the user and workstation policies.

NWADMIN32

This will install the A'dministrator program, which is essential for the creation of the ZENworks objects.

Copy Clients to Network

This will install the client software to the *sys* volume.

Check all the components you require and click the Next button. You will then be presented with a selection of options as follows:

Files

This will install all the files to the server. These files include the *nwadmin* program and its components, the Novell Application Launcher, and components and the client installation files for the three platforms.

Schema extensions

If you have already extended the schema in a previous installation, there seems little point in doing so again to the same tree. If you have not installed ZENworks to this tree before, this option must be selected. The program will check and extend the schema to cater for the new objects, which will be subsequently available.

Application objects

This will install a set of application objects that can be used to install clients, as well as some of the client software. These objects will be placed in the context where your current ID (the one which you used to log in and do the install) resides. For example, if your ID is located in a container called Support that is under the London container, then your context will be Support. London, which is where the client objects will be located. This may not be the ideal location for these objects, but you can easily move them later.

Workstation registry entries

This will update the workstation in use with correct registry entries for the *NWADMIN* program.

When you have finished selecting the components, select the tree and server to which the install will be made. Make sure the selection is correct by checking the boxes next to the servers requiring the install, and un–checking the servers that do not need it. Answer the question about language and the installation will proceed.

After the file install and schema modification are complete, the Installer will ask you which container you wish to grant rights to for workstation registration. Select the container to which you wish to register the workstations and include the sub-containers if required. If you are unsure about this step, you can leave it for later after reading Chapter 5. The task can be performed manually by running the *WSREG* program.

Installing Software Metering

To install software metering, you need to do a separate installation from the software CD-ROM (Software Metering is only available in the Full Pack). You will also need to install the NetWare Licensing Service to the server. This is done by typing the following command on the server console: `load NLS.NLM`. To load NLS automatically when the server starts, enter the same command in the server's *autoexec.ncf* startup file.

After the NLS program has been installed on the server, run the *Winsetup* program from the CD-ROM and select Install Software Metering. The install will ask various questions, including which server to install to. The installation is completed and you may start creating license certificates. See Chapter 7 for more details about Software Metering.

The NWADMIN Program

The *NWADMIN* program will be your best friend. Through this program you will have a console to create, delete, or modify objects in the NDS. The program automatically knows how to deal with objects because it uses snap-ins to support object functionality. It is important to use the latest version of the program wherever possible to ensure that any new objects can be correctly manipulated. The *NWADMIN* program also provides other functionality, such as being the master console for the Remote Management program. The program is operated by using the mouse to browse through the NDS and to operate menus at the top menu bar, or by using the keyboard. Some functionality is also available by selecting an object and using the right mouse button.

The program can be tailored to suit your preferences. The toolbar shown across the top can be configured through View → Configure Toolbar and Status Bar. There are several pages of options in there, which allow you to change buttons, status bar, etc. These preferences can be stored in a variety of places, so that they can be retrieved at a later date. To use these features, you will need to run *NWADMIN* as follows:

NWADMN32

Using no options on the command line will cause the settings to be stored in the local machine registry. This is probably what most people will want to do because they always use the program on their personal workstations.

NWADMN32 /N

The */N* option causes your preferences to be stored in your user object in the NDS. This is very useful if you tend to use different workstations, or if a workstation is being used by several support staff.

NWADMN32 /Ffilename

The */F* option causes your preferences to be registered in the specified file. For example, the following will store the settings in *f:\nwadmin.ini*: `NWADMIN32 /Ff:\nwadmin.ini`. If you don't include a path, the local Windows directory is assumed.

When you are first presented with the main screen, you will be shown a tips window and be placed in the NDS context where your user ID resides. You will find that your current context will be shown as the highest point in the tree. Your account will not actually be in the root, so you can move up the tree by either selecting View → Go up a Level or using the Backspace key (*not* the Delete key). The Delete key is very useful for getting rid of bits you don't need, but not a good key to use if you do need them. You will be warned before a delete occurs, and it is not possible to delete containers full of objects, but I have accidentally pressed this key several times, and it is heart-stopping. Be very careful what you do with the *NWADMIN* program—it is extremely useful, indeed essential, but dangerous!

The *NWADMIN* program can be operated using the mouse or keyboard. If you use the keyboard, be very careful of the Delete key. You could inadvertently delete part of your tree.

You can move up and down the tree in the browser window by using the mouse to click or double click in the right place. The mouse will expand or collapse the tree one level at a time, allowing you to see the subcontainers or objects, as shown in Figure 2-9. To create something in a container, either a subcontainer or an object, select the container with the mouse (single click) and use the right mouse button to bring up a menu where you can view or change the object details. If you wish to create a container or object, select the Create option, and you will be presented with a selection dialog box similar to Figure 2-10. Scroll through the list and select the object you wish to create.

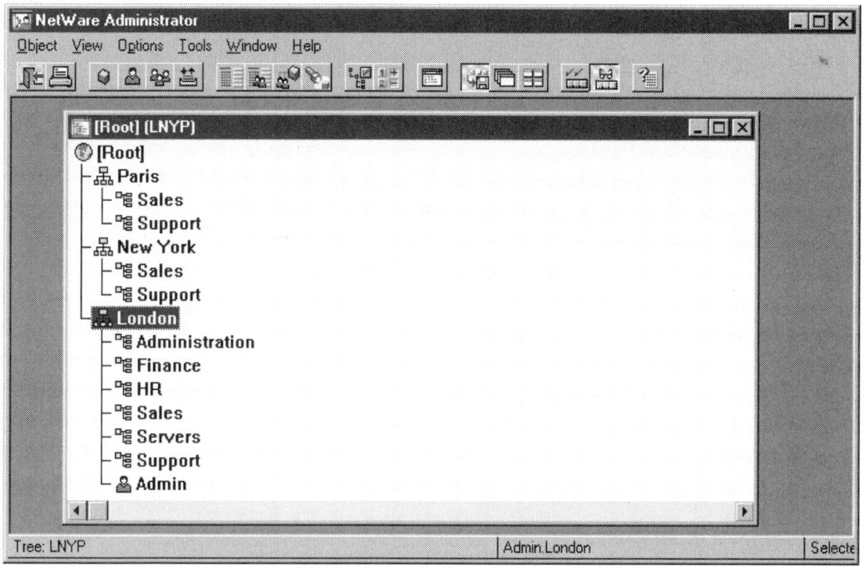

Figure 2-9. NWADMIN program main screen

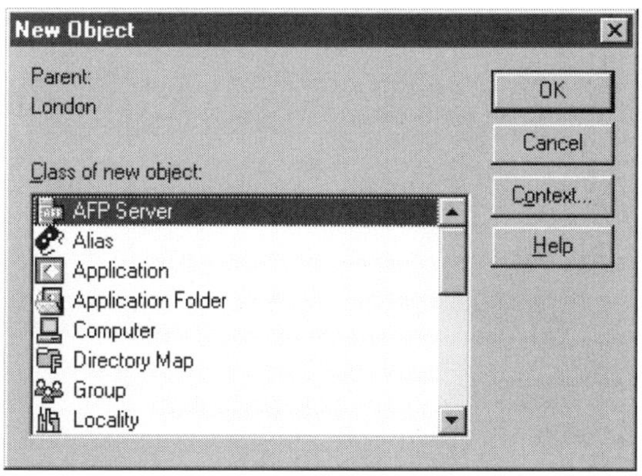

Figure 2-10. Create object selection dialog box

A Final Word

The server installation should be performed on every server from which the users run ZENworks components. As with every piece of software, patches are regularly released along with new versions. It may be a good idea to test these patches or new versions in a test tree before installing to your main tree. There may be schema modifications made during the installations that need to be understood before proceeding with the main installations. After the schema modifications have been made, they can only be reversed by installing a backup of your NDS, which is not a trivial operation. If you are testing and getting a feel for the software, then this is also probably best done in a test tree so that your eventual installation is well planned. Your test tree should reflect a structure close to the existing tree, so that any configuration issues are well understood in advance.

3

The NetWare Clients and Related Components

The NetWare clients for Windows have been designed to allow the user to connect to and use NetWare services from workstations running Windows 3.x, Window 95 or 98, and Windows NT or 2000. The clients will authenticate to a Bindery or NDS-based NetWare server and include components which, behind the scenes, fully integrate NetWare functionality into the Windows operating system, allowing users to manipulate NetWare resources transparently. This high level of integration allows for seamless inclusion of graphical user interface (GUI)-based mechanisms to support all the functionality that was available under DOS. As well as the inclusion of this functionality there is backward compatible support for NetWare-aware DOS applications. Novell has gone to a great deal of trouble to ensure that Microsoft desktop operating systems, which are the choice for most of the world's users, can be fully integrated into the Novell network operating environment.

In this chapter, I look at how to configure the client and Workstation Manager in detail. I also review how the client integrates into the operating system by analyzing the system architecture of the Windows 32-bit operating systems. This sort of detail is particularly important if you are trying to debug a problem and you need to understand how it actually works. If you find the depth of some of the material in this chapter daunting, don't worry. The architectural detail of the clients is included for debugging purposes. You will need to understand how the client should be configured and this detail should not be such heavy going.

Client Configuration

The NetWare client can be configured in a variety of ways. You may wish to configure through the Network Control Panel, through the Novell Client Installation Manager *NCIMAN.EXE*, or via the NetWare Client Configuration Policy. In each of these cases, the configuration details and the associated issues are the same.

The client configuration interface consists of a dialog containing several tabbed pages where configuration data is displayed. Some of these fields will have suggested values that can either be kept or modified, and some will need to have values entered by you. The default values for most settings are altogether adequate for the most part, and may never need to be changed, but are covered in detail later in this chapter. After the client has been installed and configured and the PC has rebooted, enter a user ID and password, then click the Advanced button to enter the NDS tree required and the context of the ID. Through the Pages list under the Advanced button, you can also configure the client to run login scripts, set login environment variables, and prepare a host of other settings.

If you have not used the client before, then set the characteristics of your NetWare environment through the Advanced button and get a feel for how it works. Enter the NDS Tree or Server, your user ID and password, and the context of your user ID. You should carefully review all of the client settings at some stage during the service development to ensure you have maximized the performance and security of your network service.

Client

From the Client tab you are able to define several important settings including the tree or server to log in to and the default context. The Windows NT/2000 client configuration page is shown in Figure 3-1. The configuration screens for Windows 95/98 and Windows NT/2000 clients are different in appearance, but contain the same configuration settings.

One of the settings, which initially seems quite straightforward, is the first network drive. This setting requires you to do some planning to ensure that the service will function in the way the user expects and to ensure that you have capacity for future services.

The first network drive setting allows you to define which drives to reserve in your organization for local devices. The problem with local drives is that the number of local devices will vary depending on the makeup of the workstation. If the first network drive is defined as the first to be available after all of the local drives, then this would vary from machine to machine, making it very difficult to predict where the network services are connected. The best way to define the first network drive value is to review the workstations in your organization and select a drive that will not conflict with any of them.

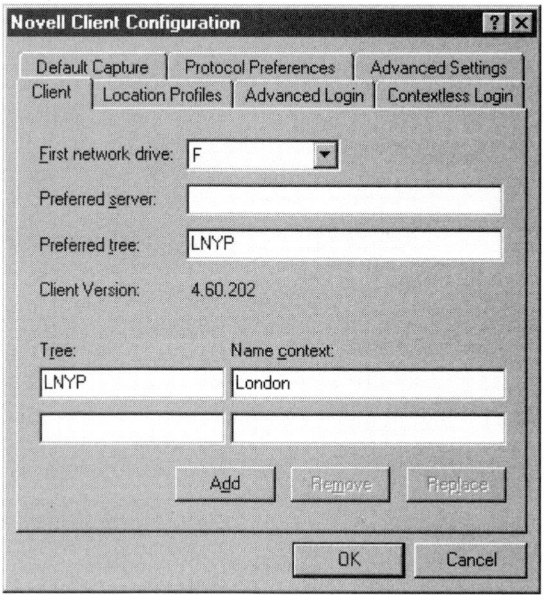

Figure 3-1. Windows NT client configuration

> It is worth taking the time to develop a plan for your workstation drive mappings. You will need to take into account all of your current requirements, your users' requirements, and what you may require in the future. This may seem like crystal ball gazing, but if you keep as many resources up your sleeve as you can, it may pay off next year.

It is generally a good policy to plan how drives will be used in your organization. Users will soon start to use services connected randomly to whichever drive they happen to select next. This will be okay until you decide to set up a new service and find that the users have mapped all the available drives, leaving you without a place to mount the new service. Therefore, it is important to have a plan dictating how the drives will be mapped in your organization. It is possible to restrict which drives can be mapped by using policies that are discussed in detail in Chapter 4, *ZENworks Policy Packages*. Table 3-1 outlines an example drive-mapping plan.

Table 3-1. Example Drive-Mapping Plan

Drive Letter	Description
A:	Local floppy disk drive
B:	Local floppy disk drive
C:	Local hard disk
D:	Reserved for local device
E:	Reserved for local device
F:	Home directory
G:	Group file share
H:	Networked applications
I:	Reserved for future networked applications
J:	Reserved for future networked applications
K: to O:	User definable drives
P: to S:	Reserved for networked CD-ROMs
T: to Y:	Reserved for future
Z:	Mapped to *sys/public* volume

From this example you can see that the local drives are planned along with the immediately obvious network services. There is an allocation of five drives for networked CD-ROM services and a provision for the users to map five of their own drives and also a reservation for future services. This plan will become a cornerstone for your network service.

Location Profiles

Workstations are generally installed in an office and that is where they stay. Location Profiles allow the user to choose which location they are currently in. This makes Location Profiles a bit confusing, because you may well conclude that the workstation is always in the same location. So why allow the user to choose a location? These profiles are useful for workstations that aren't stationary, such as portable computers. Users with portables can potentially plug their machine in anywhere and then find that they cannot log in or cannot get access to a service. This is probably because their client configuration details are inappropriate to their location.

The Location Profiles page is used by the Network Administrator to preconfigure the client for each location regularly visited by the user. When the user arrives at the remote location, he plugs in his workstation, selects the location from the client Login Dialog Box, logs in, and connects to network services successfully.

Suppose you have a user who is based in London and who regularly visits offices in Paris and New York. You may choose to add location profiles for the three office locations. If you mimic the application drive on all your main site servers and you make the connection to that drive during login, you will probably not want this connection to be made to his home site (London) but to the site he is visiting (Paris). This means that the primary application drive (drive *H:*) is connected to one of the Paris servers and not the London server, because you don't want the application to be launched through the WAN link. On the other hand, you don't want all the network redirected drives to be at the local site (Paris), because the user's personal files will probably be located in London; so drive *F:* (the user's home directory) will need to be connected to one of the London servers. You may also wish to connect a local printer, as the user will probably not want to print in London when connected in Paris.

Contextless Login

In NDS terms, a context is the path to the user object in the NDS tree. Contextless login allows users to enter their user ID and password without having to know their context and is available from NetWare 5 servers that have catalog services running. In an environment where users share workstations and where there are a large number of users whose objects are installed in different containers, the context for the user will be different. This can cause confusion amongst the users because they not only have to remember their username and password, but also their context. When contextless login is enabled and catalog services is running on the server, the user will not have to enter his context; it will be provided for him automatically when he logs in.

Advanced Login

The Advanced Login page allows you to configure how the client login box will appear to the user. These settings will allow the user more flexibility to control how and where he logs in. If your users are able to deal with these settings and your requirement is that they have this much flexibility, then you will need to make this setting available. There can, however, be problems with allowing a user this much flexibility. If the user is not expert or tends to want to explore, he could decide to fiddle with the settings, disable the login script, or simply stop the client from working. It is probably a good idea to disallow access to the Advanced button in the Login Dialog Box for most, if not all, your users. If you wish to restrict the user as much as possible and only wish him to enter a username and password, then check all of the boxes shown in the Advanced Login page.

Allowing users to select their own settings during login could cause all sorts of problems if they decide to disable the login script or change any settings. It is better to set this up for them and disallow them from this area by hiding the Advanced button.

Advanced Settings

The Advanced menu is part of the client configuration dialog and is really for advanced users; that is to say, it is not for end users, but for you. The settings under this menu all have default values which should work in your environment. It is worth looking through these settings to take a view on what you may require for you service, as shown in Figure 3-2. Some will be obvious, but some will have values that should not be changed unless you know what you are doing.

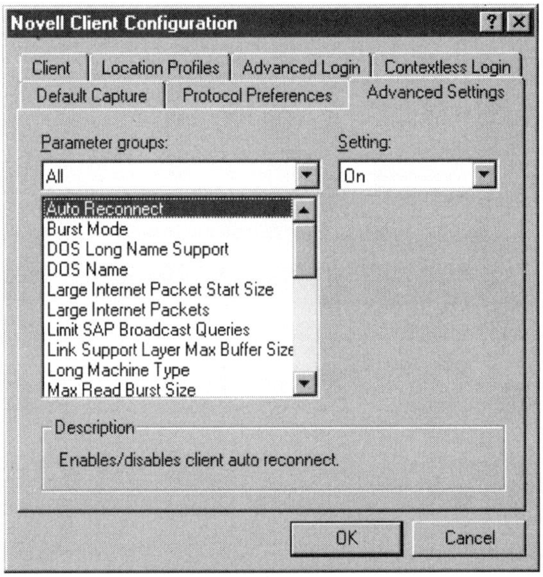

Figure 3-2. Windows NT advanced settings

The settings can vary enormously from setting environment variables to tweaking the way packets are delivered through your network. The settings include restrictions for the presentation of certain client functions on the desktop.

Don't be tempted to interfere with the settings that affect packet delivery through your network unless you are sure you understand the issues. Some of the settings are quite straightforward and some really are advanced. If possible, don't allow your users near this control panel.

The following list describes the advanced settings:

Alert Beep
: When pop-up messages are received they can alert the user with a beep. This setting will allow the beep to be on or off and is available under Windows 95/98 only.

Auto Reconnect
: The auto reconnect feature allows a client to re-establish connections to services after that service has become unavailable because of a restart or network fault. Under Windows NT/2000, the value can be either off or on, whereas under Windows 95/98, the value can be an integer from zero to five as follows:

  0 No Auto Reconnect, equivalent to off

  1 Connections to devices such as redirected drives and printers will be restored

  2 All of item 1 plus the restoration of connections to read-only files

  3 All of item 2 plus the restoration of connections to all files and any file locks

  4 All of item 3 plus the restoration of connections to all files open for write

  5 Same as 4

Burst Mode
: Burst mode improves network traffic performance by allowing multiple packets to be sent before an acknowledgment is received. If the value is set to off then an acknowledgment will be expected for each packet sent. The setting is available under Windows NT/2000 only. If your network is typically free from errors, it is certainly advantageous to have this set to on.

Cache NetWare Password
: The setting can have values of off or on and is available under Windows 95/98 only. If the value is set to on, the username and password pair is stored in memory so that if you wish to access a subsequent network resource, such as another server, you will not have to re-enter your credentials. The password is only cached for the duration of the login session.

Cancel Desktop Login
: This setting is valid under Windows 95/98 only, where it ensures that only a successful login through the client will permit access to the workstation.

Checksum
: This setting is available under Windows 95/98 and defines a checksum that can be performed on NetWare Core Protocol (NCP) packets. The values can be set as follows:

0 Disabled

1 Enabled but not preferred

2 Enabled and preferred

3 Required

Required

The checksum has an obvious overhead in that it must be calculated and inserted at one end and calculated and checked on the other end. If you have a requirement where the delivery of data needs some level of validation, then you may opt for a value of 2 or 3. If you explicitly disable the option, any packet received by the client that has a checksum will not have the checksum performed. You may wish to use this function if your network is in some way unreliable and there is no check performed on the Data Link or Network Layer protocols.

Close Behind Ticks

This setting is available under Windows 95/98 only and defines the time in ticks for the client to wait before removing a file from the cache by writing it to the disk.

Delay Writes

The Delay Write works along with Close Behind Ticks and declares that a file should remain in the cache for the time defined. The setting is available under Windows 95/98 only and is used when a file is constantly being opened and closed again.

DOS Long Name

When this option is set to on, long filenames from NetWare volumes will be visible to DOS programs. This option obviously expects that the DOS program itself supports long filenames.

DOS Name

This setting is available under Windows NT/2000 and Windows 95/98. It sets the value of the environment variable OS to a value that can be used in the login script. The value can be set to anything; the limit is five characters.

End Of Job

The End Of Job function was used prior to DOS Version 3.0 and is used to release resources when a task is complete. This value should be set to off unless you have some particularly ancient DOS programs to support. The function is available under Windows 95/98 only.

Environment Pad

Under Windows 95/98 the environment for DOS applications can be set with this function. If you have DOS programs that need lots of environment space, then extra space can be granted here. It should be noted that this is a global setting that will allocate this amount of environment for all DOS programs.

File Cache Level

This setting is available under Windows 95 and defines how the data cache works as follows:

0 Disabled

1 Read ahead and write behind

2 Short-lived caching

3 Long-lived caching

File Write Through

This option is available under Windows 95/98 only and sets all caching for file write mode to off. When the setting is set to off, the client waits for an acknowledgment that the file write is committed before continuing.

Force First Network Drive

Under NetWare, a connection must be made to the login directory on the *sys* volume during the login and logout process. This connection is made to the first network drive, which must also be set and is discussed earlier in the chapter. If this setting is set to on, this drive will be used for the process. This setting is valid for Windows 95/98 only.

Handle Network Errors

In the event that a server does not respond to a request for resource from the client an error is generated. This setting determines whether the client handles the error condition or the application that requested the resource. This setting is available under Windows 95 only and the outcome of this condition will also affect the Net Status Busy Timeout and the Net Status Timeout settings.

Hold Files

This setting is in place for old applications which use FCB_IO. These applications may wish for the files to be left open during the application execution, which is what will happen if Hold Files is set to on. It is probably best to leave this set to off unless you have applications that particularly need the file to be kept open in this way. This setting is valid for Windows 95/98 only.

Large Internet Packet Start Size

This setting is available under Windows 95/98 and Windows NT/2000, where it is designed to go with the Large Internet Packets setting. When the negotiation for the Large Packet begins, it may take several rounds before the negotiation concludes. This setting will define the initial starting point for the process to reduce the negotiation time.

Large Internet Packets

The default packet size is usually set to 576 bytes, but can be increased for performance if the network equipment will allow it. The new packet size is negotiated between the client and the server. The setting is available under Windows 95/98 and Windows NT/2000.

Limit SAP Broadcast Queries

A server can be located via a Service Advertising Protocol (SAP) broadcast or via a bindery query. When this setting is on, the server lookup is first performed via bindery lookup and then via SAP if the lookup fails. The setting is only available under Windows NT/2000.

Link Support Layer Max Buffer Size

This setting is available under Windows 95/98 and Windows NT/2000 and is primarily for use with Token Ring Networks. It can range from 638 to 24,682 bytes. The default value for this setting is 4,736 bytes and should be left at this value unless you are quite sure that you know the value can be safely increased.

Lock Delay

When a shared file needs to be accessed on the server and a lock needs to be placed on the file for some reason, the client may have to wait if the file is already locked by another client. The value specifies the time that the client will wait before giving up the lock establishment. The value is in ticks and can range from 1 to 65,535. If you receive errors from the workstation software or from SHARE then increase this value. The setting is only available under Windows 95/98.

Lock Retries

This setting is similar to the Lock Delay setting above, except that it defines the number of times the file access attempt is made. It is available under Windows 95/98 only.

Log File and Log File Size

If you wish the client diagnostics enabled, you will need to enter a value of `NWEnable Logging=True` in *System.ini*. This setting determines where the log file is to be located. The Log File Size defines the maximum size of the file. When the file becomes full the older information is flushed. The settings are available under Window 95/98 only.

Long Machine Type

This setting is available under Windows NT/2000 and Windows 95/98 and sets the `MACHINE` environment variable. This variable is useful for setting a particular machine type that may need a slightly different executable program. In this case the variable can be used in the path to the executable. The variable was originally provided for backward compatibility of DOS programs so that different versions of DOS could be provided for different machines.

Max Cache Size

This setting is available under Windows 95/98 only and relates to the other cache settings such as File Cache Level and File Write Though. The setting defines the actual maximum size of the cache used by *CLIENT32.NLM*. This is usually automatically set by the client as 25% of the free memory available during the client program load. This setting is achieved by setting the value to zero. The cache can be set to a different level if desired, but the value should not exceed 75% of total free memory.

Max Cur Dir Length

Some very old DOS programs will not allow filenames with directory paths greater than 64 bytes. Applications that require a short path will be prevented from having problems in this regard if the path is deliberately disallowed from exceeding this maximum length. The setting is available under Windows 95/98 only.

Max Read and Write Burst Size

These two settings define the maximum size for the Read or Write Window Size for a Packet Burst. They are normally set dynamically by the client according to how busy the network is. Don't change them unless you are sure of what you are doing. The setting is available under Windows NT/2000 only, but is functionally the same as Packet Burst Read and Write Window Size under Window 95/98.

Message Timeout

This setting is available under Windows 95/98 only and defines how long to wait before a broadcast message is cleared from the screen. The unit in this case is ticks and the value can range from 1 to 10,000 with 18 ticks per second. A value of 2,160 (2 minutes) seems reasonable for most users.

Minimum Time to Net

When using very slow WAN lines, a connection to a server may fail. This setting increases the wait time for a successful connection. The setting is available under Windows NT/2000 and Windows 95.

Name Cache Level

The cache in this case refers to the cache of server names held by the client. There is an overhead to holding names in cache but as always there is a trade off as performance will be degraded if the client has to constantly wait for name lookups to occur. The setting is available under Windows 95/98 only.

Name Resolution Timeout

Servers and their corresponding addresses are held by a name space provider. This setting allows you to increase or decrease the time that the client will wait for a name to address resolution from the name space provider. The setting is available under Windows NT/2000 only.

NCP Max Timeout

This setting is available under Windows 95/98 only and defines the maximum retry time for retrying a network service before sending an error message. The default setting for this is 30 seconds.

Net Status Busy Timeout

This setting is available under Windows 95/98 only and is relevant only when the Handle Net Errors setting above is set to off. This setting defines how long the client waits for a server response before putting up an error message.

Net Status Timeout

This setting is very similar to the Net Status Busy Timeout setting except that it waits for a network timeout rather than a server timeout. The timeout value is given in seconds, but the value must be set to at least four times the round trip time to the network. If the network roundtrip to the server is 5 seconds, the value will be at least 20 seconds, but will be higher if you have it set to a higher value. The default value for this setting is 30 seconds but can be set to a value up to 600 seconds. If your network or server is very slow and you need to force the client to wait for a response, then this value can be increased. The setting is available under Windows 95/98 only.

NetWare Protocol

When the NetWare client first connects to a server, it will use this order of protocols to initially establish the connection for NDS or Bindery (BIND). The default order is NDS BIND, BIND NDS, NDS, and BIND. This configuration setting is only available under Windows 95/98.

Network Printers

This setting simply sets the number of LPT printer ports available for redirection on the workstation to a maximum of nine and is only available under Windows 95/98. There is a small memory overhead to setting this value high so it may be beneficial if it is set as low as possible. Each printer port will use 103 bytes of memory, from the formula:

Memory = Num_of_Ports × (size_of_header + size_of_tail + 23 bytes)

The default value for the header is 64 bytes and for the tail 16 bytes, as discussed later in this chapter. By increasing those values, the total memory usage on the workstation per port will need to be multiplied by the number of LPT ports defined here.

NWLanguage

Set this value to your language (English if you speak English). The setting is only available under Window 95/98.

Opportunistic Locking

This setting is available under Windows NT/2000 and Windows 95/98 and when set to on will exclusively cache a file to improve performance when the opportunity arises.

Packet Burst

This setting is used by Windows 95/98 to increase network performance by reducing the number of packets sent. This is accomplished by allowing a packet Acknowledgement (ACK) to be sent only after several packets are received. If the value is set to off, an ACK will be required for each packet. The advantage to Packet Burst is clearly network throughput, but it should only be used on a reliable network such as a LAN. You may find that your WAN is very reliable as far as errors are concerned so Packet Burst may realistically be introduced in that case.

Packet Burst Read and Write Window Size

These two settings are available under Windows 95/98 and define the maximum size for the Read or Write Window. They are normally set automatically by the client according to how busy the network is. Don't change them unless you are sure of what you are doing. The settings are functionally the same as Max Read and Write Burst Size under Window NT/2000.

Polled Broadcast Message Buffers

This setting is only available under Windows 95/98 and sets the number of messages to be retained by the broadcast messenger. This setting should only be set if you have a client that needs to keep a certain number of old messages for some reason. The default value for this setting is zero.

Print Header and Tail

These settings are available under Windows 95/98 only and define the size of the head and tail of a print job that is spooled from the client. The default values to be used here are 64 bytes for the header and 16 bytes for the tail. If you wish to increase these values for some reason, such as using the printer for a particular form that is not supported in the driver, then increase the size here, but remember that it will affect the value of the network printers' total memory in use for each port.

Read-Only Compatibility

This function is present to allow a read-only file to be opened with a read/write without giving an error. The function will only allow the lock to be placed and any attempt to write to the file will produce an error. This setting is supplied for programs that insist on opening a file read/write but never need to write to it. The client will respond to the file open read/write request with a success message even though the file is actually only open for read. The function is only present under Windows 95/98.

Receive Broadcast Messages

Broadcast messages are used by the system administrator and the server to send informational or urgent messages to the workstation users and, when enabled on the client, messages can be sent from a workstation to other users on the network. This setting allows you to define which messages will be received by the workstation. The following list describes the possible values.

All

To receive messages from servers and clients

Server

To receive messages from the server only

None

To receive no broadcast messages at all

The setting is available under Windows NT/2000 only.

Remove Drive From Environment

Under NetWare, a drive can be mapped as a search drive. Search drives are used by NetWare to allow programs to be executed when not in the current directory and not in the path. The drive is connected to a NetWare volume and optionally to a directory within that volume. When the drive is connected it can be viewed with its entire path or root connected to another drive. When the drive mapping is deleted, the search mapping is usually removed also. If this setting is set to off, then the search drive will remain in the path.

Resolve Name Using Primary Connection

When this setting is on, only the Primary IP connection will be used for TCP/IP name resolution. If it is set to off all TCP/IP connections will be used for name resolution. This setting is available under Windows 95/98 only.

Search Dirs First

When you issue a `DIR` command, what appears first, files or directories? If this feature is set to on you will see the directories listed first. The setting is only available under Windows 95/98.

Search Mode

This setting is designed to assist with the location of executable files (*.exe* or *.com*) when they are not in the path. Search mode is only available in Windows 95 and can be one of the following:

Mode1

Search for the image in the search drive if there is no complete path in the application execution and the file is not in the current directory

Mode 2

Don't look in any search drives

Mode 3

Just as Mode 1 but find read-only files

Mode 5

Search on all paths

Mode 7

As Mode 5, but search for read-only files

The setting invites the possibility for users to either run programs that they shouldn't be running or programs that they didn't intend to run. This setting should be disabled (Mode 2) but the default value is Mode 1.

Send Message

As well as receiving messages on the workstation, this setting provides the user the option to send messages. This setting is available under Windows NT/2000 and Windows 95/98 and can be set to on or off.

Set Station Time

Under Windows NT/2000 and Windows 95/98 this setting will synchronize the workstation time with the NetWare server.

Short Machine Type

This is a backward compatible function that is available under Windows NT/2000 and Windows 95/98, and is used for setting the SMACHINE environment variable for DOS overlay files. The value is limited to four characters.

Show Edit Login Script Item

As well as a global login script, a user is able to have his own login script which is stored in the user object. The setting is available under Windows NT/2000 and Windows 95/98 and when set to on will show the Edit Login Script item through the Novell menu in the system tray.

Show Novell System Tray, Scheduler Icons, and Administration Menu

There are several features available from the system tray that users may wish to take advantage of. These include functions, such as drive and printer mappings. Administrative settings such as allowing the user to edit his personal login script are also included here. If you do not wish the user to have access to these items, they can be disabled here. These settings are available under Windows NT/2000 and Windows 95/98.

Shrink Path To Dot

This setting is applicable to search drives only where the value of off will permit the full path of the search drive in the path, or on when the search drive root will only be permitted.

Signature Level

This setting is available under Windows 95/98 and Windows NT/2000 and sets the security level for packet signatures by signing the first 64 bytes of the packet. The values can be:

0 Disabled

1 Enabled but not preferred

2 Preferred but will not enforce if the server does not allow it

3 Required

The server(s) should also have the appropriate level set by issuing the command: `SET NCP PACKET SIGNATURE OPTION =` *`value`*.

This setting is quite useful for protecting data on your network. If you set the value to 3, you will need to make sure that all your servers have the value 3 set also. A safe value is 2 and the default value is 1. The client's network performance will be slightly degraded as the value increases.

True Commit

This setting is available under Window 95/98 only and may be worth consideration if the client workstation handles critical data. The data will not be cached on the workstation or server, but will be written to disk immediately. There is an obvious performance overhead to having this setting on, but if data integrity is an important issue, you may consider the trade-off worthwhile.

Use Extended File Handles

This setting is available under Windows 95/98 and allows the number of file handles to be increased from the default of 170 to whatever the maximum Locks Per Connection value is set to on the server.

Use Video BIOS

This setting is valid under Windows 95/98 and relates to the speed of video for message pop-up boxes when running in DOS mode. In general, the video through BIOS is slower for graphics and faster for character-based DOS windows. The default value for this setting is off and should be left at that setting unless you are experiencing very slow or non-functioning message boxes.

There are other pages in the Client Configuration pages that really speak for themselves, such as Default Capture, which allow you to define settings for networked printers, as shown in Figure 3-3. These other settings are just as important as those complicated advanced settings; appearance and completeness are always desirable in any service delivery.

Protocol Preferences

The Windows NT/2000 and Windows 95/98 client can use the IPX transport protocol to communicate with NetWare servers. If you are using NetWare 4 or 5, you can also use TCP/IP as a transport protocol. The NetWare client for Windows NT/2000 and Windows 95/98 does not install any base transport protocols, because these protocols are supplied as part of the protocol suite within the operating system. However, they must be installed on the workstation prior to the client installation.

For many years, Novell used IPX as their mainstay network transport protocol and for this reason there are a great many IPX transport-dependant applications, both for client and for server, that required some kind of IPX transport. Novell recently committed themselves to using TCP/IP as their main transport in two products

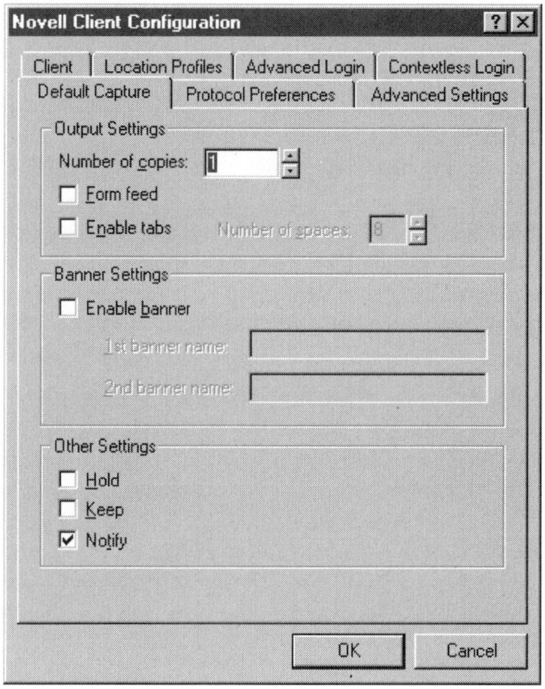

Figure 3-3. Default Capture

called NetWare IP and Pure IP. These two products are confusing because they appear to be the same, but hardly are. NetWare IP does not transmit TCP/IP on the wire, but actually encapsulates TCP/IP in IPX packets and unpacks them on the server. This is not a true IP transport and is generally recognized as such. The Pure IP product is actually a true TCP/IP transport, but is only available under NetWare 5. Many IPX-dependant applications are now IP-aware to the extent that the IPX transport is no longer required in some organizations.

In general, it is possible to use one or all of these two protocols between the workstation and the server in the following combinations:

IPX only
: This configuration will work only when IPX is installed and running on the server and IPX/SPX is installed and running on the workstation. IPX is the main protocol used by NetWare 3.x and 4.x servers and is available in NetWare 5.

IP only
: Similar to IPX only, but the workstation will not be able to talk to IPX-only servers. The Pure IP product is only available as a transport from NetWare 5 servers. Although IPX is still available if you have only NetWare 5 servers, you may want to consider TCP/IP as your only transport protocol.

IP and IPX

This will allow the client to participate in networks with servers running both protocols. This may be the desired setup for a NetWare 5 and NetWare 3 or 4 environment.

IP with IPX compatibility

This will use IP for its main transport protocol, but will communicate with servers running NetWare 5 with the migration agent installed to support IPX. This configuration is best if you wish to use Pure IP only, but have some IPX-aware applications still in use.

The use of IP on a NetWare network will probably require the use of the Service Location Protocol (SLP) as a mechanism to discover servers and other network services. The SLP does not need to be specifically routed as it uses the User Datagram Protocol (UDP) and the TCP protocol to perform discovery.

If you wish to use TCP/IP as a transport and do not want IPX, then this is the direction Novell would probably want you to go in. For those IPX-aware applications still in use with no immediate upgrade path, use IPX compatibility mode to provide the functionality without installing the IPX transport.

Layered on top of these transport protocols are transport interfaces such as NetBIOS and Windows Sockets. The interfaces allow Server Message Block (SMB) data through the NetBIOS interface and datagram services via the socket interface, as shown in Figure 3-4.

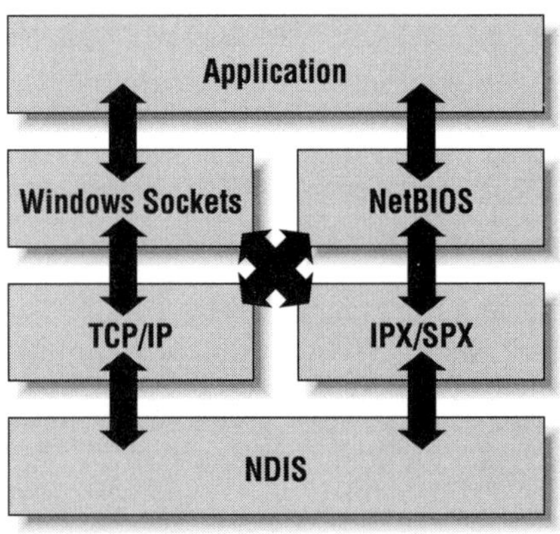

Figure 3-4. Supported protocols

The Windows NT/2000 Client

The NetWare Client for Windows NT/2000 supports authentication to NetWare servers that use NDS and Bindery. Unlike Windows 95/98, Windows NT/2000 is a secure operating system where processes running in user mode, which is where the user's application runs, are secured from unsupported access to processes running in kernel mode, which is where the operating system and its components run. The NetWare client provides 16- and 32-bit libraries and interfaces that run in user mode. These libraries pass compliant information to the Windows NT Executive services running in kernel mode.

Windows NT/2000 Client Architecture

The Windows NT/2000 system architecture is shown in Figure 3-5. Unlike DOS and Windows 3.x, Windows NT/2000 was designed from the ground up with network services fully built into its architecture. The NetWare client has to interface with the complex executive services layers running in kernel mode. To achieve full integration with the Windows NT/2000 operating system, the Client software meshes into the system architecture to provide full, integrated NetWare services to the workstation. These services provide support for the following areas:

- Integration of the NetWare filesystem into the Windows NT filesystems architecture
- Integration into the Windows NT Networking architecture
- Provision for NetWare print services
- Authentication to NetWare and Microsoft authentication systems through the NetWare Graphical Identification and Authentication Module (*NWGINA*), which replaces the Microsoft GINA (*MSGINA*)

The Windows NT I/O Manager is part of the executive services and dictates how all the input and output in the operating system is managed. This includes requests from the user in user mode for resources and applications in user mode requiring resources. The I/O Manager performs several functions, and the following are relevant to the discussion:

Filesystem drivers and redirectors

There is accommodation for more than one filesystem driver in the operating system and, in general, most workstations will have a NTFS filesystem driver (*NTFS.SYS*) and a CD-ROM driver (*CDFS.SYS*) in use. These drivers also provide a redirector as part of the device driver architecture. The redirector takes the request for data from the mapped network drive and converts it to a format that can be accepted by the I/O manager. The NetWare Client provides support for a new filesystem driver called the NetWare File System driver (*NWFS.SYS*) also with a built-in redirector.

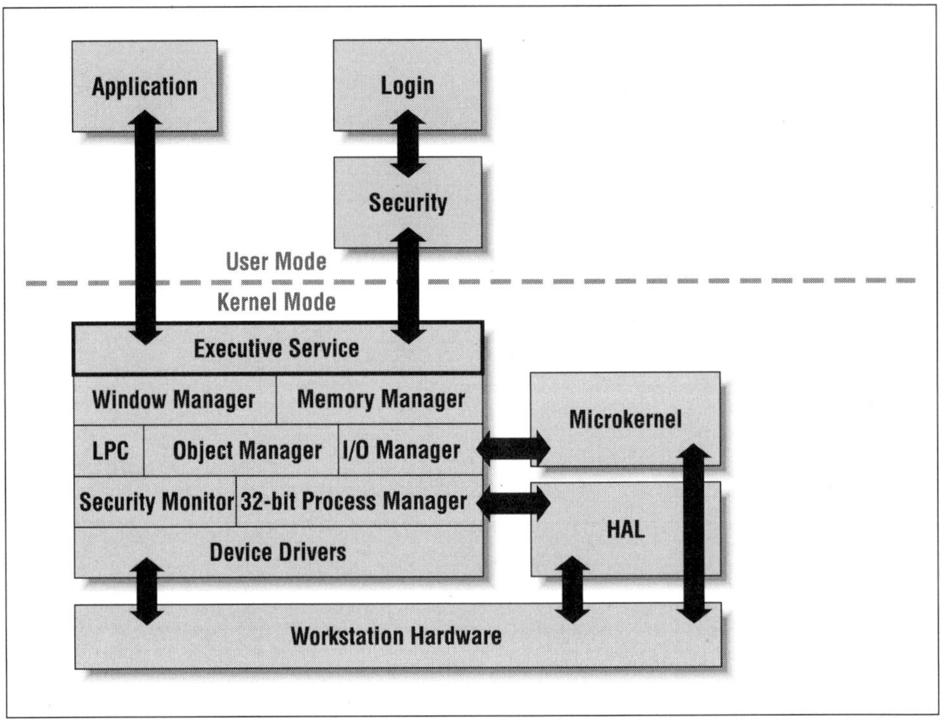

Figure 3-5. Windows NT architecture

Multiple Universal Naming Convention Provider (MUP)
The MUP resolves Universal Naming Convention (UNC) paths and determines which redirector should be used to provide the service.

Transport Driver Interface (TDI)
This is an interface provided for filesystem drivers to communicate with available transport protocols to provide the service.

NetWare Filesystem Integration

The NetWare filesystem (NWFS) and redirector interface directly with the I/O Manager, which is part of the Executive Services running in kernel mode. There is also built-in support for applications running in user mode with modules running to cater to 16- and 32-bit programs requiring appropriate access to the NetWare filesystem. The NWFS communicates with the MUP and the TDI, as shown in Figure 3-6, to provide a fully integrated filesystem component.

The client installation contains no new transport protocols, but uses the Windows NT IPX/SPX and TCP/IP built-in protocols.

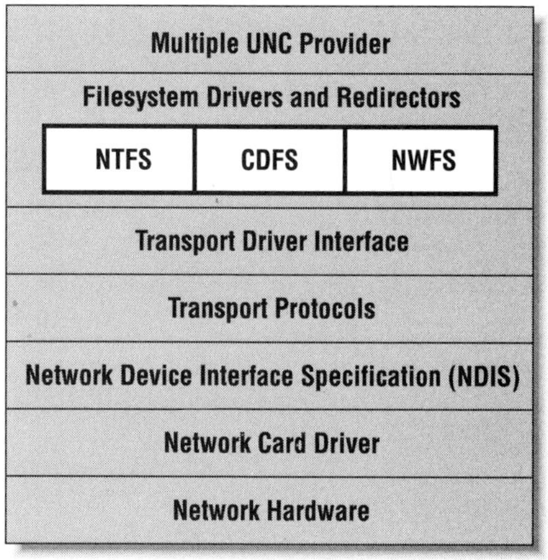

Figure 3-6. The I/O Manager

Windows NT/2000 Support for Open Datalink Interface

The Windows NT/2000 transport protocols use NDIS as the interface to network hardware. This interface provides a standard through which all network communication can occur, providing reliable support to the I/O Manager and other services.

The Windows NT/2000 client gives provision for Open Datalink Interface (ODI) via the NDIS network layer, by providing the ODI support layer below it, as shown in Figure 3-7. The ODI functionality should only be used if you require backward compatibility for ODI-aware applications. There are very few ODI drivers available for Windows NT/2000 and you should certainly consider using the NDIS layer exclusively unless you have a very specific case requiring ODI functionality.

NetWare Aware Application Support

The Windows NT/2000 virtual DOS machine can provide backwards compatible support for API calls to Virtual Load Modules (VLM) and IPX from DOS programs, through a Terminate and Stay Resident (TSR) program that is loaded from *AUTOEXEC.NT*. These TSRs intercept the API calls and route them through the 32-bit client libraries running in user mode and pass them to the I/O Manager. These VLM and IPX support modules are also used to support backward compatibility in 16-bit Windows programs.

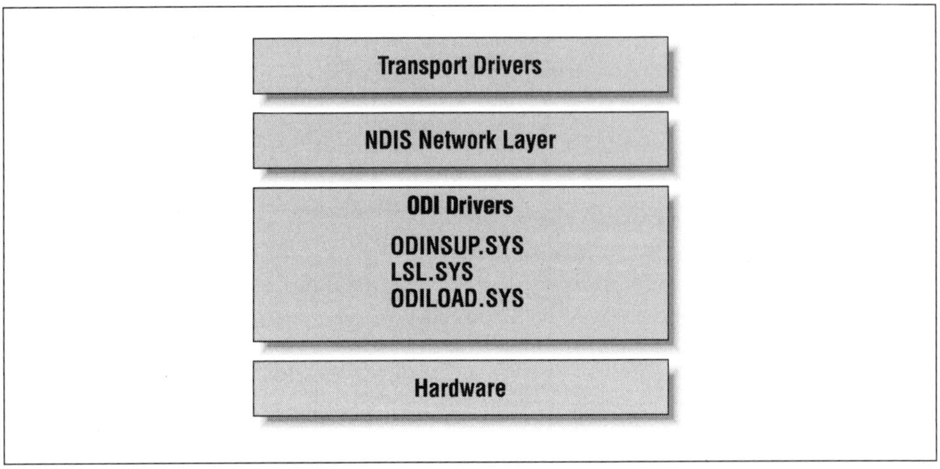

Figure 3-7. ODI support layer

Windows 32-bit applications requiring NetWare API calls are passed directly to the Novell 32-bit client libraries running in user mode, as shown in Figure 3-8.

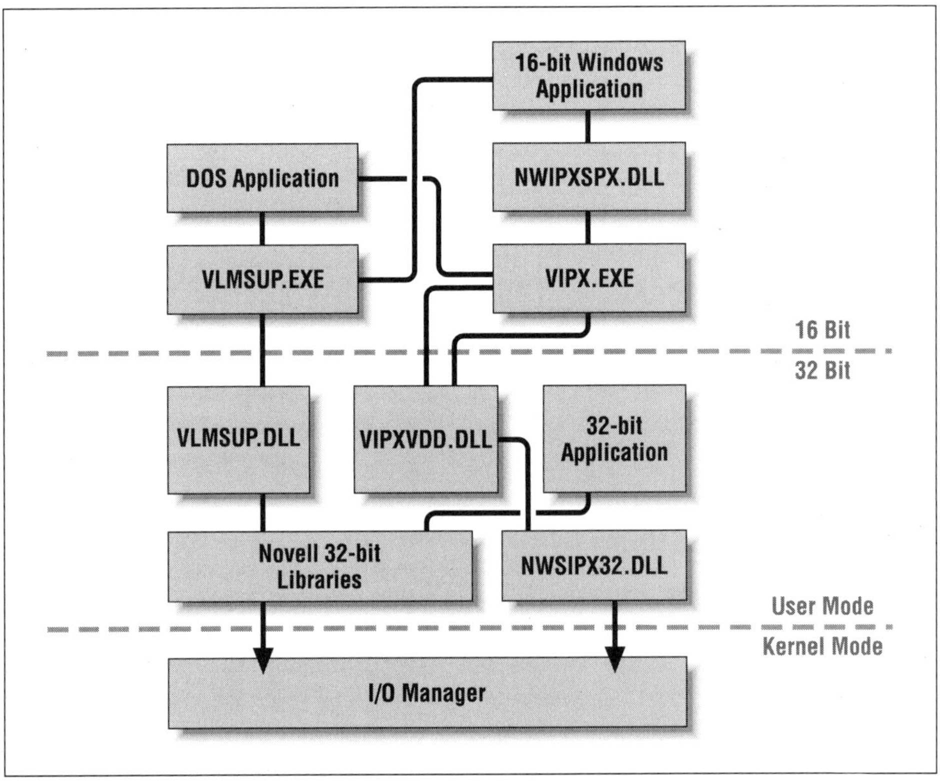

Figure 3-8. Windows NT application support

The Login Process

The normal login process under Windows NT/2000 uses a Graphical Identification and Authentication (GINA) component called *MSGINA.DLL*. This provides the user with a mechanism to enter the login details to authenticate to a Microsoft network. The NetWare client installs a new GINA called *NWGINA.DLL*, which replaces the Microsoft GINA as the Login Dialog Box greeting the user when he first logs in. The authentication GINA used for this purpose is stored in the registry location shown in Table 3-2.

Affected keys
HKEY_LOCAL_MACHINE\Software\Microsoft\WindowsNT\CurrentVersion\Winlogon

Table 3-2. The Login GINA

GINA	Value Name	Data Type	Value
Microsoft	GinaDLL	REG_SZ	MSGINA.DLL
NetWare	GinaDLL	REG_SZ	NWGINA.DLL

During the machine boot process, the Winlogon process reads this registry key and launches the GINA. The GINA requests the user to enter the login username and password pair that is passed to the NDS for authentication. After this authentication has occurred to the NDS, a subsequent authentication must be made to Windows NT. At this stage, the username and password pair are compared in the local machine and, if matched, allow the user into the workstation. The process of local authentication is carried out by Winlogon, which opens the workstation's SAM database with the username and password pair used for NetWare authentication. If the username and password pair do not match, the user is asked for a valid pair for the workstation. Access to the workstation will not be granted unless a valid pair is established.

If the Workstation Manager is running on the workstation and a Dynamic Local User policy is enabled in the NDS and associated with the user, a username and password will be created on the workstation. This allows the user to gain access to the workstation without a local user ID and password. The operation of the Workstation Manager is discussed later in this chapter and the Dynamic Local User Policy is discussed in Chapter 4.

The Network Provider

Windows NT/2000 permits a number of network service providers to exist within the network architecture. To accomplish this, each service provider must have its own network provider. The Microsoft provider is called NTLM, which services requests for LAN Manager functionality. This provider handles requests for Server Message Block (SMB) to LAN Manager-compliant servers, which underpins higher level services such as file and printer sharing. The Novell Network Provider for NT (*NOVNPNT*) sits alongside the NTLM, providing services to NetWare servers, which fully integrates into the Windows NT/2000 desktop environment.

Network-aware applications can use several mechanisms to establish a route to a resource, such as server or printer information. One such mechanism is a UNC connection, which routes through the MUP. The other is the Windows Networking API (WNet), which routes through the Multiple Provider Router (MPR). The MPR routes specific requests for Microsoft services through the NTLM provider (*NTLM.DLL*) and NetWare services through NetWare Provider (*NOVNPNT.DLL*). These service requests pass either through the Workstation Service or the Novell 32-bit client libraries, both running in user mode. The request is then passed directly to the appropriate filesystem redirector, as shown in Figure 3-9.

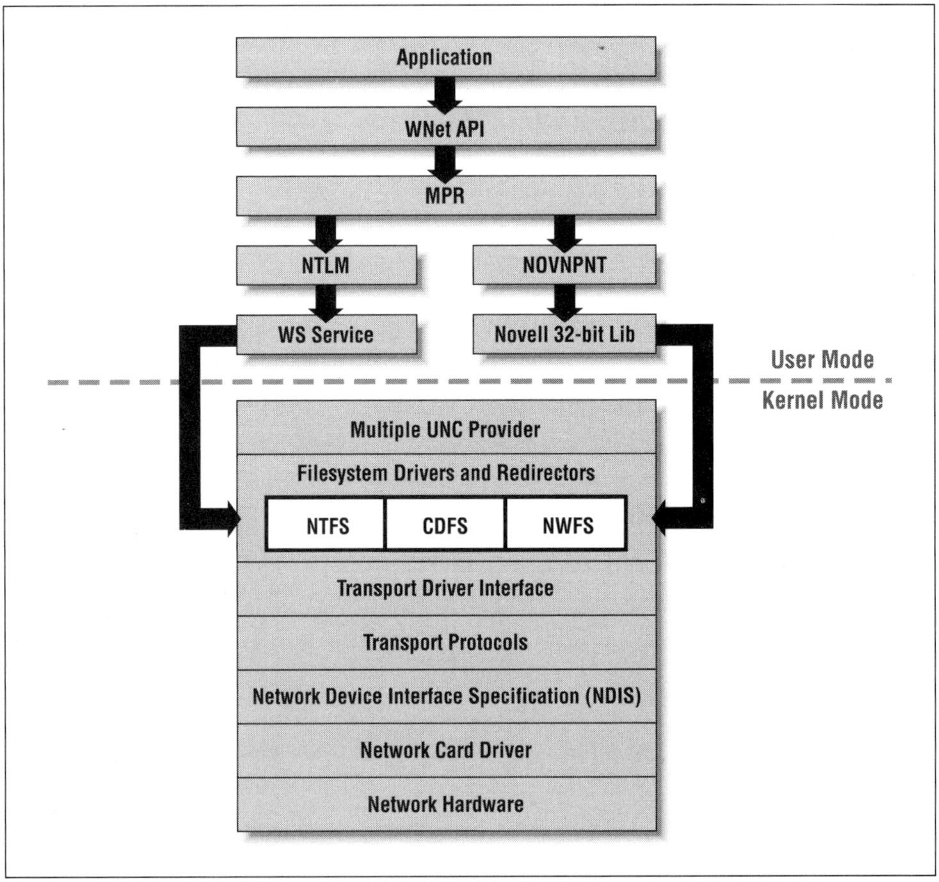

Figure 3-9. WNet application handling

The WNet integration allows applications such as Network Neighborhood and My Computer to handle NetWare service requests such as authentication, browsing, and drive mapping. It is also a very useful tool for getting NetWare volume information by right-clicking a volume icon and selecting Properties, as shown in Figure 3-10.

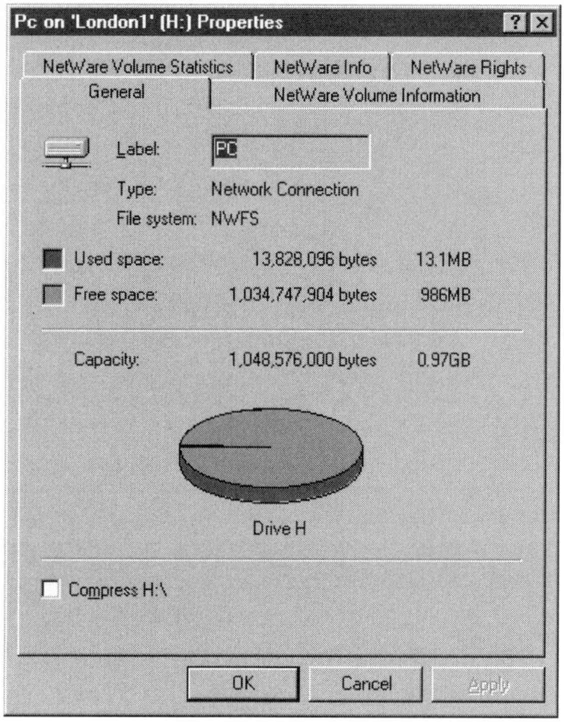

Figure 3-10. NetWare volume properties

Managing NetWare filesystem trustee rights and attributes is much easier through the GUI than having to use the *RIGHTS*, *GRANT*, and *REVOKE* commands from the Windows NT DOS command line. The attribute of a file can be viewed or modified through checkboxes when the File tab is visible. The rights function is more complicated, but you are essentially able to set effective rights to files or directories. This is accomplished through the rights page shown in Figure 3-11, by adding, modifying, or removing multiple trustees to the file and by assigning rights to the trustee. It is not possible (for security reasons) to modify Supervisor rights, although they are viewable in the page shown in Figure 3-12. Supervisor rights must be set through the *NWADMIN* program.

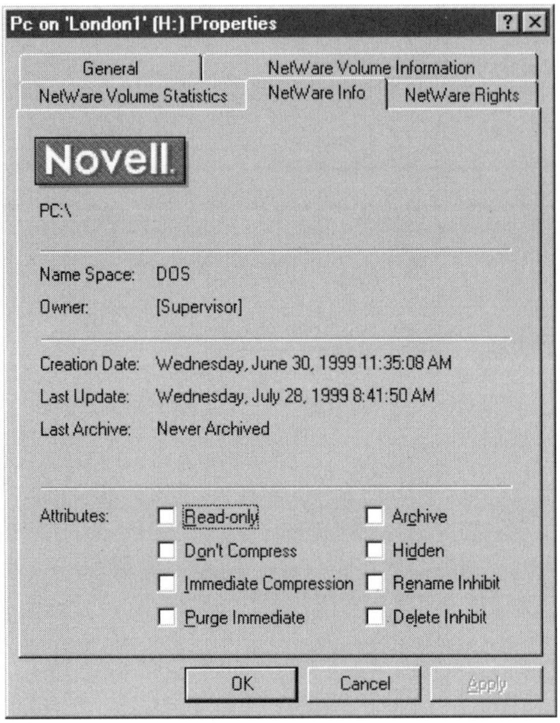

Figure 3-11. NetWare rights

The Print Provider

The functionality for print services is similar to the Network Provider discussed earlier in that it also uses the WNet API. The print job is passed through the Windows NT/2000 printer interface and then on to the Print Provider Router. The job is handed to the NetWare Spooler (*NWSPOOL.DLL*) and subsequently down through the network stack, as shown in Figure 3-13.

The Windows 95/98 Client

The Windows 95/98 client provides similar NetWare integrated functionality to that provided under Windows NT/2000 described earlier. However, the Windows 95/98 system architecture is quite different from Windows NT/2000 and, as a result, the integration is accomplished in a different way. The client is fully able to communicate with NetWare NDS and bindery-based servers and does so in a similar way to Windows 3.x; indeed, the code is based on the Windows 3.x 32-bit client.

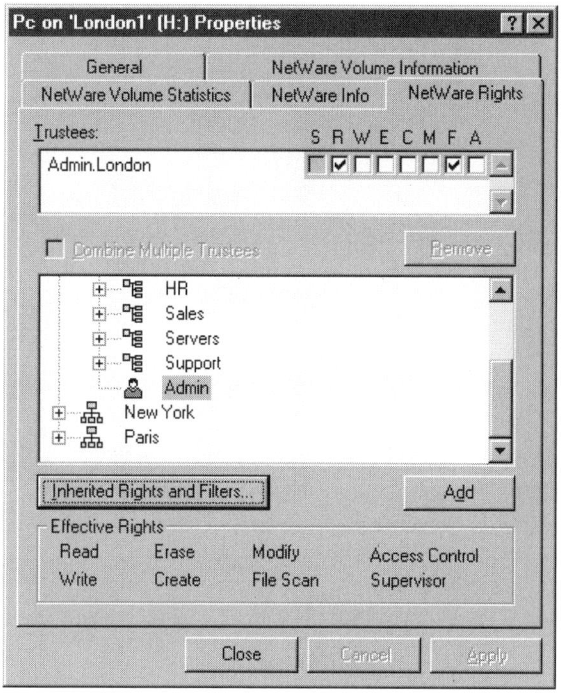

Figure 3-12. Trustee rights

Windows 95/98 Client Architecture

Windows 95/98 is a 32-bit operating system, which, unlike Window 3.1 and DOS, has networking built into the system architecture. The NetWare client for Windows 95/98 will not install any transport level network drivers and can use either NDIS or ODI LAN drivers for communication to the network hardware.

The client architecture of Windows 95/98 is shown in Figure 3-14 and is different from the Windows NT/2000 architecture. NT uses a redirector and filesystem driver whereas the Windows 95/98 client is more similar to the Windows 3.1 client, which also uses the NetWare I/O Subsystem (NIOS). This subsystem uses WNet APIs to handle its networking requirements. The Windows 95/98 operating system has full support for 16-bit applications by providing a 16-bit API to WNet, which is passed to the 16-bit user interface, *user.exe*. It is then handed on to the Multiple Provider Router (MPR). The application API functionality is discussed in the section "The Login Process."

The NetWare client is implemented as an interrupt 21 shell. Because there is no workable API operating above the IFS manager, the NetWare client intercepts

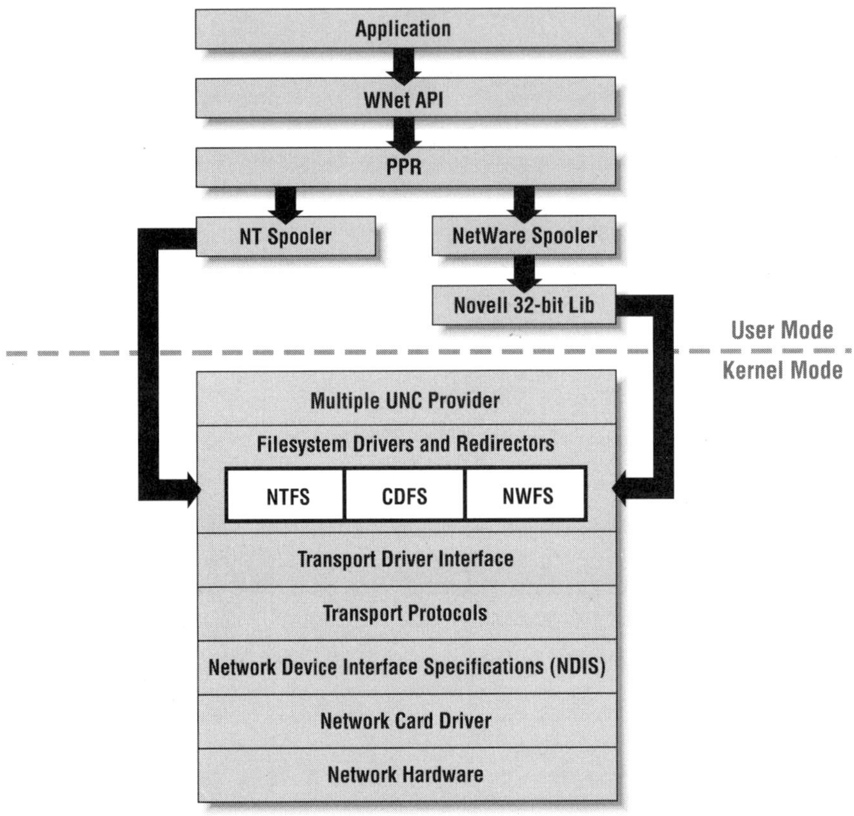

Figure 3-13. The Windows NT Print Provider

interrupt 21 and processes the information to ensure that any NetWare resource requests are routed through NetWare Client NIOS and any Microsoft requests through the IFS manager. The NetWare client provides the following functions:

- Support for the NetWare filesystem to Windows 95/98
- Integration into the Windows 95/98 Networking architecture
- Provision for NetWare print services
- Authentication to NetWare through the NetWare login GUI

NetWare Filesystem Integration

Microsoft uses filesystem drivers to provide filesystem redirection. These drivers are implemented as virtual (VXD) device drivers which are written in assembler

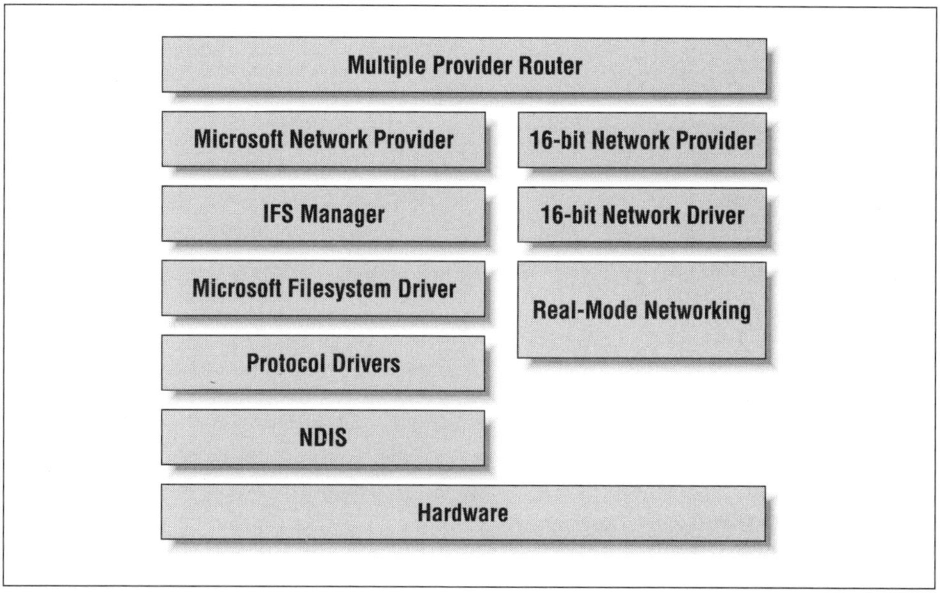

Figure 3-14. Window 95/98 architecture

and execute at ring zero. This is the mechanism used by Intel to gain access to resources in protected mode.

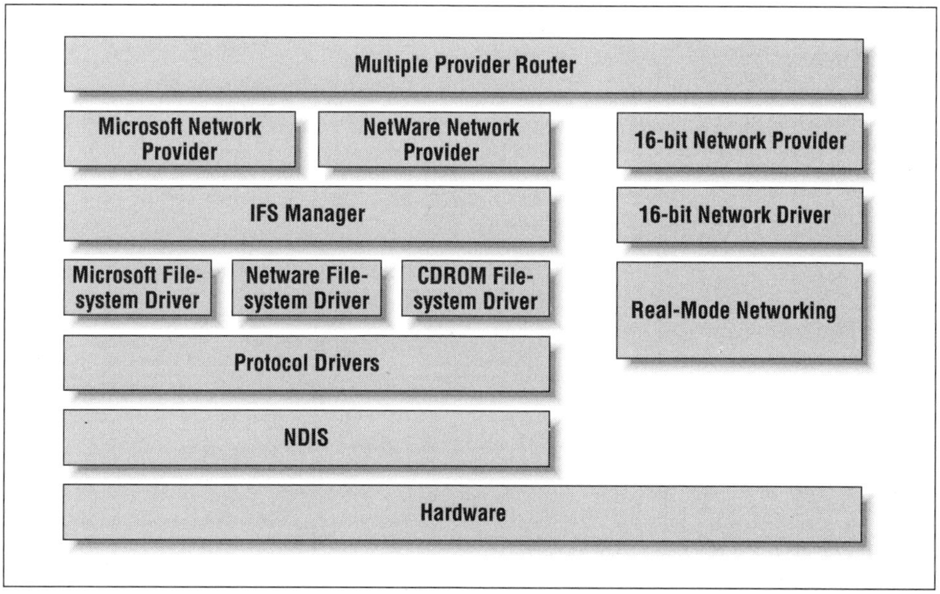

Figure 3-15. Microsoft and NetWare filesystem drivers

The Microsoft 32-bit redirectors use a Virtual Memory cache, implemented as a device driver that therefore runs in protected mode. This driver (*VCACHE.VXD*) is a wider ranging and smarter version of the Windows 3.x *SMARTDRV.SYS*, providing a dynamic memory pool and support for CDFS filesystems previously managed by *MSCDEX.EXE*, as shown in Figure 3-15.

The client for Windows 95/98 Network provider does not use the *VCACHE.VXD* for its memory management. It instead uses a separate cache provided by the NIOS interface. The NIOS is loaded through a Virtual Device Driver (*LOADER.VXD*), giving all the NLMs in the client kit access to extended memory. This includes the *NIOS.NLM* I/O Manager and the *CLIENT32.NLM* client requester that is responsible for all filesystem functionality and service tracking.

The Microsoft networking functionality is provided by a protocol called *Server Message Block* (SMB). This protocol allows services to be provided from Microsoft Servers and is also used for peer-to-peer communications. The NetWare equivalent of this is the NetWare Core Protocol (NCP). It is installed as part of the 32-bit Windows 95/98 client and works through the session multiplexor for the provision of NetWare file services.

Windows 95/98 Support for Open Data Interface

Under Windows 95/98, the Microsoft-provided ODI support module exists as a shim below the NDIS layer between it and the network hardware. After the Client 32 Software has been installed, the support for ODI is provided by placing an ODI driver beside the NDIS layer. This driver shim communicates between the Link Support Layer (LSL) and the network hardware, as shown in Figure 3-16. There is also provision in this model for NDIS support with the provision of a shim above the NDIS layer to provide LSL to NDIS translation.

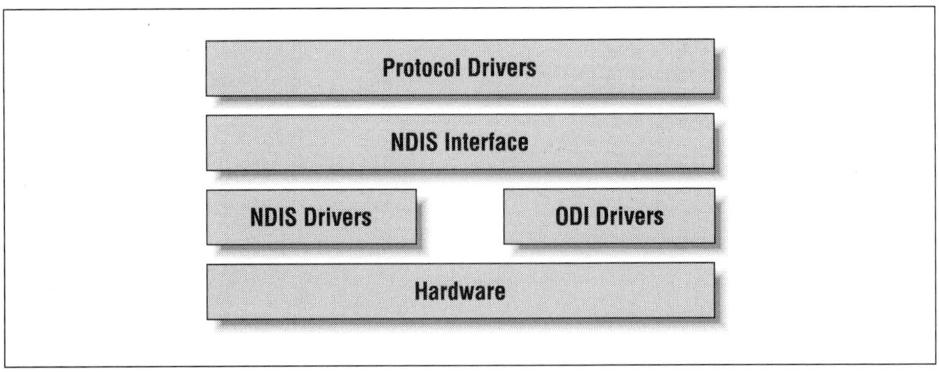

Figure 3-16. ODI support in Windows 95/98

Support for 16-bit ODI drivers is provided for with the provision of a layer between the LSL and the 16-bit real-mode driver. This is provided via a 32- to 16-bit translation NLM, which is an ODI driver as far as LSL is concerned, but actually provides an interface between the two layers.

Application Support

Windows 95/98 is Microsoft's direct replacement for DOS and Windows 3.x and, because of this, it not only has to be able to handle 32-bit applications, but 16-bit applications, even catering to DOS real-mode demands as well. This places challenges not only on the operating system, but also on the NetWare client's backward compatible support provision.

The Login Process

The login process under Windows 95/98 is not strictly necessary, but if the Microsoft client is installed in the network stack, then it will be presented to the user during the boot process. This client provides the user with a mechanism to enter the login details to authenticate to a Microsoft network.

After the NetWare Client has been installed, a new GUI login utility (*LOGINW95.EXE*) is presented to the user allowing authentication to a bindery or NDS NetWare network. There is provision for login script execution and support for Workstation Manager desktop management. The NetWare GUI login utility is similar to the Microsoft client in which you can simply cancel the login and gain access to the local system. This feature can be disabled through the use of a policy that can be forced on the user provided the policy is enabled as described in Chapter 4, and provided the Workstation Manager is running on the workstation as described in "The Workstation Manager," later in this chapter.

During the Windows 95 boot process, the NetWare login program automatically starts asking the user for login credentials. The user enters his username and password, which is then passed to the network provider for authentication. Upon successful login to NetWare, the username and password pair is cached and subsequently used for access to the Windows 95 workstation. Access to the Windows 95/98 operating system can be made a great deal more secure by using a policy to force authentication before access is granted. These policies are discussed in detail in Chapter 4. The program will then start to search the tree for a policy associated with the user and, when it is found, allows the Workstation Manager to execute it.

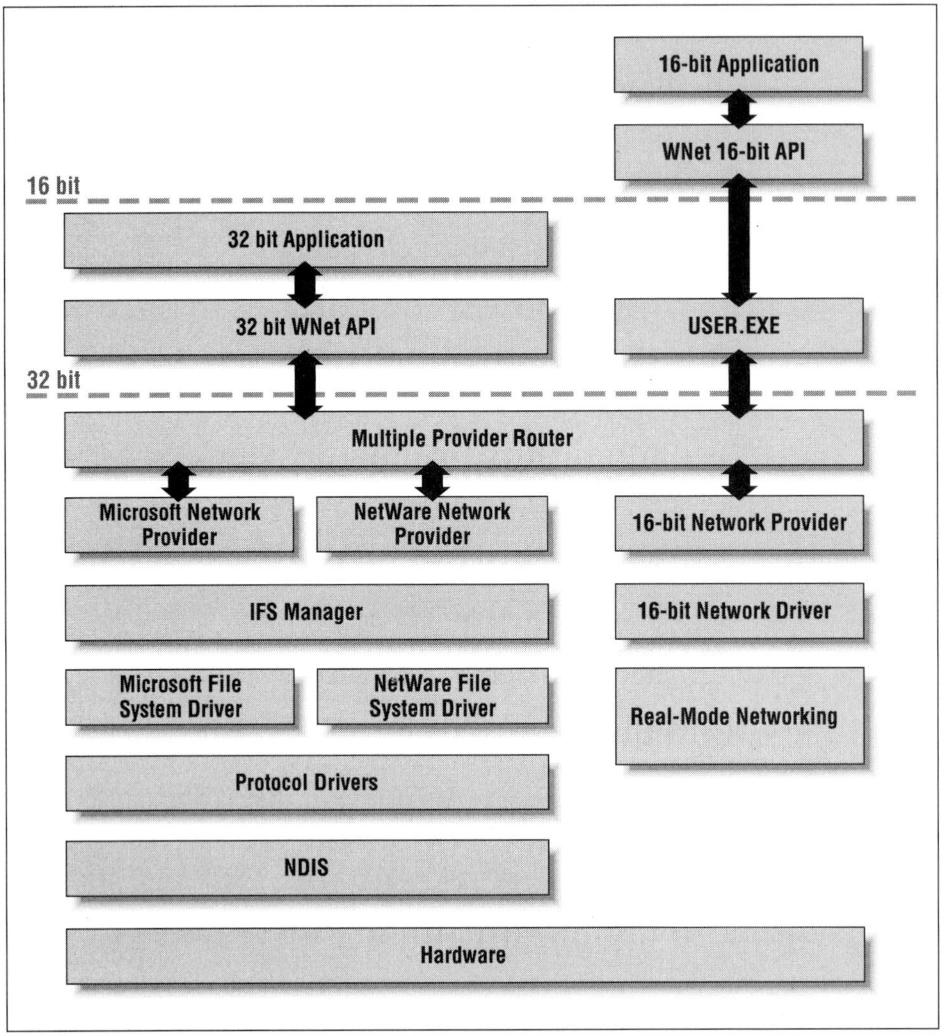

Figure 3-17. Windows 95/98 application handling

The Network Provider

The Windows 95 networking architecture allows for more than one provider of network services. In order for NetWare services to be fully accessible, the client installation installs provider software allowing NetWare services to be fully integrated into the desktop environment. Under Windows NT/2000, the provider specifically requires WNet functionality to support the provision of desktop integration. In the case of Windows 95/98, this is supported because most services under Windows 95/98 are supplied via WNet anyway.

The Windows 95/98 provider allows utilities such as My Computer, Network Neighborhood, and the Windows Explorer to be fully functional with NetWare services including:

- NetWare network browsing for servers and trees
- NetWare authentication to servers and trees available in the Browse window
- Drive mapping via server volume browsing, including map root and search drive mapping
- Printer browsing and capturing

The connection and execution of services via standard UNC pathnames is also supported via applications and shortcuts. The NetWare volume information is also available by right clicking a volume icon and selecting Properties. This is very similar to the tool available under Windows NT/2000, shown earlier in Figure 3-10.

The DOS utilities for managing NetWare filesystem trustee rights and attributes is provided for via a GUI. This is also made visible by right clicking a volume, folder, or file in the browser window. The attribute of a file can be viewed or modified by selecting the File tab. The GUI rights function is available and, as with Windows NT/2000, allows you to set effective rights to files or directories by selecting the Rights tab, which is similar to that shown earlier in Figure 3-11. Trustee rights can also be assigned through the GUI by adding, modifying, or removing multiple trustees to the file, similar to that shown in Figure 3-12. As with Windows NT/2000, it is not possible to modify Supervisor rights, although they can be seen within the page. Supervisor rights must be set through the *NWADMIN* program.

The Print Provider

Windows 95/98 does not require a physical device port such as LPT1 to be redirected for printing to occur via a network print queue. The printer can be added in the standard way via the Add Printer function, allowing you to browse the NDS and select an already installed print queue. Select a print driver in the usual way and the printer will be set up.

The Windows 3.x Client

Windows 3.x is an addition to DOS that allows GUI programs to be run in extended memory. The architecture of Windows 3.x had no allowance for networking until Windows 3.11 for Workgroups arrived, and then networking was really only an add-on for Microsoft networking.

The NetWare Windows 3.x client is a 32-bit protected-mode interface that adds networking functionality without using real memory. The client does not require a

DOS network layer, but provides a protected environment similar to the NetWare server architecture. There is provision for NetWare Loadable Modules (NLMs) that are loaded into extended memory.

Windows 3.x Client Architecture

The Windows 32-bit client is built around the NetWare I/O Subsystem (NIOS), and provides an interface between the client 32-bit protected-mode environment and the operating system. This component (*NIOS.EXE*) is loaded to provide the flat-memory environment for the NLM launcher. The NIOS subsystem requires a memory manager (*HIMEM.SYS*) to be present on the workstation as it does not have its own memory manager.

There are clear advantages to using the 32-bit Client because of the way it uses extended memory rather that the DOS components in real memory. This is particularly the case where the workstation has devices requiring device drivers loaded into real memory such as CD-ROM and multimedia devices. The addition of these devices, together with the standard DOS network stack, place exceptional requirements on the memory below 1 MB. The result of an overloaded real memory is that you may be able to load Windows, but can run very few programs.

Because the NIOS system loads the network stack into extended memory, you will need to ensure that the machine has sufficient memory to allow for this and any Windows requirements.

The Windows 3.x Client 32 communicates to network services using the ODI. The network components are loaded into extended memory and include a Link Support Layer, an IPX protocol support module, Virtual Load Module along with TCP/IP, and several others that you may optionally load to support configuration (see Figure 3-18).

The Client 32 Requester is a major component which supports a host of functions, all of which are contained in *CLIENT32.NLM*. This mode provides support for file redirection, print services, NDS and bindery support, along with NETX and VLM-aware DOS application support.

The Workstation Manager

During the client installation, discussed in Chapter 2, *The ZENworks Installation*, one of the installation options is a component called the Workstation Manager which runs on the client. This component faithfully carries out your work. The tasks performed by the Workstation Manager vary from creating and deleting accounts on the local NT Workstation, making changes to the registry, and running inventories to collect hardware or software information.

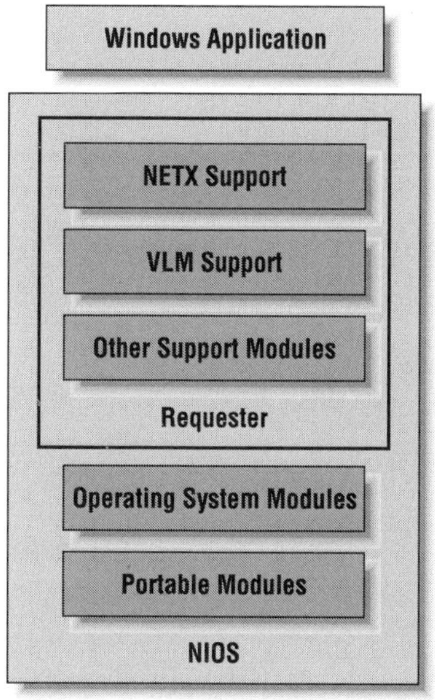

Figure 3-18. NIOS architecture

The work carried out by the Workstation Manager is centrally configured in the NDS policy objects associated with the operating system platform. These policy objects target either users or workstations according to the type of work being done. All work done by the Workstation Manager under Windows NT/2000 is run with System privileges so that the user has no need for any extra workstation rights. The policy objects are covered in detail in Chapter 4.

The Login Process

During the user login process, the NWGINA will check the user object for a policy associated with it. If the policy is present, it will be opened and any work to be performed will be inserted into the schedule to be executed at the appropriate time. If a policy is not found for the individual user object, then any group objects associated with the user will be checked for associated policies. If the user is a member of more that one group, the first group to have a policy will have the policy obeyed and all other groups with associated policies will be ignored. If no groups are found with associated policies, the user's parent container will be checked and then the parent above that and so on until the search reaches the root of the tree.

The Workstation Manager has a few configuration details, as shown in Figure 3-19. These details allow you to enable the Workstation Manager and to enter the trusted tree. The Workstation Manager is enabled when you install it. If for any reason you wish to disable it, say, for some test purpose, you may do so here rather than uninstalling the component.

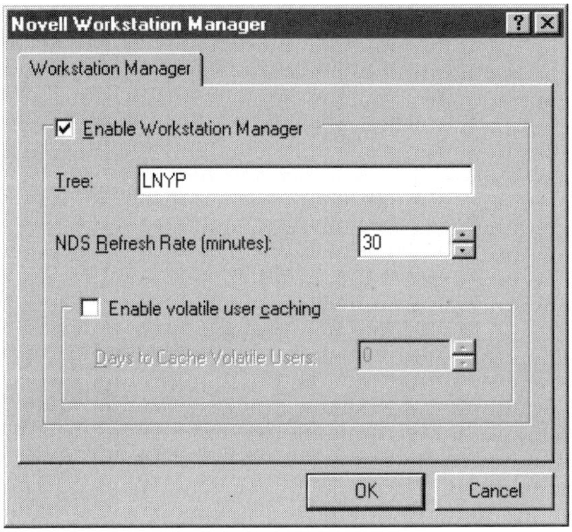

Figure 3-19. The Workstation Manager configuration page

The trusted tree is a very important concept. You must indicate which trust is granted to which tree. The work carried out by the Workstation Manager is run with system privileges and only the work defined by you should be allowed to be carried out. A good example of this is account creation under Windows NT/2000 via Dynamic Local User. When this policy is enabled in the Windows NT/2000 User Policy, the Workstation Manager will create the account on the workstation, allowing you to log in.

While this is an essential part of the Windows NT/2000 workstation authentication process, it can be seen as a potential security loophole for Windows NT/2000 workstations, if the trusted tree setting is allowed to be modified by users. The security of the system can be compromised if another NetWare tree was installed by a user within your organization. If the user is able to modify the trusted tree setting, then he may be able to gain privileged access to the workstation. The user would only have to enter his tree from the NetWare Login Dialog Box and have a policy obeyed that grants access with Administrator privileges. The best way of avoiding this problem is to define a trusted tree in the Workstation Manager dialog box and protect it from the users. In addition, it is beneficial to disallow the users from seeing the Advanced button in the Login Dialog Box.

The trusted tree is important for Windows NT/2000 users. It must be protected against users who may modify the tree name to attempt to gain privileged access to the NT Workstation. In general Windows NT users are given user access to the workstation. Any attempt to assign greater rights to the user could breach the security of your NT workstations.

The login process begins with the operating system, the NetWare client, and then the Workstation Manager. We shall examine the whole process for Windows NT/2000, Windows 95/98, and Windows 3.x to help understand how it works.

Operating system boot

The three operating systems in question boot in different ways, but during that process the client GUI login screen is called to accept the username and password pair.

Authentication

The username and password pair are sent to the NDS and the user object is opened to check if the password is correct. If it is correct, a success message is sent to the client. If not, an error is returned and displayed to the user. The error message will depend upon whether the password was wrong or the user ID does not exist.

Policy check

The NetWare client will check to see if there is a policy package associated with the user and the workstation. If a policy package is found, it will be opened and the contents executed by the Workstation Manager, including creating a local NT account for the user if Dynamic Local User is set in the policy package (see Chapter 4 for more details about Dynamic Local User). In some cases, the work to be performed on the client is not scheduled to run during login, but at another scheduled time or event. In this case the task is stored in the scheduler to be performed by the workstation later. If the Workstation Manager is not installed or is not running, then the policy contents will be ignored. In the case of Windows NT/2000, if the user ID and password matches a local credential set, the user will be logged in. If the credential set is not valid on the workstation, the user will have to enter a valid user ID and password for the workstation before he is allowed to continue the login process.

Continue boot

After the Workstation Manager has finished, the boot process continues and any registry modification made by the Workstation Manager through policies in the policy packages will be valid and enforced when the user shell is executed.

Complete login

The login script is executed and, if the script is executed synchronously, this will have to complete before the user shell is executed and the workstation desktop is built.

If you wish to use policies in the policy packages to force the workstation desktop into a presentable state or to permit authenticated login to Windows NT/2000, you must install and enable the Workstation Manager.

The Help Requester

The Help Requester is basically a tool to enable the user to contact or send problems to the Helpdesk. There are 16-bit and 32-bit versions of the program, allowing it to be used on all supported platforms. The program is opened when the user executes the program, which should be placed in a useful location such as the desktop. The user is presented with a window similar to that in Figure 3-20. This window presents details about who to contact on the Helpdesk and the contact details. There is also a mechanism to allow the user to send a message or query via email.

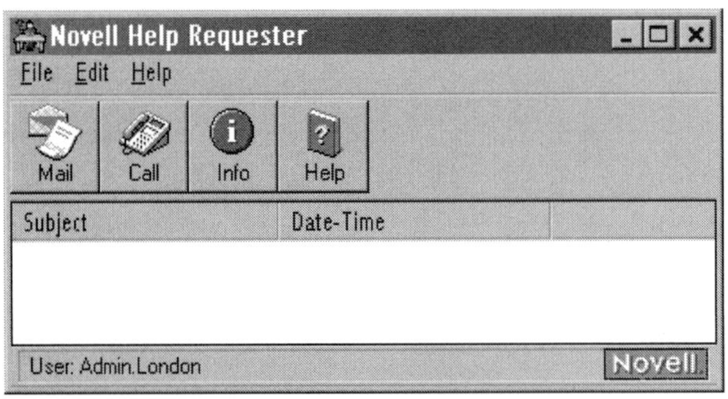

Figure 3-20. The Help Requester

The configuration details for the Helpdesk are stored in the NDS through a policy package. The policy governing the use of the Help Requester can be configured differently by associating a different policy package for each group of users. More details about how to configure the Help Requester can be found in Chapter 4.

Users frequently have trouble finding out who to contact about a problem, and when they do contact the Helpdesk, they are unable to tell the Helpdesk operator who they are (in NDS terms). This information is available to the user through the Info button. The contact details are displayed, as configured in the policy package, along with the user's login details.

If the user (or you) decides that the best way to get appropriate help is by raising a trouble ticket via an email, then a message can be prepared and sent to a preconfigured email address. The user is able to select a subject line to summarize the problem, which is also preconfigured in the policy package. This will allow the trouble ticket to flow through the Helpdesk email processor (if the function is supported by your Helpdesk software) to the correct software support person. To make use of the email functionality, you will either have to be using Groupwise email or have a MAPI configured agent installed to forward the message.

A Final Word

The ZENworks client is an important and complex part of the product which should give very little trouble. If you do have problems with the client, understanding how it works is really the only way of troubleshooting and fixing the problem. When something goes wrong it is usually for a logical reason. Try to analyze what is actually going on, and you will usually find that the problem is quite straightforward.

4

ZENworks Policy Packages

ZENworks policy packages have been engineered to help you manage two essential components: the user and the workstation. In most organizations these components account for a significant portion of the work performed by the IT department. When managing these components, a balanced view needs to be taken regarding how much to restrict and how much to allow, but in general it is probably best to restrict as much as possible. The degree to which you do either will be defined by the requirements derived from you IT strategy. In this chapter we will review the management of both users and workstations on Windows NT/ 2000, Windows 95/98, and Windows 3.x. A policy package is a set of rules which governs the basis upon which a user is granted access to workstations and the way the workstation is presented to the user. There is a policy package for each platform which governs the user (user policy package) and for each platform that governs the workstation (workstation policy package), each of which exists as a separate type of NDS policy package object. There is also a policy package, which improves the performance overhead associated with policy packages (container policy package), by restricting policy searches within the NDS.

> Do not be confused between ZENworks policy packages and Windows policies. Policy packages contain a series of policies, some of which are not covered by any Windows policies. Windows policies can be implemented as a policy within a policy package, and are specifically referred to as user and computer policies.

Policy packages will allow you to restrict and manage your workstations and users by configuring policy package objects within the NDS and associating these objects to a user or workstation. The policy package is implemented at some time while the user is using the workstation (usually at login time), by the Workstation Manager, which is running on the workstation. The policy package can also be actioned by some event trigger, such as the logout process or at other scheduled times. Any changes to the policy package will automatically be replicated to the associated users or workstations without having to make a personal visit, because all the configuration details are contained centrally within the NDS policy package object.

Policy packages are a very important and powerful feature of ZENworks. It is through these objects that most of the desktop management features are enabled. It is worthwhile spending time considering and planning the use of these objects, regardless of the size of your organization. The Windows NT policy package is valid for Windows 2000 as well as Windows NT, but you will need to ensure that the Windows NT/2000 client is installed on the workstation.

NDS Considerations

As far as the NDS is concerned, users and workstations are very similar in function. This is because the NDS is supplying a service to both of these objects via the policy packages. If you have installed a policy package, which is associated with users, the closer this policy is to that user the better. This is also true of workstation objects, which should also be close to the policy packages associated with them.

If your NDS is partitioned by WAN infrastructure, it is likely that the users and workstations will be distributed in containers at the remote office. In this case you may have very similar policy packages located in different containers which target users and workstations in those remote offices. You should also implement a Container policy package to ensure performance is not degraded. For all policy packages the following rules should be used:

Container policy location
: The container policy should be created at the highest level required for that associated user or workstation, and no higher. This will allow you to set the search characteristics appropriate for the group of users or workstations being targeted.

User policy
: This policy should be created as close to the user objects as possible in order to reduce NDS search time. Improve the performance further by using a container policy as well.

Workstation policies
: The workstation policies should be placed as close as possible to the workstations objects. A container policy to improve performance is desirable here also.

NDS performance is affected if you do not give careful consideration to the location of policy packages. Policies are a crucial part of the desktop management features of ZENworks and will probably affect a large number of your users, if not all of them. It is worth giving careful consideration to their placement in the NDS.

Creating Policy Packages

To create a policy package you will need to be attached to a server with equivalent ADMIN privileges in order to run the *NWADMIN* program. The location of a policy package can affect NDS performance if the location is not carefully considered. The issues surrounding ZENworks objects and the NDS is discussed in detail in Chapter 2, *The ZENworks Installation*, and above in the previous section. All work performed on policy package objects must be performed through the *NWADMIN* program, which is available for Windows NT/2000 and Windows 95/98. This program will not work under Windows 3.x.

When you have decided on a location, select the container where the policy packages are to be created and press the INS key. When you are presented with the Create Object dialog box select Policy Package and you will be presented with the Policy Package Wizard shown in Figure 4-1. Select the package to be created and give it a name. This name should reflect the purpose of the object (although it can be renamed later). If the policy package is being created to govern access for the Finance Department who use Windows NT/2000, call it, say, NT User Finance. If the policy is to grant Administrator access to NT Workstation, call it Windows NT user Administrator, etc. After finishing this screen, you are able to select which policies in the policy package to implement and configure, or you can leave them unchecked and modify the policies later.

It is entirely likely that you will have more than one policy package, but it is not possible to have more than one policy package per user or workstation governing a singe platform. For instance, it is possible to have a Windows NT policy and a Windows 95/98 policy associated with a user, but not two Windows NT policy packages for the same user. During the login process, the workstation client will search for the policy package governing that platform for the user. If the user is using Windows 95 and there is more than one Windows 95 policy package associated with the user, then which should be used? In reality, the *NWADMIN* program will not permit a second policy package association of the same type with the same user or workstation.

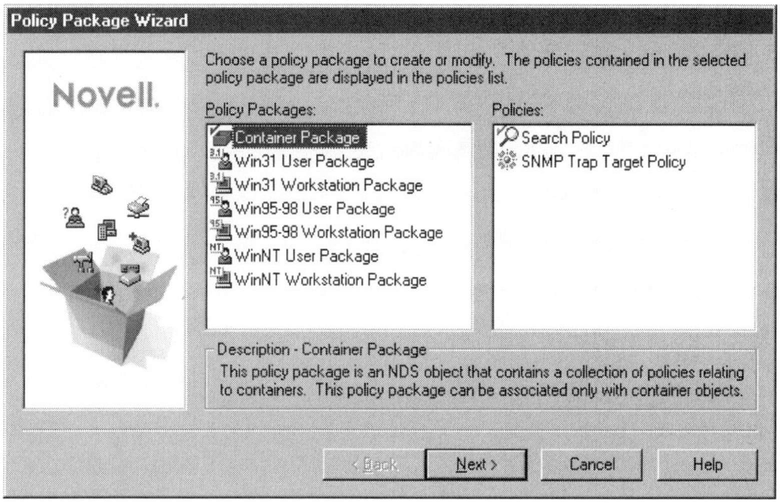

Figure 4-1. The Policy Package Wizard

Minimum Recipe for NDS-Authenticated Access to Windows NT/2000 Workstation

1. Install and configure the client on the workstation.
2. Install the Workstation Manager on the workstation and configure it to use your NDS tree.
3. Set up a Windows NT user policy in the NDS, which authenticates access using NetWare credentials, via Dynamic Local user. Associate the user policy with a user ID.
4. Reboot the workstation and log in with that user ID.

To modify the contents of the policy package, select the policy package object and press the Enter key. You are now shown a view of the policy package in Figure 4-2, which is a Windows NT user policy package. Click the Associations button on the right and a page will appear allowing you to define which user/workstation, group of users/workstations, or container with which to associate the policy package. The association is very important as it dictates which user or workstation will be affected by the policy package. The association is a task to be left for last after all the policies within the policy package have been closely examined. You may wish to just associate a test ID or test workstation initially in order to perform testing.

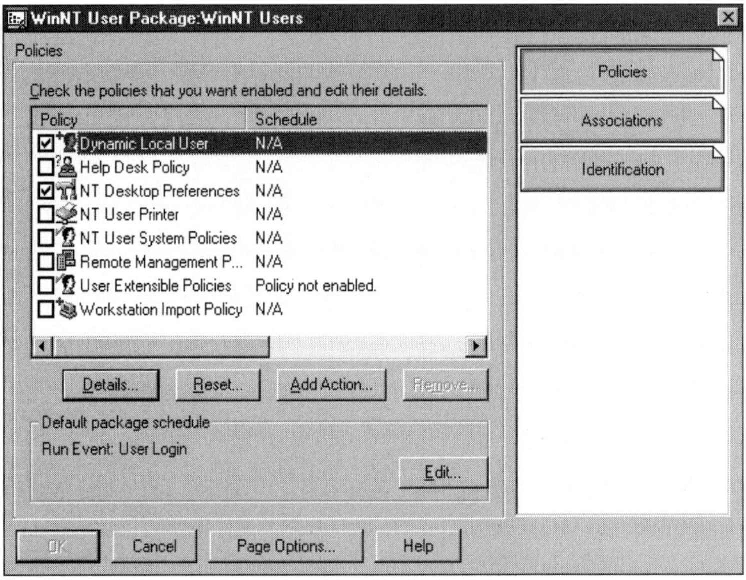

Figure 4-2. The NT user policy package

The Windows NT user policy package is shown in Figure 4-2 with the Full Pack installed. In the center of the Policy Viewer is the list of policies available. This list will vary according to which policy package platform is being viewed and which pack (Starter Pack or Full Pack) you have installed. The details of which policies are available in each pack is discussed in Chapter 2. The policies will be enabled by checking the boxes beside them.

Each policy has configuration settings within, which vary greatly according to which policy is being viewed. These settings are accessed via the Details button. The settings and the issues surrounding them will be the main focus in this chapter.

Adding Actions

As well as the actions listed in the policy packages, you are also able to add your own *action*. An action is a task or series of tasks that you require to be performed on the workstation. This action can be either a *.exe* or *.dll* file. The action will be carried out at scheduled times, as explained in the next section. Actions are a very useful way of carrying out housekeeping tasks, such as disk defragmentations, virus checking, tidying the local hard disk, etc. Actions are really no different than policies within the policy package. Policies are actions or a series of actions that are implemented by the workstation manager.

The Policy Scheduler

If you installed the Workstation Manager on the workstation as part of the install process, then the ZENworks scheduler will be running on the workstation (Windows NT/2000 and Windows 95/98 only). The scheduler is operated from within the policy package and can be modified from the main window by clicking the Edit button. The default schedule is shown in Figure 4-3, where the selected item within the policy has a policy schedule type set to Event. The Event in this case is User Login. This event is reasonable in most cases, because most policies require the action to be performed at that time. It is usually possible to change the event to something else or to change the action to occur at a different time rather than be event driven.

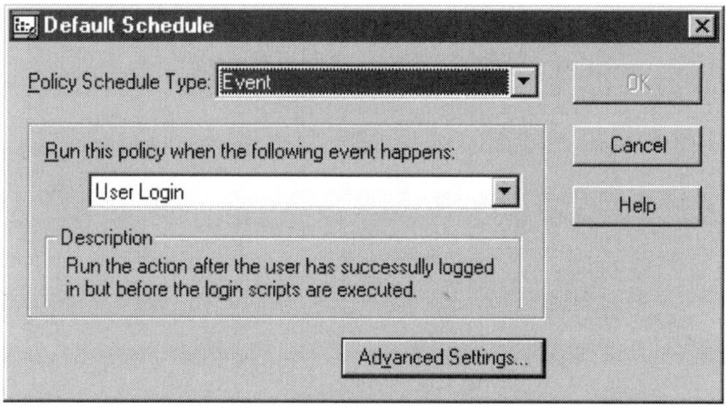

Figure 4-3. The NT user scheduler options

The Scheduler provides a series of hooks called events, which can be used to perform the action at a time more suited to your requirements. The most obvious event is a User Login. The problem with User Login is that a great deal is scheduled to happen during this event and the user will soon get fed up if you schedule too many actions in that slot. Where possible, it may be wise if you can schedule actions for later. There are several good candidates for this later time, including when the screen saver is active, which obviously implies that the user is not using the workstation, or when the workstation is locked. These seem obvious choices for work, which can be rescheduled. Another good event to make use of is shutdown. You may want to perform a series of tidy up routines, backups, quota checks, or whatever at this time.

> If you schedule too much work to occur during login, the users will complain, "Why does it take so long to login?" As a general rule, if you can schedule the work to occur at a later time, then do it!

The Scheduler can also be set to run a specific action at specific times. The times available are daily, weekly, monthly, and yearly. These times are useful for very routine jobs such as inventory. You may, for example, only wish to collect the hardware inventory every month, because it really isn't going to change much on a daily basis.

The Package Scheduler is highly configurable and more settings are available after pressing the Advanced Settings button, as shown in Figure 4-4. Within this set of pages you will be able to set options to cater for such things as completion. What should be done after the action has completed? Another area to consider is what to do if a fault occurs. Should the scheduler keep trying to run the job indefinitely or just reschedule it? You may wish to allow the action to occur with full system rights. To do this, use the Impersonation option and set it to System. The insecure system is very similar to system, but allows the action to interact with the user during execution. This can be considered dangerous because the user will be able to affect the course of an action which is running privileged, which is why it is referred to as "Insecure."

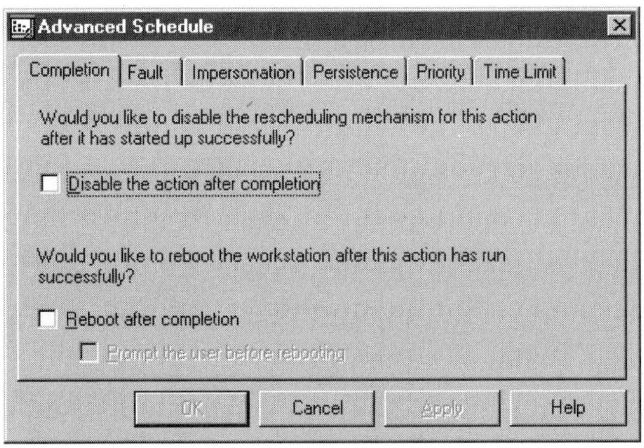

Figure 4-4. Scheduler Advanced settings

Windows NT Dynamic Local User

Windows NT/2000 is a secure operating system requiring some kind of authentication to grant access to the system. The ZENworks user policy package Dynamic Local User grants access to the NT Workstation and defines the criteria by which the user may use it. If you wish to use Windows NT/2000 Workstation on your desktops, then you will probably have to implement this policy package or you will not be able to grant access to users, unless you either use a Windows

NT/2000 Domain Controller or create local accounts on each workstation. In either of these latter cases, you will end up with multiple authentication domains to manage. The Windows NT-specific policy Dynamic Local User is designed to grant access to the secure NT workstation and can do so without creating new authentication domains.

Use Dynamic Local User to grant access to Windows NT/2000 by authenticating to the NDS. The account is created on the Workstation and can either remain or be removed after logout.

From the Details page in the policy package, shown in Figure 4-5, you are able to configure settings to allow you to either use the NetWare credentials or define an account to be used each time. If there is an existing account on the system that you wish to use, then managing existing accounts is the obvious choice, but this option can be useful for other reasons. In this case, the policy package is also particularly useful for tidying up after a crashed session, when used in conjunction with the Volatile User. This option will remove the account when the user logs out. This seems a sensible choice for a large network of shared systems with a large number of users (such as a university), but because the user is recreated each time she logs in, she will be assigned a new Security Identifier (SID). Any files left on the local workstation will not be owned by her when she logs back in again, even though she has the same username. The solution to this, of course, is for users to save personal work on a network volume and not the hard disk. The final step is to select a Windows NT local group to place the user into. The default value is the local group users, but you can select a different one or even a selection of them. If the policy package is particularly specialized, you can create a local group with specific rights using the Custom button, which will create the group on the workstation and place the user into that group.

Each Windows NT user is assigned a unique identification number called a Security Identifier (SID). When a user is deleted from the system, the SID is never re-used for reasons of security. All files on an NTFS file system that are owned by the user are identified by their SID and not by their username. If you use Dynamic Local User and remove the account after the user has logged out, the user will no longer own any files saved to the NT Workstation when she next logs into it.

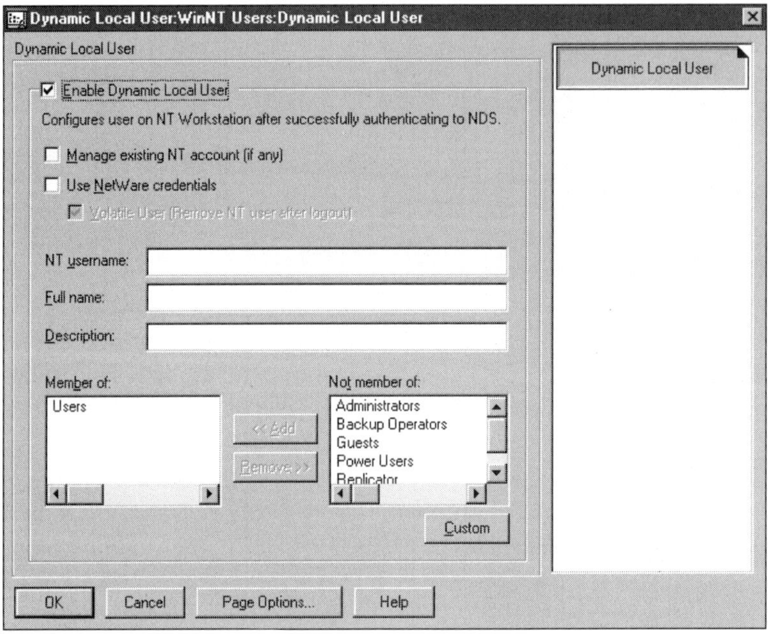

Figure 4-5. Windows NT Dynamic Local User

The Helpdesk Policy

The Helpdesk policy is available in the Windows NT, Windows 95/98, and Windows 3.x user policy packages. It defines the configuration of the Help Requester, which is discussed fully in Chapter 3, *The NetWare Clients and Related Components*. The Details button will reveal two pages, which are selectable from the Information and Configuration buttons on the right. The information page supplies the user with contact details such as email address and phone number. The Configuration page allows you to enable the Help Requester and configure the mechanism for sending help requests or trouble tickets via email. This is particularly useful if your Helpdesk software accepts Helpdesk requests and automatically files them within the database. If your Helpdesk system also automatically routes trouble tickets to a particular IT specialist or group according to the subject line, then these subject lines can be entered here, where they can be selected by the user. There is potential for the user to select the entirely wrong subject here, especially if there are a lot of them. It may be wise to present the user with just a few subjects to avoid confusion.

The Desktop Preferences Policy

Desktop Preferences define standards for the user's desktop environment and are available under Windows NT/2000 and Windows 95/98. This policy is used both to disable functionality (see also user and system policies), and to set corporate image and standards. The policy consists of two sections covering the Control Panel and the Roaming Profile.

Control Panel

The Control Panel page, shown in Figure 4-6, will allow you to define settings that standardize and/or hide some of the control panels. This is achieved by centrally defining what those settings should be and forcing them on the user during the login process. In general the settings are the same or similar to the control panels already available within the operating system. One of the main differences is the absence of test buttons and areas, for the keyboard and mouse. To access the control panels, use the mouse to double click on the icon.

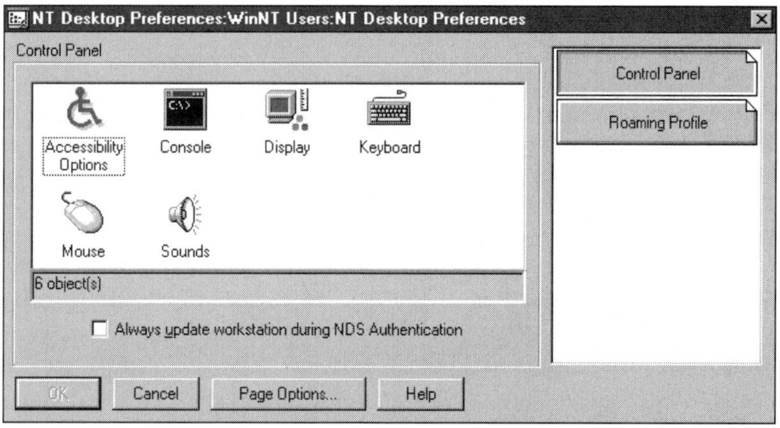

Figure 4-6. Windows NT Control Panel

Roaming and Mandatory Profiles

A Roaming Profile is a mechanism to allow the user to store his personal settings on a network server (see Figure 4-7). This way, the settings can be easily backed up, but more importantly, it also allows the user to have those settings available regardless of where he may be logged in. In reality, of course, it is not the profile that roams, it is the user, but it follows the user and allows him to carry the settings around with him. The profile consists of not only the user's HKEY_CURRENT_USER contained in the file *ntuser.dat* (for Windows NT/2000) or *user.dat* (for Windows 95/98), but also other settings such as the contents of his personal desktop and favorites list. Some of these features will not be automatically available and will need to be enabled in the user system Windows ZAK policy in order for them to actually work.

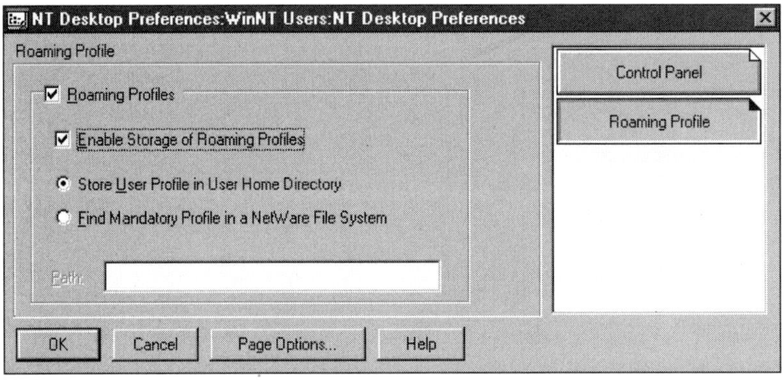

Figure 4-7. Windows NT Roaming Profiles

It is important to note that Windows NT 4, Windows 2000, and Windows 95/98 profiles are incompatible with each other because their HKEY_CURRENT_USER file structure is different. It is for this reason that those who use both platforms will have the profiles stored separately at the top level of their home directories. The Windows NT 4 profile is stored in a directory called "Windows NT 4 Workstation Profile," the Windows 2000 profile is stored in "Windows NT 5 Workstation Profile," and the Windows 95/98 profile is simply stored at the top level of the home directory. In addition, any files stored on the desktop or in the recent document list after logging into Windows NT 4 will not be present within their Windows 2000 or Windows 95 environment. This will be true for some of the other roaming features as well. The profile is cached on the local hard disk for the entirety of the login session and then copied back to the home directory during the logout process. In the event that the user has never logged into that operating system before, a copy of the default profile is taken from the current workstation and used as a basis to create a profile for the user. It is therefore also important that all of the workstations have an appropriate default profile installed.

You will probably need to implement profiles in some way. Regardless of whether you intend to use Mandatory Profiles or Roaming Profiles, you will probably need one or the other.

There is also allowance for another type of profile called the Mandatory Profile. This profile is intended more to restrict the user rather than allow flexibility. In this case, the system administrator designs a profile that is suitable for all users and makes it available on the network file server where it is shared by all users associated with the policy that implements it. When a user logs in, the profile is copied to the local hard disk for the login session, but is not copied back during the logout process.

The NT User Printer Policy

This policy is available only through the Windows NT user policy package. The NT user printer policy allows you to remotely install printers on remote workstations, and to set a default printer in the list for the user. There is a similar policy for Windows NT and Windows 95/98 workstations, which is discussed later in this chapter. From the Add dialog box, select a print queue via the NDS browser. If it is the first printer installed, no driver will be associated with the queue. If there is already at least one printer in the list, the driver associated with the last queue will be used. If you wish to add or change a driver, click the New Driver button and select a driver to associate with the queue (you may need to insert the Windows NT/2000 or 95 CD-ROM or a OEM driver disk). This operation can only be performed on a Windows NT/2000 machine for a Windows NT/2000 policy as the drivers will be copied from the workstation currently being used and will also be true for Windows 95/98 policies. The device driver will be stored on the server, so that when the user selects the printer, the appropriate device driver can be installed on his behalf. You can also specify what the NetWare printer settings are for the printer.

About User and Computer System Policies

When Windows 95 finally arrived onto the world market, a growing realization emerged that this operating system would bring a great deal more power, flexibility, and stability to the user, but also a great deal more system work for IT support. Microsoft introduced the Zero Administration Kit (ZAK), which is designed to keep the power and stability of the system but also to remove flexibility. The concept of a Taskstation, a workstation that essentially runs only one program, and an Appstation, a workstation that runs just a couple of programs, was introduced. There is actually a great deal to be said for this way of thinking for an environment where a user has been known to inadvertently break the installation by fiddling with components that are better left for IT support. ZAK is achieved in several ways: Mandatory Profiles, which were mentioned earlier, and extended computer and user policy settings. These policy settings are shown by *poledit* as default user policies and local computer policies and are shown in Figures 4-8 and 4-9. The *poledit* program examines the user policy and the computer policy separately but within the same window. ZENworks also treats these two policy types separately but they have to be examined and set from the workstation and user policy packages.

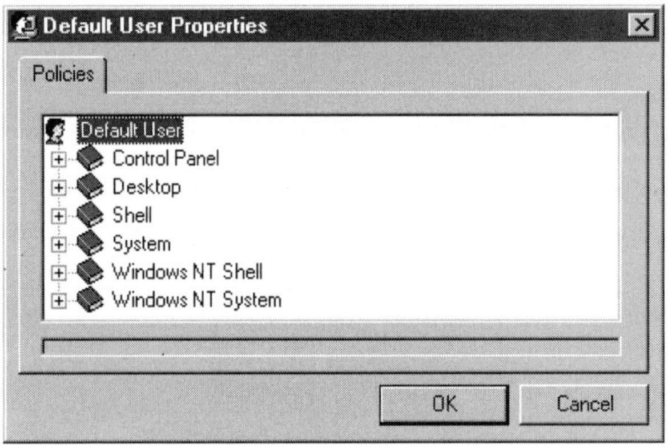

Figure 4-8. Microsoft User Policy Editor

Microsoft introduced computer and user policies to help the system administrator provide more flexibility in the provision of a corporate implementation of Windows NT/2000 workstation and Windows 95/98. By using the Policy Editor (*poledit*), the system administrator is able to create policy files to introduce new features, although more often to disable functionality. These policy files are loaded during the user login process and contain instructions to set registry keys, which cause the operating system to make the restrictions defined by you. These restrictions should not necessarily be seen as a degradation of the system, but more of a mechanism to cater for the removal of unnecessary, undesirable, or unwanted features of the operating system as defined by your system planning requirements.

User and workstation policies are implemented for a reason—okay, they are being used to implement your requirements, but more fundamentally, they are almost always a restriction for the user. Restrictions associated with workstations will affect the look and feel of that workstation, but the results will only be *felt* by the user (the workstation doesn't care). It is important to be clear about the reason for the restriction. Do you wish the restriction to simplify the system or to protect the system (or both)? In the coverage of these System policies, we will look at these user and computer policies from both points of view. These policies can be misread very easily—it is important to understand what the policy is asking. It is

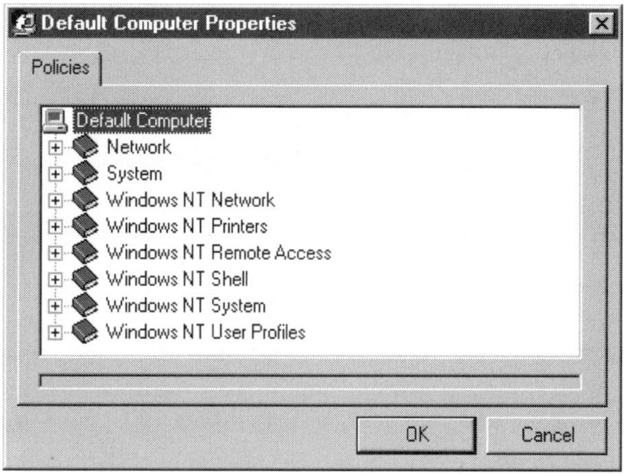

Figure 4-9. Microsoft Computer Policy Editor

important that you test your policies carefully because they can sometimes have unexpected results. In general, user and computer system policies have three possible settings:

Enable (box is checked)
: Enable the policy for either the workstation or the user. If you have more than one policy package governing more than one group and you enable a policy for one group, you may need to disable it for the other, depending upon the reason for the policy package.

Disable (box is white)
: This is an explicit disablement of the policy. If you have more than one policy package governing more than one group and you disable a policy for one group, you may need to enable it for the other.

Ignore (box is gray)
: This is the default setting for all polices when they are first created. If you have two groups of users—say "expert" and "not expert"—and you use two policy packages to control their access, the "ignore" setting may actually be inappropriate. This will be the case when both groups are using the same workstation and the setting is stored on the workstation. When the restricted user logs in and the policy is enabled, the expert user may get the enabled state if her policy is configured to ignore it. Ignore settings are much quicker to parse than the enabled and disabled state, so it is probably best to leave them as ignore unless you clearly want to enable or disable.

For any given platform, if you enable or disable a policy in one policy package, you must decide what the setting should be for all other similar policy packages. You should either enable or disable them, but don't leave them in the ignore state, or you may get unpredictable results. However, leaving them ignored is best if the policy is not altered by other policy packages.

User system policies are available in the Windows NT and Windows 95/98 policy packages. These policies stay with the user as long as she is logging in to the same authentication domain. The user system policies are the same as those available using the Windows Policy Editor, except that in addition it includes the ZAK policies as well. While there are similarities between the Windows NT user policies and those for Windows 95/98, there are significant differences. This is also the case for the computer system policies where similarities and differences require them to be reviewed together where possible, but where differences occur the targeted operating system will be noted. The policies either make a change to a registry key or they create new keys to implement the desired state. The registry keys targeted by the policy are provided for convenience and for ease of debugging. If you implement a policy and it doesn't work, check that the registry key has been set as expected.

Windows 95/98 and NT User System Policy Packages

Windows NT/2000 is a secure operating system in which there is a clear distinction made between a user and an administrator. The user is still, however, able to make changes to some areas. These policies allow you to restrict the user further to cover areas where you prefer the user not to be. There are many Windows NT user system policies available with the main policy areas shown in Figure 4-10. It is probably less confusing to study and decide on one area at a time to avoid confusion.

Windows 95/98 makes no distinction between users and administrators, as far as the local operating system and the filesystem are concerned. Areas such as the Network Control Panel and the System Control Panel may well be considered inappropriate places for users to be messing about. It is for this reason that policies are important on these platforms. These policies, even if you implement all of them, will not provide the level of security and control that is provided under Windows NT/2000, but they will remove or restrict certain key areas of the system. The Windows 95/98 user system policies are shown in Figure 4-11 and contain a host of possible settings. Take a section at a time and decide how they can assist your desktop management.

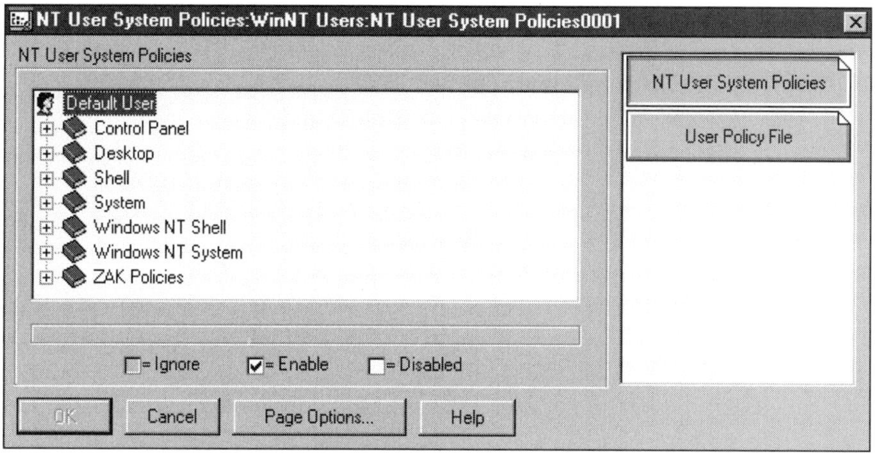

Figure 4-10. Windows NT user system policies

Use policies to increase the security of Windows 95/98 by removing system features such as control panels, which you feel are not for the user to be interfering with.

Control Panel Policies

Control panel policies rather unsurprisingly restrict the workstation control panels, but most of these will probably be already restricted from the user under Windows NT/2000 because they are protected by operating system security. Under Windows 95/98 there are more policies restricting the control panels because the user will normally have full control over them.

Display restrictions

From the point of view of the IT management, the look of the desktop is important. This can be particularly true for a service launch where a subsequent change to the desktop may be inappropriate and unpopular. In general it is better to deliver the service with appropriate settings already made than to take them away after the service delivery.

The desktop customization in its simplest form consists of colors and backgrounds but also screen resolutions and settings, which can cause problems if the user makes changes deliberately or otherwise. The Settings tab is both useful and dangerous. Each user has her own requirements for the screen resolution, color depth, and monitor refresh rate. Unfortunately these settings are stored in HKEY_LOCAL_MACHINE. This means that when a user changes any of these settings, the next user will have hers as well. There is currently no way that the screen settings can roam with users. This is a control panel, which probably should be restricted in some way if your users share machines.

Another problem area is screensavers, which seem harmless enough and indeed they can certainly save the monitor from harm, but they also have drawbacks. Screensavers can action code, they can demand a password to access the system, they can log the user off, or worse. If your environment demands more than one user per PC then a screensaver could cause trouble! If a user sets a screensaver password and leaves the workstation, then he has potentially taken possession of the machine. You may wish to enable the control panel screensaver policy to remove the ability to change the screensaver and force one of your own via desktop preferences.

> If an "expert" user changes the screen resolution, a "less expert" user attempting to use the same workstation may have trouble if he cannot change it back. There is no mechanism to allow the screen settings to roam with the user, or to force default settings for each login. If you hide the Settings tab, users will have to use the settings preset by you. Neither of these options are ideal.

Affected keys

HKEY_CURRENT_USER\Software\Microsoft\Windows\CurrentVersion\Policies\System

Table 4-1. Modified Keys from Windows 95/98 and NT Display Policies

Policy	Value	Data Type	Enable	Disable
Deny Access to Display Icon	NoDispCPL	REG_DWORD	1	0 or no value
Hide Background Tab	NoDispBackgroundPage	REG_DWORD	1	0 or no value
Hide Screensaver Tab	NoDispScrSavPage	REG_DWORD	1	0 or no value
Hide Appearance Tab	NoDispAppearancePage	REG_DWORD	1	0 or no value
Hide Settings Tab	NoDispSettingsPage	REG_DWORD	1	0 or no value

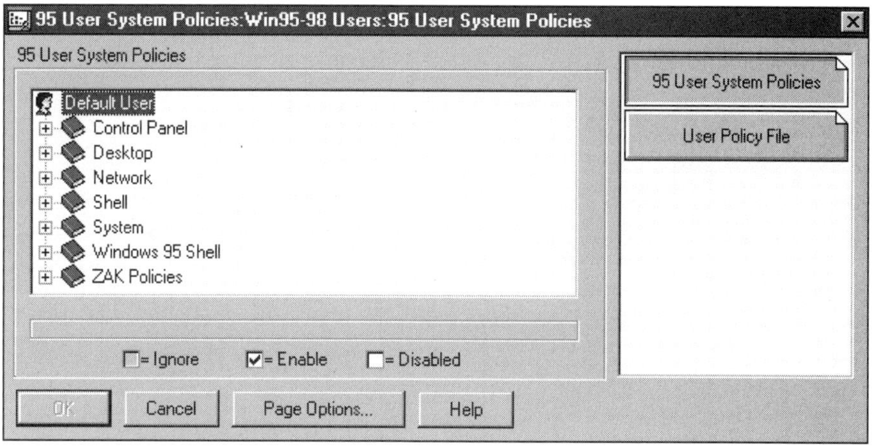

Figure 4-11. Windows 95/98 user system policies

Network restrictions

This policy is available in the Window 95/98 user policy only. The Network control Panel allows the addition or removal of the network device, network protocols, network services, and their properties. This is usually an area that the user is normally able to enter, but should be disallowed from doing so. There are several options in this policy which range from disabling the control panel altogether to just hiding some of the pages.

> The Network control panel is a dangerous place for users to venture into. If you disable it altogether (by enabling the policy), the user will not be able to fiddle with it, but don't forget to disable the policy for your ID or nobody will be able to see the control panel.

Affected keys

HKEY_CURRENT_USER\Software\Microsoft\Windows\CurrentVersion\policies\Network

Table 4-2. Modified Keys from Windows 95/98 Network Policies

Policy	Value	Data Type	Enable	Disable
Disable Network Control Panel	NoNetSetup	REG_DWORD	1	0
Hide Identification Page	NoNetSetupIDPage	REG_DWORD	1	0
Hide Access Control Page	NoNetSetup-SecurityPage	REG_DWORD	1	0

Password restrictions

This policy is available in the Window 95/98 user policy only. Local password caching is a hangover from Windows for Workgoups, where the machine password was stored on the local machine, and the functionality is still present with Windows 95. It is strongly recommended that password caching be disabled, as the cached passwords are very easy to crack. The setting that configures password caching and others is stored in the Password control panel. Users will probably not need to go in here, so it is a good idea to hide it from them.

Affected keys

HKEY_CURRENT_USER\Software\Microsoft\Windows\CurrentVersion\Policies\Network

Table 4-3. Modified Keys from Windows 95/98 Password Policies

Policy	Value	Data Type	Enable	Disable
Disable Passwords Control Panel	NoSecCPL	REG_DWORD	1	0
Hide Change Passwords Page	NoPwdPage	REG_DWORD	1	0
Hide Remote Administration Page	NoAdminPage	REG_DWORD	1	0
Hide User Profile Page	NoProfilePage	REG_DWORD	1	0

Printer restrictions

This policy is available in the Window 95/98 user policy only. When a user selects a printer from the control panel and examines the properties of it, several options will become available, including the Details page, which will allow the user to change the printer port and the device driver and their settings. Once you have configured a printer to work, it is unlikely that the user will need to make any changes.

Affected keys

HKEY_CURRENT_USER\Software\Microsoft\Windows\CurrentVersion\Policies\Explorer

Table 4-4. Modified Keys from Windows 95/98 Printer Policies

Policy	Value	Data Type	Enable	Disable
Restrict Printer Settings	NoPrinters	REG_DWORD	1	0
Hide General and Details Page	NoPrinterTabs	REG_DWORD	1	0
Disable Deletion of Printers	NoDeletePrinter	REG_DWORD	1	0
Disable Addition of Printers	NoAddPrinter	REG_DWORD	1	0

System restrictions

This policy is available in the Window 95/98 user policy only. In general, the System control panel is not a place where users should be making changes. This policy, when enabled, will allow you to restrict the System control panel by disallowing access to certain pages such as the Device Manage page. In most user populations, about 90% of the users wouldn't know what to do with this page and the other 10% shouldn't be allowed to touch it. There are some useful policies in here which will allow you to keep the users from breaking their own workstations.

Affected keys

HKEY_CURRENT_USER\Software\Microsoft\Windows\CurrentVersion\Policies\System

Table 4-5. Modified Key from Windows 95/98 System Policies

Policy	Value	Data Type	Enable	Disable
Hide Device Manager	NoDevMgrPage	REG_DWORD	1	0
Hide Configuration Page	NoConfigPage	REG_DWORD	1	0
Hide File System Page	NoFileSysPage	REG_DWORD	1	0
Hide Virtual Memory Page	NoVirtMemPage	REG_DWORD	1	0

Desktop Policy

This is a cosmetic policy, but a useful one if you wish to define desktop standards and disallow the user from changing them. These policies are available in Windows NT and Windows 95/98 user policies. They refer to wallpaper settings and color schemes, and are enforced by the registry keys below.

Affected keys

HKEY_CURRENT_USER\Control Panel\Desktop

Table 4-6. Modified Keys from Windows 95/98 and NT Desktop Policies

Policy	Value	Data Type	Enable	Disable
Wallpaper Name	Wallpaper	REG_SZ	Path to Wallpaper	0 or no value
Tile Wallpaper	TileWallpaper	REG_SZ	1	0 or no value

Affected key

HKEY_CURRENT_USER\Control Panel\Appearance

Table 4-7. Modified Key from Windows 95/98 and NT Color Scheme Policies

Policy	Value	Data Type	Enable	Disable
Color Scheme	Current	REG_SZ	Scheme Name	0 or no value

Network Policy

These policies are available in the Windows 95/98 user policy only. The policy is designed to prevent users from starting peer-to-peer networking services. If it is your policy to disable this function then enable this policy.

Affected keys

HKEY_CURRENT_USER\Software\Microsoft\Windows\CurrentVersion\Policies\Explorer

Table 4-8. Modified Keys from Windows 95/98 Share Policies

Policy	Value	Data Type	Enable	Disable
Disable File Sharing Controls	DisableFileSharingCtrl	REG_DWORD	1	0
Disable Print Sharing Controls	NoPrintSharingControl	REG_DWORD	1	0

Shell Restrictions Policy

If you have decided to use the Explorer Shell, but wish to restrict either for safety, security or just for simplicity, then there are some useful options here. They are available in Windows NT and Windows 95/98 user policies. The policies include Remove Run from the Start Menu and disabling the settings function from the Start menu. These functions certainly restrict the user, but do not prevent. If you remove Run from the Start menu, users will still be able to run programs, but not through this mechanism. These policies are designed to limit the Start menu. If you wish to use them in conjunction with other policies to really restrict the user, then this is a section you should look at.

There are pitfalls in these policies in that they may produce unpredictable results or responses form the users. A good example of this is the policy "Hide Network Neighborhood." This seems like a good way of restricting the users. But this policy will disable UNC pathnames to services. These policies seem like a good idea, but you need to test the results carefully.

If you don't wish users to poke around local or mapped drives, one of the ways of stopping them is to hide the drive. It is also quite possible, of course, to use or mount the drive from a DOS command prompt, so careful planning is required to implement such a policy. This is probably a useful policy if you plan the use NAL to launch applications, because it prevents users from finding the application themselves if they are stored on a network volume. The issue is particularly important if you plan to use the software metering option in ZENworks. In this case, the meter will not work unless the application is launched through NAL.

Affected keys

HKEY_CURRENT_USER\Software\Microsoft\Windows\CurrentVersion\Policies\Explorer

Table 4-9. Modified Keys from Windows 95/98 and NT Shell Restrictions

Policy	Value	Data Type	Enable	Disable
Remove Run from the Start Menu	NoRun	REG_DWORD	1	0 or no value
Remove Folders from Settings in the Start Menu	NoSetFolders	REG_DWORD	1	0 or no value
Remove Taskbar from Settings on Start Menu	NoSetTaskBar	REG_DWORD	1	0 or no value
Remove Find Command from the Start Menu	NoFind	REG_DWORD	1	0 or no value
Hide Drives in My Computer	NoDrives	REG_DWORD	1	0 or no value
Hide Network Neighborhood	NoNetHood	REG_DWORD	1	0 or no value
No Entire Network in Network Neighborhood	NoEntireNetwork	REG_DWORD	1	0 or no value
No Workgroup Contents in Network Neighborhood	NoWorkGroupContents	REG_DWORD	1	0 or no value
Hide All Items in the Desktop	NoDesktop	REG_DWORD	1	0 or no value
Disable Shutdown Command	NoClose	REG_DWORD	1	0 or no value
Don't Save Settings on Exit	NoSaveSettings	REG_DWORD	1	0 or no value

System Policy

The system is this case refers to the operating system, which in general is not something that needs to be tweaked on a per user basis, but here are some exceptions. This policy is available in Windows NT and Windows 95/98 user policies, and will prevent users from fiddling with the machine registry. Do users need to look at or make changes to the registry? Not as a general rule! This policy will not prevent users from doing things to the registry—it will just disable the standard tools. By enabling this policy, the users will be prevented from running *Regedit* and *Regedt32* but not from running some other program which does the same thing, or from executing a *.reg* file.

Affected key

HKEY_CURRENT_USER\Software\Microsoft\Windows\CurrentVersion\Policies\System

Table 4-10. Modified Key from Disable Windows 95/98 and NT Registry Editing Tools

Policy	Value	Data Type	Enable	Disable
Disable Registry Editing Tools	DisableRegistryTools	REG_DWORD	1	0 or no value

Run Only Allowed Windows Applications

If you really want to restrict the users, then this policy will do that, although it may have a high maintenance overhead. If this policy is disabled, the user will be able to run what she likes. If the policy is enabled, you will be given the opportunity to enter a list of allowed programs. These policies are available in Windows NT and Windows 95/98 user policies.

If you want to restrict the user to a specific set of programs, this is the place to do it! Enable the policy in all platform policy packages for the users to be restricted, then disable it for those not being restricted.

Affected key

HKEY_CURRENT_USER\Software\Microsoft\Windows\CurrentVersion\Policies\Explorer

Table 4-11. Modified Key from Disable Windows 95/98 and NT Run Only Allowed Windows Applications

Policy	Value	Data Type	Enable	Disable
Run Only Allowed Windows Applications	RestrictRun	REG_DWORD	1	0 or no value

Affected key

HKEY_CURRENT_USER\Software\Microsoft\Windows\CurrentVersion\Policies\Explorer\RestrictRun

Table 4-12. Modified Key from Disable Windows 95/98 and NT Run Only Allowed Windows Applications

Policy	Value	Data Type	Enable	Disable
Run Only Allowed Windows Applications	Incrementing number starting with 1	REG_SZ	Application name	No value

MS-DOS Options

These policies are available in the Windows 95/98 user policy only. If you have decided to eliminate the MS-DOS prompt from the user, then this is how it is best done. If you wish to keep the MS-DOS functionality, but allow only protected mode applications, then real-mode applications will not be permitted on the workstation. In general it is always better to use protected mode where possible.

Affected key

HKEY_CURRENT_USER\Software\Microsoft\Windows\CurrentVersion\Policies\WinOldApp

Table 4-13. Modified Key from MS-DOS Options

Policy	Value	Data Type	Enable	Disable
Disable MS-DOS Prompt	Disabled	REG_DWORD	1	No value
Disable Single Mode MS-DOS Applications	NoRealMode	REG_DWORD	1	No value

Windows NT Shell/Windows 95 Shell

This is really an extension to the Shell policies discussed earlier. These policies are available in Windows NT and Windows 95/98 user policies, but will be called Windows NT Shell in the Windows NT policy and Windows 95 Shell in the Windows 95/98 policy.

Custom user interface

This policy is available in the Windows NT user policy. The default user interface for Windows NT is *explorer.exe.* If you wish to implement a very restricted taskstation or appstation, then you will need to specify a shell with which to restrict the user. When this policy is enabled, you will be prompted for a mapped drive or UNC path to the new shell. One such shell available is the Novell Application Launcher *nal.exe*, which will be discussed in detail in Chapter 6, *The Novell Application Launcher.* If you disable this policy, the user will be offered the standard *explorer.exe.*

Custom folders

It is possible to customize certain areas such as the Start menu via this set of policies, which is available under Windows NT and Windows 95/98. Central management and control of certain areas is probably a good idea. It is certainly a great relief to be able to make changes to these areas without having to visit every workstation. By making changes to the Custom folders, you will be able to replicate the changes throughout the network. You will be able to control a series of areas within this area, the most important being the Start menu/Programs folder. This is certainly an area that would benefit from a centralized folder. If you enable this policy, you will need to enter a mapped drive or UNC path to the custom folder. You may also wish to enable the Hide Start Menu Subfolders option as well, or you will find that you have two Program folders—one local and the other remote. If this is your intention, that's fine, but if not, then enabling this policy will remove the local Program folder. If it is disabled, then the local Program folder will remain.

Affected key

HKEY_CURRENT_USER\Software\Microsoft\Windows\CurrentVersion\Policies\Explorer

Table 4-14. Modified Key from Disable Windows 95/98 and NT Hide Startmenu Subfolders

policy	Value	Data Type	Enable	Disable
Hide Start Menu Subfolders	NoStartMenuSubFolders	REG_DWORD	1	0 or no value

Affected keys

HKEY_CURRENT_USER\Software\Microsoft\Windows\CurrentVersion\Explorer\User Shell Folders

Table 4-15. Modified Key from Disable Windows 95/98 and NT Shell Folders

Policy	Value	Data Type	Enable	Disable
Custom Program Folders	Programs	REG_SZ	Path to folder	No value
Custom Desktop Icons	Desktop	REG_SZ	Path to folder	No value
Custom Startup Folder	Startup	REG_SZ	Path to folder	No value
Custom Network Neighborhood	NetHood	REG_SZ	Path to folder	No value
Custom Start Menu	Start Menu	REG_SZ	Path to folder	No value

Restrictions

As well as customizing the Windows NT/2000 shell, you can also restrict it by disabling certain functions. The All Users component of the user profile contains a variety of common components, one of which is the Common Program group. When the Remove Common Program Groups from Start Menu policy is enabled, the All User menu becomes hidden. This option is useful when you have implemented custom folders to store your application shortcuts, or if you use the Novell Application Launcher.

Another useful policy is to restrict the user by disallowing her ability to map network drives. This is achieved through the Remove the Map Network Drive and Disconnect Network Drive policy.

One particularly devious feature of Windows NT/2000 in a networked environment is link-file tracking. Windows shortcuts use absolute and relative path names. When a user clicks on a shortcut, the absolute path is attempted first, then the relative. When this policy is enabled, the absolute path will be ignored and only the relative attempted. This is very useful when rolling out Windows NT/2000 from an image file. The problem with link-file tracking is that local applications such as *calc.exe* will not run from the local machine if the Disable Link File Tracking policy is not enabled. The Windows NT and Windows 95 Resource Kits come with a utility called *scut.exe* that will sort out the link-file tracking, as well.

Affected keys

HKEY_CURRENT_USER\Software\Microsoft\Windows\CurrentVersion\Policies\Explorer

Table 4-16. Modified Keys from Windows NT Shell Restrictions

Policy	Value	Data Type	Enable	Disable
Use Only Approved Shell Extensions	EnforceShellExtensionSecurity	REG_DWORD	1	0 or no value
Remove File Menu from Explorer	NoFileMenu	REG_DWORD	1	0 or no value
Remove Common Program Groups from Start Menu	NoCommonGroups	REG_DWORD	1	0 or no value
Disable Context Menus for the Task Bar	NoTrayContextMenu	REG_DWORD	1	0 or no value
Disable Explorer's Default Menu	NoViewContextMenu	REG_DWORD	1	0 or no value
Remove the Map Network Drive and Disconnect Network Drive options	NoNetConnectDisconnect	REG_DWORD	1	0 or no value
Disable Link File Tracking	LinkResolvedIgnoreLinkInfo	REG_DWORD	1	0 or no value

Windows NT System

These are miscellaneous policies, which are mostly related to the logon process and are available in the Window NT user policy only. Some of the useful features in this policy include running the logon script synchronously. Windows NT/2000 will usually allow the logon script to be executed simultaneously with the loading of the User shell. When this policy is enabled, the User shell is prevented from loading until the logon script has finished executing.

If you decide to parse *autoexec.bat*, be careful to ensure the commands are valid, as an incorrect setting can crash the Windows NT/2000 Windows On Windows

(WOW) 16-bit subsystem. If you experience *wowexec* errors, look for errors in startup files or crashed 16-bit programs.

Affected keys

HKEY_CURRENT_USER\Software\Microsoft\Windows\CurrentVersion\Winlogon

Table 4-17. Modified Keys from Windows NT Logon Policies

Policy	Value	Data Type	Enable	Disable
Parse Autoexec.bat	ParseAutoexec	REG_SZ	1	0 or no value
Run Logon Scripts Synchronously	RunLogonScript	REG_DWORD	1	0 or no value

Affected keys

HKEY_CURRENT_USER\Software\Microsoft\Windows\CurrentVersion\Policies\System

Table 4-18. Modified Keys from Windows NT Task Manager

Policy	Value	Data Type	Enable	Disable
Disable Task Manager	DisableTaskMgr	REG_DWORD	1	0 or no value

Affected keys

HKEY_CURRENT_USER\Software\Microsoft\Windows\CurrentVersion\Explorer\Tips

Table 4-19. Modified Keys from Windows NT Welcome Tips

Policy	Value	Data Type	Enable	Disable
Show Welcome Tips at Logon	Show	REG_DWORD	1	0

ZAK Policies

These are policies related to the Zero Administration Kit (ZAK). This kit is available from Microsoft and, among other things, sets policies that have been incorporated into the Windows NT and Windows 95/98 user policies.

User profiles through system policies

When a user logs in, her profile is cached to the local hard disk and is copied back during the logout process. Any data stored within the profile has to be copied through the network twice for every login session. A lot of data stored in the profile slows the login/logout process, so you may wish to consider which of these should be used. Unless these policies are enabled, the application data and favorites, etc., will not be part of the profile and will be lost between login sessions.

Affected keys

HKEY_CURRENT_USER\Software\Microsoft\Windows\CurrentVersion\Explorer \User Shell Folders

Table 4-20. Modified Keys from Windows 95/98 and NT ZAK System Policies

Policy	Value	Data Type	Enable	Disable
Appdata	Appdata	REG_DWORD	1	0 or no value
Favorites	Favorites	REG_DWORD	1	0 or no value
NetHood	NetHood	REG_DWORD	1	0 or no value
PrintHood	PrintHood	REG_DWORD	1	0 or no value
Send to	Send to	REG_DWORD	1	0 or no value

Internet Explorer security

If you use Microsoft Internet Explorer, you can force the user to accept security when receiving certain files. These policies are available in Windows NT and Windows 95/98 user policies. They include the ability to secure the workstation by removing the ability to accept active components such as ActiveX and Java. If you are concerned about the security of the workstation in this regard, then you can disable these elements of the browser, but be warned that active scripts are fast becoming an essential part of many Internet web sites. You may instead wish to be notified when active content is downloaded by setting the Active Content Security Level, which is described in Table 4-22.

Affected keys

HKEY_CURRENT_USER\Software\Microsoft\Windows\CurrentVersion\Internet Settings

Table 4-21. Modified Keys from Windows 95/98 and NT IE Security Policies

Policy	Value	Data Type	Enable	Disable
Allow Downloading of ActiveX Contents	Code Download	REG_SZ	YES	NO
Enable ActiveX Controls and Plugins	Security_RunActiveX-Controls	REG_DWORD	1	0
Run ActiveX Scripts	Security_RunScripts	REG_DWORD	1	0
Enable Java Programs	Security_RunJava-Applets	REG_DWORD	1	0

Table 4-22. Internet Explorer Security Levels

Security Level	Description
High	When active content is detected, the user is warned and the content disallowed.

Table 4-22. Internet Explorer Security Levels (continued)

Security Level	Description
Medium	When active content is detected, the user is given the option to download it.
None	When active content is detected, the user is not notified and it is downloaded.

Affected keys

HKEY_CURRENT_USER\Software\Microsoft\Windows\CurrentVersion\Explorer \User Shell Folders

Table 4-23. Modified Keys from Internet Explorer Security Levels

Policy	Value	Data Type	Enable	Disable
High	Trust Warning Level	REG_SZ	High	No, or other value
Medium	Trust Warning Level	REG_SZ	Medium	No, or other value
None	Trust Warning Level	REG_SZ	No Security	No, or other value

Drive restrictions

This set of policies will allow you to hide a selection of local or network drives from the users. These policies are available in Windows NT and Windows 95/98 user policies. When the Show Only Selected Drives policy is enabled, you will have the opportunity to select which drives will be hidden. In the case when you will be selecting the drives, which you do not require through the GUI, this is straightforward, but it may be useful to define how the registry key is derived.

The key is defined by setting the registry key to a decimal or hexadecimal number, which corresponds to a 26-bit binary string, with each bit representing a drive letter:

```
11111111111111111111111111
ZYXWVUTSRQPONMLKJIHGFEDCBA
```

The above configuration corresponds to a decimal value of `67108863d` and will hide all drives. If you wish to hide only drive *F:*, you would make the 6th lowest bit a 1, set all the rest to 0, and then convert the binary string to decimal `32` or to hexadecimal `20`.

Affected keys

HKEY_CURRENT_USER\Software\Microsoft\Windows\CurrentVersion\Policies\Explorer

Table 4-24. Modified Keys from Windows 95/98 and NT Hide Drives

Policy	Value	Data Type	Enable	Disable
Show Only Selected Drives	NoDrives	REG_DWORD	Value in Hex	No value

Windows load

These policies are available in Window NT and Windows 95/98 user policies. When this policy is enabled, you will be able to specify programs to be loaded during the shell startup process. I tend to use NAL to load programs during startup, but if you don't plan to use it, then the program can be loaded here instead.

Affected keys

HKEY_CURRENT_USER\Software\Microsoft\Windows\CurrentVersion\Windows

Table 4-25. Modified Keys from Windows 95/98 and NT Load

Policy	Value	Data Type	Enable	Disable
Windows Load	Load	REG_DWORD	Path	No value

Windows NT and 95/98 Computer System Policies

Windows NT computer system policies are designed to remove functionality and define default settings. Notice the similarities between the policy in Figure 4-12 and that for *poledit* computer policies in Figure 4-9. These policies differ slightly from user policies in that they sometimes require a reboot of the workstation in order to take effect.

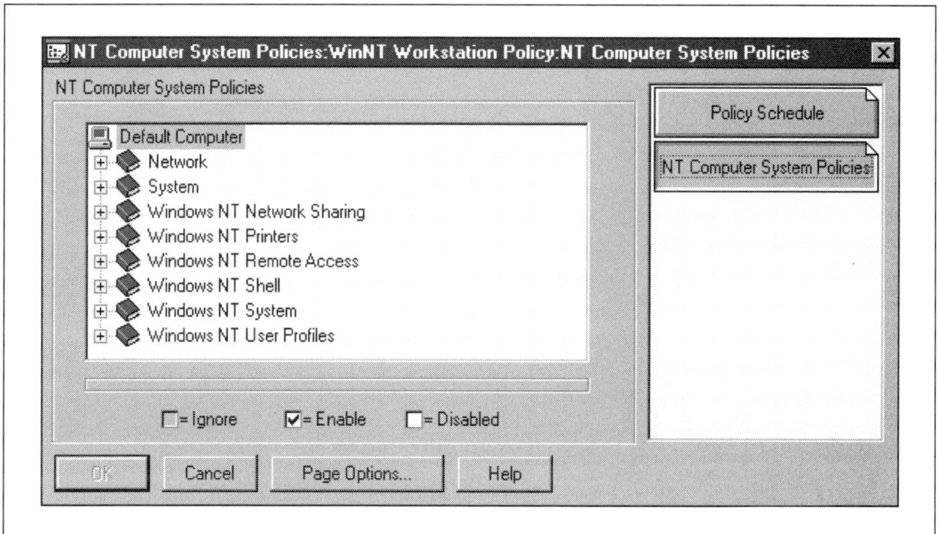

Figure 4-12. Windows NT computer system policies

Windows 95/98 users are generally able to use/abuse the system as much as they please as there are no built-in security features to prevent them from doing so. Several areas such as those pertaining to passwords and authenticated access should be seriously considered. If your workstations are connected to the Internet, you may wish to require access to the workstation only if successful authentication occurs, in order to manage users who use the network or Internet inappropriately. These policies will restrict the system in some crucial areas. The policies are targeted at the workstation, but the user will still be affected. The policies will either add registry keys or modify the value of existing keys.

> Windows 95/98 computer system policies can help secure the workstation from inappropriate use and force authentication from the NDS before access is granted to the system.

Network

There are a number of policies affecting the network.

System policies update

This policy is available in Windows NT and Windows 95/98 computer system policies (see Figure 4-13), but is called system policies update in the Windows NT computer system policy and update in the Windows 95/98 policy.

Affected keys

HKEY_LOCAL_MACHINE\ System\CurrentControlSet\Control\Update

Table 4-26. Modified Keys from Windows 95/98 and NT Network Remote Update

Policy	Value	Data Type	Enable	Disable
Update Mode	UpdateMode	REG_DWORD	1 = Automatic 2 = Manual	0 or no value
Update Path	NetworkPath	REG_SZ	Path	0 or no value
Display Error Messages	Verbose	REG_DWORD	1	0 or no value
Load Balancing	LoadBalance	REG_DWORD	1	0 or no value

User level access control

When this policy is enabled, users are only given access to the workstation with user level security after authentication from a NetWare NDS or NT Server—you will also need to enter the server name and type of authenticator. The policy is only available in the Windows 95/98 computer system policies.

Affected keys

HKEY_LOCAL_MACHINE\System\CurrentControlSet\Services\VxD\FILESEC

Table 4-27. Modified Keys from Windows 95/98 User Access Control Enable

Policy	Value	Data Type	Enable	Disable
User Level Access Control Enable	Start	REG _DWORD	1	No value
Automatic	StaticVxD	REG _SZ	filesec.vxd	No value

Affected keys

HKEY_LOCAL_MACHINE\Security\Provider

Table 4-28. Modified Keys from Windows 95/98 User Access Platform Type and Server

Policy	Value	Data Type	Enable	Disable
Platform	Platform_Type	REG _DWORD	3=NetWare 2/1=Microsoft	No value
Server	Container	REG _SZ	Server name	No value

Affected keys

HKEY_LOCAL_MACHINE\System\CurrentControlSet\Services\VxD\NWSP

Table 4-29. Modified Keys from Windows 95/98 User Access NetWare Security Provider

Policy	Value	Data Type	Enable	Disable
Platform	StaticVxD	REG _SZ	nwsp.vxd	No value
Server	Start	REG _DWORD	0	No value

Affected keys

HKEY_LOCAL_MACHINE\System\CurrentControlSet\Services\VxD\MSSP

Table 4-30 . Modified Keys from Windows 95/98 User Access Microsoft Security Provider

Policy	Value	Data Type	Enable	Disable
Platform	StaticVxD	REG _SZ	mssp.vxd	No value
Server	Start	REG _DWORD	0	No value

Logon

These policies are available in the Window 95/98 computer system policy only. There are several policies here, which should be given careful consideration. The Logon Banner policy, when enabled, will allow you to enter some text, which will be displayed during the logon process. This text is typically a legal notice defining the basis upon which a user is allowed to use the workstation. Legal notices are important in most organizations to ensure that the user is aware of the terms by which they are given access to the workstation and network.

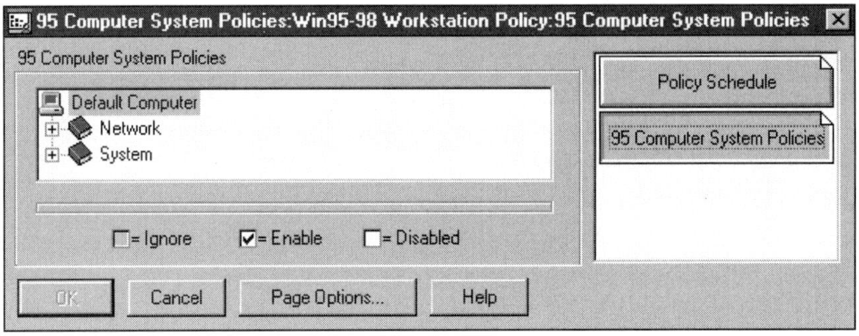

Figure 4-13. Windows 95/98 computer system policies

The Require Validation from Network for Windows Access policy is quite important. Users are normally able to use a Windows 95/98 workstation without using a password or giving authentication. When this policy is enabled, the user will have to authenticate to a network server before access is granted to the workstation. The user will be able to use the workstation without a password if this is disabled.

In a network environment, it is probably not a good idea to grant access to workstations without proper authentication. User IDs and passwords should be given access to a workstation and the password should be secret. It is not a good idea to have passwords visible in any way nor should they be cached on the workstation. Passwords should also be of a reasonable length (at least six characters).

Affected keys

HKEY_LOCAL_MACHINE\Software\Microsoft\Windows\CurrentVersion\Winlogon

Table 4-31. Modified Keys from Windows 95/98 Logon

Policy	Value	Data Type	Enable	Disable
Logon Banner	LegalNoticeCapition	REG _SZ	Text	No value
Require Validation from Network for Windows Access	LegalNoticeText	REG _SZ	Text	No value

Passwords

These policies are available in the Window 95/98 computer system policy only. The policies under this heading are quite important from a security point of view and they should all be considered. Password visibility should be disallowed and minimum passwords should also be considered. The local caching of passwords is also not recommended.

Affected keys

HKEY_LOCAL_MACHINE\Software\Microsoft\Windows\CurrentVersion\Policies\Network

Table 4-32. Modified Keys from Windows 95/98 Passwords User

Policy	Value	Data Type	Enable	Disable
Hide Share Passwords with Asterisks	HideSharePwds	REG _DWORD	1	0 or no value
Disable Password Caching	DisablePwdCaching	REG _DWORD	1	0 or no value
Require Alphanumeric Windows Password	Requirealphanum	REG _DWORD	1	0 or no value
Minimum Windows Password Length	MinimunPwdLen	REG _DWORD	Value between 1 and 8	0 or no value

Dialup networking

This policy is available in the Window 95/98 computer system policy only. When this policy is enabled, dial-in will not be permitted on the workstation. This will not disable the workstation's ability to dial-up through a modem.

Affected keys

HKEY_LOCAL_MACHINE\Software\Microsoft\Windows\CurrentVersion\Policies\Network

Table 4-33. Modified Keys from Windows 95/98 Disable Dial-in

Policy	Value	Data Type	Enable	Disable
Disable Dial-in	NoDialIn	REG _DWORD	1	0 or no value

File and print sharing

These policies are available in the Window 95/98 computer system policy only and relate largely to peer-to-peer networking. The peer-to-peer networking idea started in Windows 3.11 for Workgroups and is still present in Windows 95/98 today. There are times when this functionality can be useful, but in general it is probably best if it is disabled. If your users require a common area for sharing then this is best provided on a network server rather than sharing the workstation filesystem. They will still have the same functionality, but the service will be better (if a user shuts down his workstation then the files are no longer visible) and the files can be backup up centrally. There are issues to do with security around this also in that the central NDS authentication is more appropriate for granting access to network resources. Printer services can similarly be provided better via a print queue on the server.

Affected keys

HKEY_LOCAL_MACHINE\System\CurrentControlset\Services\NcpServer\Parameters

Table 4-34. Modified Keys from Windows 95/98 Disable File SAP Advertising

Policy	Value	Data Type	Enable	Disable
Disable SAP Advertising	Use_Sap	REG _DWORD	0	1

Affected keys

HKEY_LOCAL_MACHINE\Software\Microsoft\Windows\CurrentVersion\Policies\Network

Table 4-35. Modified Keys from Windows 95/98 Disable File and Print Sharing

Policy	Value	Data Type	Enable	Disable
Disable File Sharing	NoFileSharing	REG _DWORD	1	0 or no value
Disable Print Sharing	NoPrintSharing	REG _DWORD	1	0 or no value

SNMP

The Simple Network Management Protocol (SNMP) allows the workstation to be monitored from an SNMP management station. The issues are similar to those mentioned under "System" below except that an additional registry key can be set for Windows 95/98.

Affected keys

HKEY_LOCAL_MACHINE\System\CurrentControlSet\Services\SNMP\Parameters\RFC1156Agent

Table 4-36. Modified Keys from Windows 95/98 SNMP MIB RFC 1156

Policy	Value	Data Type	Enable	Disable
Internet MIB (RFC 1156)	sysContact	REG _SZ	Text	No value
Internet MIB (RFC 1156)	sysLocation	REG _SZ	Text	No value

System

The system policies differ under the two platforms but only because the run section has more options under Windows 95/98.

SNMP

These settings allow for the configuration of the Simple Network Management Protocol (SNMP). These policies are available in Windows NT and Windows 95/98 computer system policies, but are set under Network SNMP in the Window 95/98 computer system policy. The policy enables communities and permitted managers of the workstation.

Affected key

HKEY_LOCAL_MACHINE\System\CurrentControlSet\Services\SNMP\Parameters\ValidCommunities

Table 4-37. Modified Key from Windows 95/98 and NT SNMP Communities

Policy	Value	Data Type	Enable	Disable
Communities	Incrementing integer starting with 1	REG_SZ	Text of valid community integer	Invalid community number

Affected key

HKEY_LOCAL_MACHINE\System\CurrentControlSet\Services\SNMP\Parameters\PermittedManagers

Table 4-38. Modified Key from Windows 95/98 and NT SNMP Managers

Policy	Value	Data Type	Enable	Disable
Permitted Managers	Incrementing integer starting with 1	REG_SZ	Text of valid community integer	Invalid community number

Affected key

HKEY_LOCAL_MACHINE\System\CurrentControlSet\Services\SNMP\Parameters\TrapConfiguration\Public

Table 4-39. Modified Key from Windows 95/98 and NT SNMP Community Traps

Policy	Value	Data Type	Enable	Disabled
Traps for Public Communities	Incrementing integer starting with 1	REG_SZ	Text of valid community integer	Invalid community number

Run

These policies are available in Windows NT and Windows 95/98 computer system policies and when enabled will allow you to centrally define programs, which should be run during the login process.

Affected key

HKEY_LOCAL_MACHINE\Software\Microsoft\Windows\CurrentVersion\Run

Table 4-40. Modified Key from Windows 95/98 and NT Run Applications

Policy	Value	Data Type	Enable	Disable
Run	Application Name	REG_SZ	Path	No value

User profiles

This policy allows the use of roaming profiles on the Windows 95/98 workstation when enabled.

Affected keys

HKEY_LOCAL_MACHINE\Software\Microsoft\Windows\CurrentVersion\Policies\Network\Logon

Table 4-41. Modified Keys from Windows 95/98 User Profiles

Policy	Value	Data Type	Enable	Disable
Enable User Profiles	UserProfiles	REG _DWORD	1	0 or no value

Network path for Windows setup

When an extra option is installed on the workstation, the system looks for the setup files from the location it was originally installed from, i.e., a CD-ROM drive. When this policy is enabled, you are able to specify an alternate location for these files such as a network share. The value entered can be either a connected drive or a UNC path. When disabled, the setup path will be set to the original install. This policy is only available in the Windows 95/98 computer system policy.

> If you copy the Windows install directory to a directory on the network, it means that you will not have to carry the CD-ROM around with you all the time. This seems like a good idea, but if you install a piece of software that would normally prompt you to put the Windows CD-ROM in to copy some files, this prompting will not occur when the Windows install is on the network. Why does this matter? Well, after installing files from say, the Windows 95 CD-ROM, you should reinstall the Service Pack, in case there are patches to be applied. There are therefore pros and cons to having the Windows install files stored on the network. One solution is to have the files available, but only after deliberately mounting the drive—that way you know when to apply the service pack. The other obvious solution is to apply the Service Packs to the Windows install directory.

Network path for Windows tour

This policy allows you to change the location path to the Windows tour program when enabled. The value entered can be either a connected drive or a UNC path and must end with *tour.exe*. This policy is only available in the Windows 95/98 computer system policy.

Affected keys

HKEY_LOCAL_MACHINE\Software\Microsoft\Windows\CurrentVersion\Setup

Table 4-42. Modified Keys from Windows 95/98 Setup and Tips Path

Policy	Value	Data Type	Enable	Disable
Network Path for Windows Setup	SourcePath	REG _DWORD	Path	No value
Network Path for Windows Tour	TourPath	REG _DWORD	Path	No value

Windows NT Network Sharing

These policies are available in the Windows NT computer system policy only, and are designed to restrict the networking functionality of the system. Peer-to-peer networking is possible under Windows NT/2000 but requires privileges to set up. If you don't plan to use peer-to-peer then you may as well remove the browser and server service on the workstation. Peer-to-peer networking can usually be replaced by a common area for sharing files on a network server, which is regularly backed up.

When a drive or directory is shared, the share may be hidden by placing a $ symbol at the end of the share name. By default the root of the Windows NT/2000 partition is shared as C$ and an ADMIN$ share is also enabled. By enabling the Create Hidden Drive Shares policy these hidden drive shares will be created.

Affected keys

HKEY_LOCAL_MACHINE\System\CurrentControlSet\Services\LanManServer\paramaters

Table 4-43. Modified Keys from Windows NT Network Sharing

Policy	Value	Data Type	Enable	Disable
Create Hidden Drive Shares (workstation)	AutoShareWks	REG_DWORD	1	0
Create Hidden Drive Shares (workstation)	AutoShareServer	REG_DWORD	1	0

Windows NT Printers

These policies are available in the Windows NT computer system policy only and are similar to the issues discussed previously with regard to peer-to-peer networking, except that it concentrates on printer sharing rather than file sharing. If users wish to share a printer, it is probably best to use a print queue to perform the service rather than use peer-to-peer printing.

Affected keys

HKEY_LOCAL_MACHINE\ System\CurrentControlSet\Control\Print

Table 4-44. Modified Keys from Windows NT Printers

Policy	Value	Data Type	Enable	Disable
Disable Browse Thread on This Computer	DisableServer-Thread	REG_DWORD	1	0 or no value
Scheduler Priority	SchedulerThread-Priority	REG_DWORD	1>Normal 0=Normal	ffffffff
Beep for Error Enabled	BeepEnabled	REG_DWORD	1	0

Windows NT Remote Access

These policies are for the configuration of Remote Access on a client workstation and are available in the Window NT computer system policy only.

Affected keys

HKEY_LOCAL_MACHINE\System\CurrentControlSet\Services\RemoteAccess\Parameters

Table 4-45. Modified Keys from Windows NT Remote Access

Policy	Value	Data Type	Enable	Disable
Max Number of Unsuccessful Authentication Retries	AuthenticateRe-tries	REG_DWORD	Retries in hex	No value
Max Time Limit for Authentication	AuthenticateTime	REG_DWORD	Time (secs) in hex Default =120	No value
Wait Interval for Callback	CallbackTime	REG_DWORD	Time (secs) in hex Default =2	No value
Auto Disconnect	AutoDisconnect	REG_DWORD	Time (mins) in hex Default =20	No value

Windows NT Shell

It is possible to customize certain areas such as the Start menu via this set of policies. Central management and control of certain areas is probably a good idea. It is certainly a great relief to be able to make changes to these areas without having to visit every workstation. By making changes to the Custom folders, you will be able to replicate the changes throughout the network. The Start menu/Programs folder is certainly an area that would benefit from a centralized folder. If you enable the Custom Programs Folder policy, you will need to enter a mapped drive or UNC path to the Custom folder, but you will find that you have two Program folders—one local and the other remote. If this is your intention, that is fine, but if not, then enabling the Hide Start Menu Subfolders policy will remove the local program folder.

If you plan to use the NAL to manage the Start menu items then you may want to ignore the custom menus, because NAL will manage this area much better. These policies were originally designed by Microsoft to help manage the Start menu in a Microsoft domain. They can be used in the same way in a NetWare environment if you prefer. The policies are available in the Windows NT computer system policy only.

Affected keys

HKEY_LOCAL_MACHINE\Software\Microsoft\Windows\CurrentVersion\Explorer\UserShellFolders

Table 4-46. Modified Keys from Windows NT Custom Shared Folders

Policy	Value	Data Type	Enabled	Disabled
Custom Program Folders	Common Programs	REG_EXPAND_SZ	Path	No value
Custom Desktop Icons	Common Desktop	REG_EXPAND_SZ	Path	No value
Hide Start menu subfolders	Common Start Menu	REG_EXPAND_SZ	Path	No value
Custom Startup Folder	Common Startup	REG_EXPAND_SZ	Path	No value

Windows NT System

These policies are available in the Window NT computer system policy, and are policies for the workstation specifically for logon such as Logon Banner and file-system tuning.

Logon

The Logon Banner policy is useful for permanent text such as a legal message detailing the basis upon which the user is allowed to use the workstation. It is probably a good idea to have such a banner for legal reasons.

The Do Not Display Last Logged On User Name policy is very useful. I would advise anyone using a Windows NT/2000 workstation to enable this very useful policy, particularly for workstations that are shared between several people. More account lockouts are caused by the disablement of this policy than for any other reason. Why do users never read what is on the screen in front of them? If you allow the last username to be displayed, when the next user comes along, he will just type in the password without entering the username. This will result in a password failure. The user will then try the password again and again, until he realizes what he has done, and will then get it right. Unfortunately this may lock the user ID of the previous user, because it was his ID that had the password wrong. If you have a lot of shared workstations, it would be a good idea to clear the username of the last login.

Affected keys

HKEY_LOCAL_MACHINE\Software\Microsoft\WindowsNT\CurrentVersion\Winlogon

Table 4-47. Modified Keys from Windows NT Logon Polices

Policy	Value	Data Type	Enable	Disable
Logon Banner	LegalNoticeCaption	REG _SZ	Text	No Value
	LegalNoticeText	REG _SZ	Text	No Value
Enable Shutdown from Authentication Dialog Box	ShutdownWithoutLogon	REG _SZ	1	0
Do Not Display Last Logged on User Name	DontDisplayLastUser-Name	REG _SZ	1	0
Run Logon Scripts Synchronously	RunLogonScriptSync	REG _SZ	1	0

Filesystem

Options for the NTFS filesystem only. These policies are available in the Window NT computer system policy only, and include rules for the creation of filenames and filesystem performance improvements for read-only files.

Affected keys

HKEY_LOCAL_MACHINE\System\CurrentControlSet\Control\FileSystem

Table 4-48. Modified Keys from Windows NT File System Options

Policy	Value	Data Type	Enable	Disable
Do Not Create 8.3 Filename for Long Filenames	NtfsDisable8dot3Name-Creation	REG_DWORD	1	0 or no value
Allow Extended Characters in 8.3 Filenames	NtfsAllowExtended-Characterin8dot3name	REG_DWORD	1	0 or no value
Do Not Update Last Access Times	NtfsDisableLast-AccessUpdate	REG_DWORD	1	0 or no value

Windows NT User Profiles

These policies are available in the Window NT computer system policy only and seem to be fairly innocent. The Delete Cached Copies of Roaming Profiles policy is quite straightforward. When this policy is enabled, the user's roaming profile is removed from the workstation during the logout process. If you have a lot of users sharing workstations, it may be beneficial to remove the profiles to tidy up.

The Automatically Detect Slow Network Connections doesn't seem like an important policy, but it can create confusion. When the user logs in, his profile is downloaded from the server (when roaming profiles are enabled). In the event that a slow network is detected, the user will be asked if his profile should be downloaded or a locally cached copy should be used. A slow network is usually read as being a WAN link or a modem link. There are circumstances where this can happen on a LAN also, though. This is usually caused by either a network fault, a very busy network, or an unresponsive server. All in all, it causes confusion to the users who don't know what the statement means or how to answer it. There are more settings that you may wish to consider along with this policy, such as the Slow Network Connection Timeout and the Timeout for Dialog Boxes.

Affected keys

HKEY_LOCAL_MACHINE\Software\Microsoft\WindowsNT\CurrentVersion\Winlogon

Table 4-49. Modified Keys from Windows NT User Profiles

Policy	Value	Data Type	Enable	Disable
Deleted Cached Copies of Roaming Profiles	DeleteRoamingCache	REG _DWORD	1	0 or no value
Automatically Detect Slow Network Connections	SlowLinkDetectEnabled	REG _DWORD	1	0 or no value
Slow Network Connection Timeout	SlowLinkTimeout	REG _DWORD	Value in Hex	0 or no value
Timeout for Dialog Boxes	Show	REG _DWORD	Value in Hex	0 or no value

Windows 3.x Computer System Policy

The Windows 3.x computer system policies do not have nearly the functionality that Windows 95/98 and Windows NT/2000 do, but there is the ability to manage files on the workstation that is quite sophisticated and worth enabling if you have a number of Windows 3.x systems. The Windows 3.x client must have the Windows 3.x workstation manager (*WM3X.EXE*) installed at the end on the network startup script (*STARTNET.BAT*) in order to activate the file management.

Within this policy you will be able to indicate a file or list of files to be managed, as shown in Figure 4-14. These files can be either ASCII or binary files and the process is slightly different, depending upon which type of file you indicate. In the case of a binary file, you will need to indicate the source path and the destination path for the file. This file will then be downloaded to the workstation. The ASCII file type is useful for managing *.ini* or *.bat* files. In this case, you will also need to enter the destination path, but the source will be visible and editable within the object.

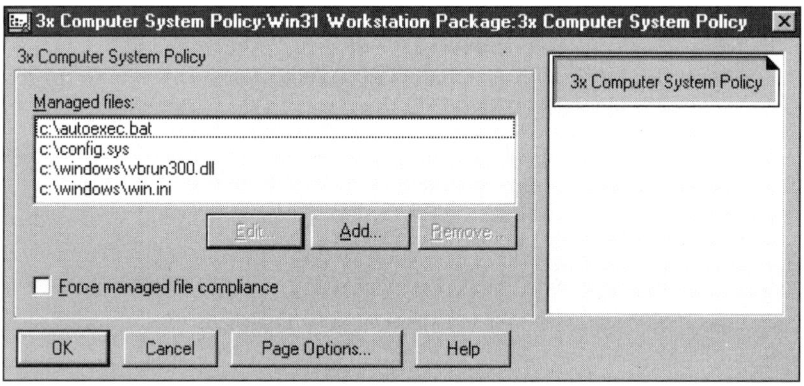

Figure 4-14. Windows 3.x managed files

The files are generally downloaded to the associated workstation only once, allowing a user to modify them at will. By checking the Force Managed File Compliance box, the files on the workstation that are being managed will be checked and replaced as necessary each time the workstation is started up.

Client Configuration Policy

The NetWare Client Configuration policy allows the network administrator to force standard configuration settings on the NetWare client installed on Windows NT/2000 and Windows 95/98 workstations (see Figure 4-15). In the case of Windows

NT/2000, the user will not (usually) have rights to modify these settings, but the Windows 95/98 user will. In either case, any change you have decided to make after installing the client on numerous workstations can be made via this policy without having to revisit all the workstations again. If you have both operating systems installed, the policy will have to be enabled in the Windows NT/2000 workstation and the Windows 95/98 workstation policy packages.

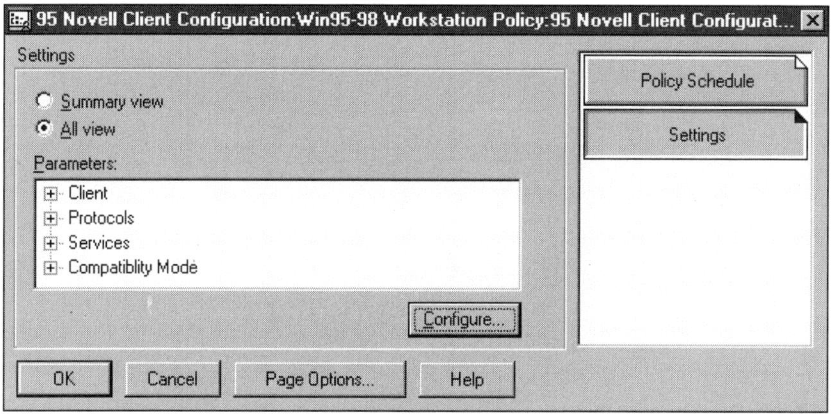

Figure 4-15. NetWare Client Configuration policy settings

The client configuration can be scheduled at a particular time or event. This schedule will allow the enforcement of this policy to differ from the schedule associated with the policy package. The policy allows you to indicate the settings for each workstation associated with it.

Within the policy you are able to select which parameters are to be distributed and under what circumstances. The default distribute option is distribute always, but other options are also available which allow you to distribute if the default is set or not set.

Computer Printer Policy

The Computer Printer policy allows the network administrator to add and configure printers on Windows NT/2000 and Windows 95/98 workstations. These policies are available for both platforms and are very similar. If you wish to take advantage of these policies on both platforms, the policy will have to be enabled in the Windows NT/2000 workstation and the Windows 95/98 workstation policy packages. It is essential to realize that when creating a Windows NT Computer Printer policy you must do so from a Windows NT/2000 workstation (see Figure 4-16). Similarly, for a Windows 95 Computer Printer policy, you must do so from a Windows 95/98 workstation. The associated drivers will be sourced from the workstation you are using when creating the policy. This policy is very useful when you have installed a new printer on your network, which you then wish to make available to all or a group of users. When the printer is installed, it will be available to all the workstations associated. The driver will be installed and configured automatically according to how you have configured it in the policy.

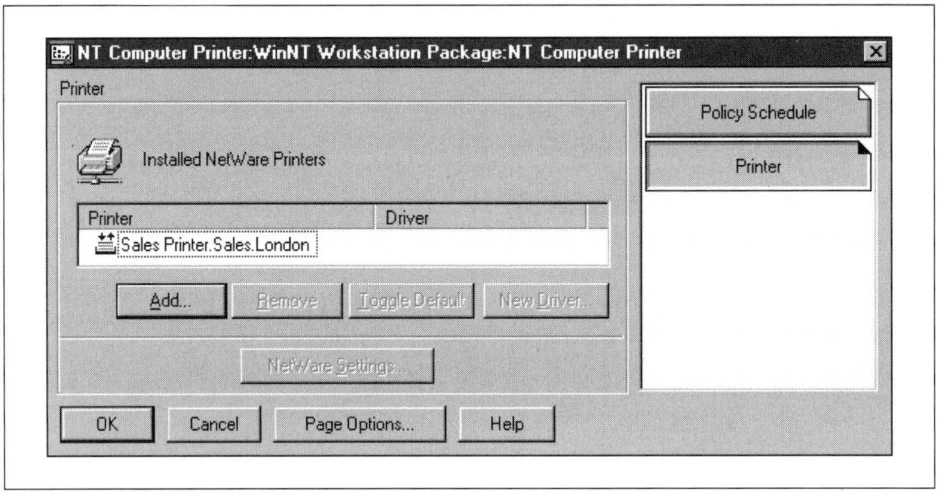

Figure 4-16. Windows Computer Printer policy

The policy will allow you to select an NDS print queue and associate an appropriate printer driver with it. This is all done for you because the printer selection is performed in the same way as if you were installing and selecting a local printer. The driver is then copied to the network volume where it is retrieved later when the user selects the printer. It is important to install all the drivers needed on your own workstation, then apply the Service Packs, because a patch may need to be applied to the driver. The service patch will replace or patch the driver and this updated driver will be uploaded to the server.

RAS Configuration Policy

The Remote Access Service (RAS) Configuration policy allows the network administrator to define standard configuration settings for the RAS control panel on Windows NT/2000 and Windows 95/98 workstations. To use the policy on both platforms, you will need to configure it in both the Windows NT workstation policy package and the Windows 95/98 workstation policy. The workstation scheduler will not execute any action until the dialup is complete and the connection made. When creating a RAS Configuration policy, you must do so from the platform for which it is being targeted, e.g., the NT workstation RAS policy must be configured from an NT workstation and likewise for Windows 95/98.

As with the previous policy, you must perform the RAS policy work after you have installed all the service packs and hot fixes available for the particular operating system. There may be patches that should be applied to distributed network version here as well.

Remote Management Policies

The ZENworks Remote Management product itself—what it does and how—is discussed at length in Chapter 8, *Remote Management*. This section will review the enforcement of the Remote Management client configuration settings for a user or a workstation. The Remote Management facility has five functional areas: General, Remote Control, Remote View, Remote File Transfer, and Remote Execute. There are minor differences between the user policy and the workstation policy in this regard in that the workstation policy has slightly more functionality.

User Remote Management Policies

The Remote Management policy applies to Windows 95/98 and Windows NT user policy packages. It must be configured in both places if you wish to enforce the policy for users on both platforms. The policy is also available in the Windows 3.x policy packages except that the Remote File Transfer is not present. The policies have issues of security that must be carefully considered in order that the user does not feel that an invasion of privacy has taken place. The options available are as follows:

General
: The General tab contains functionality that allows the IT operator to chat in real time with the user and perform remote diagnostics on the workstation.

Remote Control
: Remote Control allows the user's workstation to be taken over by the IT operator and has configuration to ensure security by allowing the user to give permission for a remote control or giving an audible or visible signal. Remote Control will allow the IT operator to see the workstation desktop and take over the keyboard in a read-write fashion.

Remote View
: Remote View is very similar to Remote Control, except that it is read-only; the IT operator can only see what the user is doing and cannot take over the workstation with the keyboard or mouse.

Remote File Transfer
: Remote File Transfer allows the IT operator to transfer files to the user's workstation. There is also an option to allow this to happen only with the user's permission.

Remote Execute

Remote Execute is similar to Remote File Transfer, except that it allows for a remote file execution; again, there is an option for user permission to be granted before this can take place.

Workstation Remote Management Policy

This section reviews the enforcement of the Remote Management Client Configuration settings on a workstation (see Figure 4-17). The Remote Management policy applies to Windows 95/98 and Windows NT workstation policy packages. It is also applicable to the Windows 3.x Computer policy except that Remote File Transfer is not available.

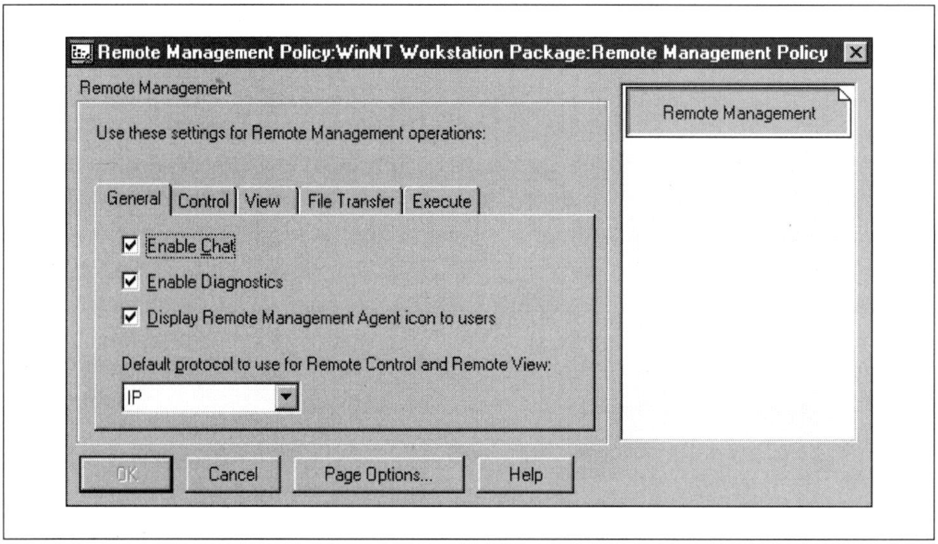

Figure 4-17. Windows Workstation Remote Management settings

Workstation Remote Management has the same dialog queries as the User Remote Management with the addition of general policy, which in this case has extra functionality to make the Remote Control agent visible or invisible and also which protocol to use to communicate with the user.

In the event that a Remote Management policy is in force for a user and a workstation at the same time, the following rules will dictate the state of the Remote Management process with respect to discrepancies between configuration settings:

- If either of the Remote Management policies has the Enable Remote Management setting disabled, that policy will take precedence.
- If either of the Remote Management policies has the Prompt User for Permission setting enabled, that policy will take precedence.

- If either of the Remote Management policies has the Give Audible Signal setting enabled, that policy will take precedence. If there is a difference between the times the signal is given, the smallest interval will take precedence.
- If either of the Remote Management policies has the Give Visible Signal setting enabled, that policy will take precedence. If there is a difference between the times the signal is given, the smallest interval will take precedence.

Restrict Login Policy

This policy allows and disallows selected users from accessing the associated workstation. This policy applies to Windows 95/98 and Windows NT workstation policy packages and will need to be implemented in both policy packages if both platforms are restricted.

The policy window in Figure 4-18 shows where a user can be granted access or denied access. You can browse the NDS to select a user, group of users, or container of users. If this policy is enabled, then all user objects not specifically granted access will be denied. If you do not grant access to anyone, then no one will be able to use the workstation. A user cannot be granted access if she is specifically denied access; therefore the user must be in one or the other columns (or neither), but never both.

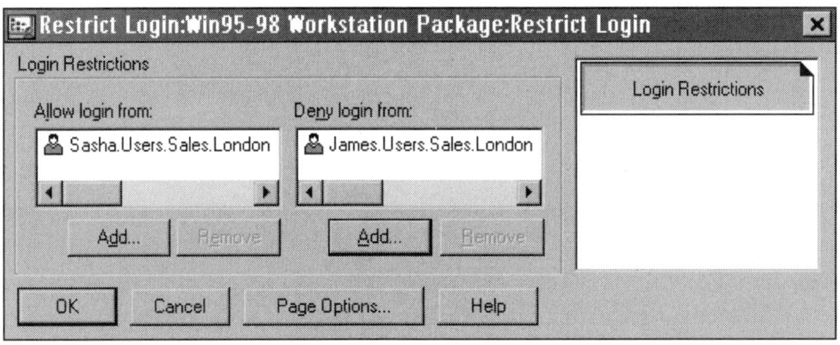

Figure 4-18. Windows Restrict Login policy

Search Policy

The search policy is only available in the container policy package and is the only policy in that package. The search policy speeds up login time by enhancing the way a user object finds its associated policies. If a user object initiated a search through the entire tree, which includes slow network links, the login time would be unacceptable. This policy can therefore be particularly useful for minimizing WAN traffic caused by policy package searches.

The policy allows you to set the search limits to be performed by "ring fencing" the area to be searched to a specific area. This search area can be defined by indicating a container or partition to search in:

[Root]
: Search for policies up to the root of the tree.

Selected container
: Search up to the selected container (defined later) for the policies as shown in Figure 4-19.

Partition
: Search up to the container, which forms the root of the local partition.

Object container
: Search only up the object's parent container.

Search Level
: Indicate the number of levels you wish the search to perform up to. The default is zero, which will only allow a search in the current container. A positive value will allow searches up the tree to that value and a negative value will search containers below the current container to that value.

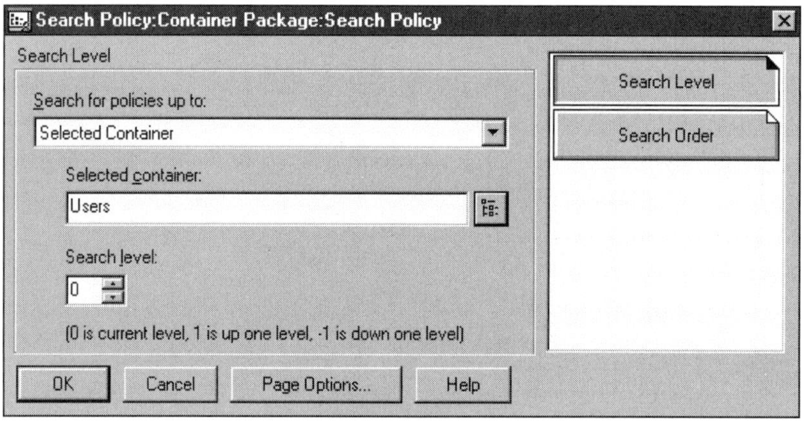

Figure 4-19. Container Search policy

You can specify the order, which will be used by the system to search for associated policy packages. There are three possible entries:

Object
: Must be either a user or a workstation.

Group
: Will usually be a group of users or group of workstations.

Container
: Will only be effective if the container has either users or workstations (or both) in it.

By default the search order is object, group, container. You can increase or decrease the priority of these items to suit your requirements.

Extensible Policies

These policies are very similar to the system policies discussed earlier. The extensible policies are available in the Windows NT and 95/98 user policy packages (user extensible policies) and the Windows NT and 95/98 computer policy packages (computer extensible policies).

The Microsoft *poledit* program uses configuration files to build the policy browse tree and to associate each leaf or policy in the tree with one or more registry keys. The files are referred to as *.adm* files. The *poledit* program was originally supplied with a *common.adm* file (common to Windows NT/2000 and Window 95/98), a *Windows.adm* file (for Windows 95/98), and a *winnt.adm* (for Windows NT/2000). These files had a section for the computer (class machine) and a section for the user (class user) that correspond to the user and computer system policies.

When Microsoft launched the Zero Administration Kit (ZAK), some of the functional restrictions were provided through extra *.adm* files that made restrictions for users and computers. Novell implemented some of these features in the system policies, but they did not provide any flexibility to add extra features via *.adm* files.

When *poledit* is used to read an *.adm* file, a series of policies are selected to be implemented by the system administrator who is running the program. When the process of selecting the policy and choosing the policy settings is complete, these settings are saved in a policy file which has the extension *.pol.* These policy files are used in a Windows NT networking environment to enforce policies, because the policy file (usually *config.pol*) is downloaded and implemented when each user logs in. Novell's implementation of system and user policies, whilst very powerful in the way they have been integrated into the NDS, has limitations because they cannot use the new *.adm* files that were introduced in the ZAK, unless a policy file (*config.pol*) was used to implement them.

Novell has now made up for this lack of flexibility by providing a mechanism for the importation of *.adm* files through extensible policies. The policy, shown in Figure 4-20, shows a Windows NT/2000 user policy package with the *Offic97.adm* Extensible policy loaded and shown in the righthand pane. If you were to look at a Windows NT/2000 computer extensible policy you would see a default computer icon rather than a default user one.

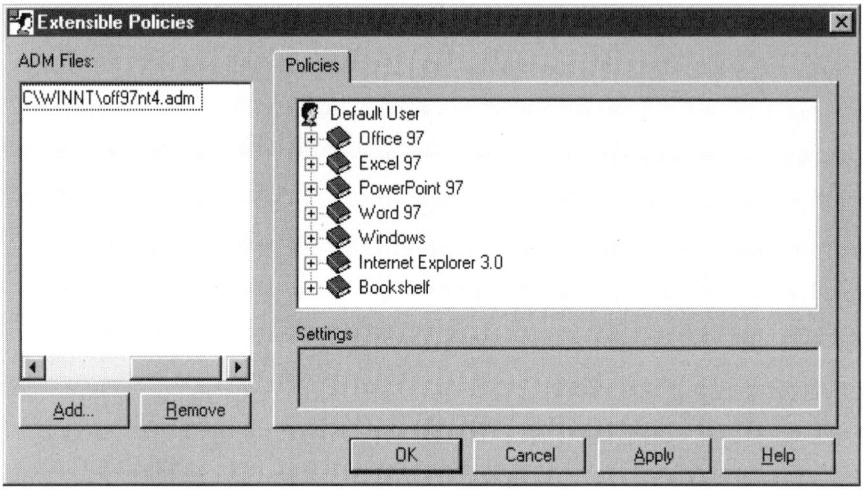

Figure 4-20. Windows NT user Extensible Policies

The policy details are not stored in the object in the same way that the system policies are, so you will need to ensure that the *.adm* files are available at all times by placing them on a network volume. It may be best to use a UNC path to the files if you have a lot of servers.

There is no particular reason why you could not create your own *.adm* files to use in this manner except that they are not easy files to write. The *.adm* file is a simple text file, but because the writing of these files is not obvious, you may wish to read how this can be done elsewhere.

Workstation Import Policy

If you wish to take advantage of workstation objects to provide associations to other objects such as application objects or to collect inventory, then you will need to enable this policy. Workstation objects are discussed at length in Chapter 5, *Workstation Objects and Inventory*, so we will not dwell on them here. Workstation import policies are available within the Windows 3.x, Windows 95/98, and Windows NT user policy packages, where they are found to be similar and are therefore treated together in this section.

The policy allows you to specify where you wish to locate the workstation objects in the NDS, and will allow you to specify this in the following ways:

Associated object container

The user policy package will be associated with a particular user or container. This option specifies that the object should be placed in that container.

Selected container

This option allows you to enter the container where the workstations should be placed in the field marked "Path." Note that the path in this case is an NDS context path and not a disk or UNC path.

User container

Workstation objects will be placed in the same container where the user object who initially registered the object resides.

There is also a mechanism that allows you to specify how the workstation will be named in the NDS. There are a variety of components to be selected in which their values are concatenated into a string, thereby making the workstation name. The most obvious are Computer Name, DNS Name, and Network Address, as shown in Figure 4-21.

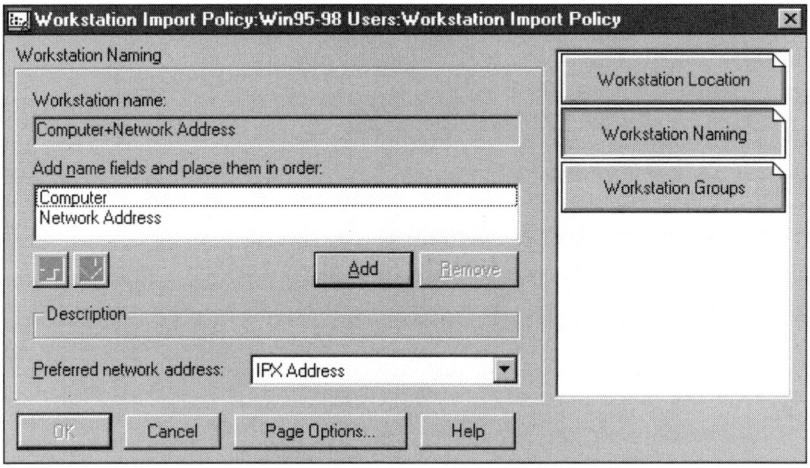

Figure 4-21. Workstation import policy naming

After the workstation is imported, you may wish to make it a member of an existing group. You can define this group in the object so that it will appear in the group without any manual intervention. The workstation may be a member of more than one group.

Workstation Inventory Policy

Traditionally, workstation inventories have consisted of data collected manually and entered manually into a database. The database becomes out of date quickly, unless you can afford the time to check and correct it. Most hardware inventories suffer from this problem because a static system was employed to solve a dynamic problem. Software inventories suffered even more from this problem because users are less likely to change hardware than software. The ZENworks inventory system (Figure 4-22) collects data at a frequency defined by you and stores the inventory data in a Sybase database that is located on one or more servers. Workstation inventory is available on Windows NT and Windows 95/98 workstation policy packages.

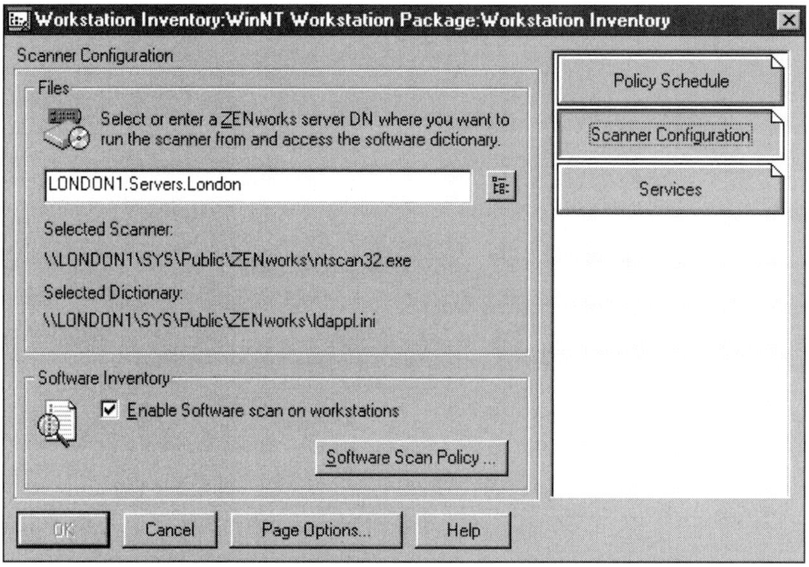

Figure 4-22. Workstation inventory policy

The window illustrated in Figure 4-22 shows the main configuration for the policy. You will need to indicate where the scanner software is located. In the case shown, the scanner is set to a Windows NT/2000-specific scanner program (*ntscan32.exe*) because it is a Windows NT workstation policy. If you enable the policy in a Windows 95/98 Computer policy package, the scanner will be *winscan.exe*.

If you wish to use the Software Inventory function, you need to configure it so that the software you wish to be recognized is selected, as shown in Figure 4-23. You may wish to select all of the software in the list, but remember that the inventory process will take longer if the selected list is long. The list shown is the file *ldappl.ini*, which is shown in the window in Figure 4-23.

The software recognition program will go through the hard disk(s) of the workstation and attempt to recognize the installed software by the size of one of the main

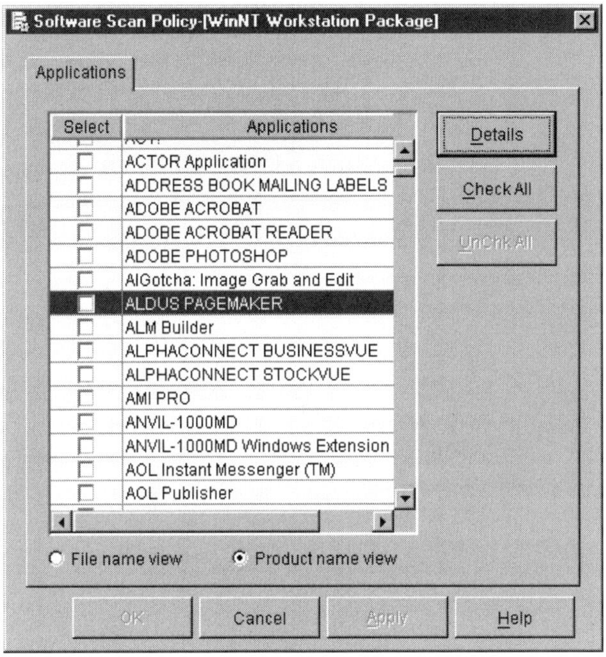

Figure 4-23. Software Inventory configuration

application files, as shown in Figure 4-24. This file could be a *.dll* file (as in Figure 4-23) or an executable file.

A sample from the *ldappl.ini* is shown below:

```
<I>,ACTOR.EXE,149328,Actor,2
<I>,ACTOR.EXE,150480,Actor,3
<I>,ACTOR.EXE,150672,Actor,3.1p
<I>,ACTOR.EXE,227696,Actor,4
<I>,ACTOR.EXE,415744,ACTOR Application,1 0 0 1
<I>,ALDIM3.DLL,213616,ALDUS PAGEMAKER,5
<I>,ALDIM3.DLL,245216,Adobe Pagemaker {German},5.0a
<I>,ALDIM3.DLL,281504,Adobe.Pagemaker+Enh.{Europe},5.0a
```

From this list it is quite obvious that a software package can be added, even allowing for different versions or different releases of the same version (different languages), by editing this file; however, this is *not* the recommended way of modifying the list, as detailed in Chapter 5. You will also need to specify where the inventory gatherer and storer NLMs are running and where the Sybase database is installed. This configuration can be set through the Services button.

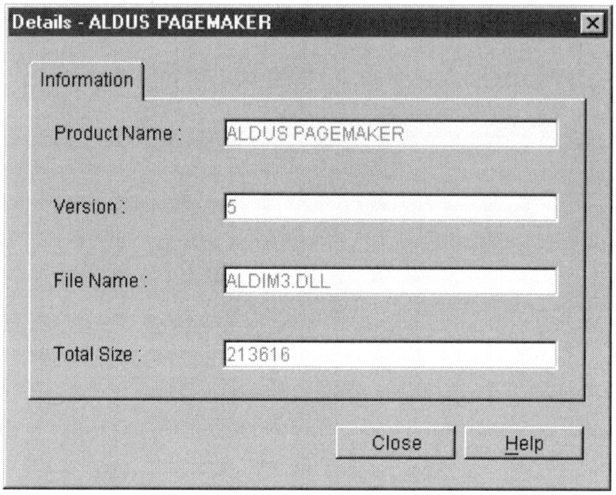

Figure 4-24. The Software Recognition program

A Final Word

Policy packages are very useful objects. They are the cornerstone for desktop management within ZENworks and should be used whenever necessary. Be careful: there is an obvious maintenance overhead to having too many of these objects. There has been a lot of discussion in this chapter about object placement, which is an important issue, but if you feel undecided about this issue, just create the object in the most sensible place and start using it. These objects are not anchored permanently in the NDS, and you can always move or recreate them later if you decide their location is wrong.

There is a lot of information to digest about these objects, so it may be appropriate to limit what you decide to do or use in the first instance. Careful consideration should also be given to system and user policies and how to employ the enable, disable, and ignore settings in your environment. There is certainly an argument for installing these objects in a test tree initially and limiting the number of objects and settings to a minimum. Use a test client workstation and ramp up the configuration settings until you have achieved a solution that fits your requirements. It is also very important to make notes of what you do; when the real installation occurs in the main tree, you can perform the configuration with minimum problems.

Finally, beta test your solution to sympathetic and influential users who can give you some constructive feedback about your implementation. The users are far less likely to complain about your workstation and desktop if they helped to design it.

5

Workstation Objects and Inventory

ZENworks allows workstations as well as users to be represented in the NDS by providing an object for each workstation. Like users, workstations have names, and the name given to the workstation object is quite flexible. The acknowledgment that workstations have requirements just as users do is quite unique in the server world of distributed systems, yet the concept is very important to allow the needs of modern distributed systems to be properly supported.

Workstations not only have an identity, but they also have contents and characteristics that need to be managed. This means that every workstation has hardware characteristics and software characteristics that make up the unique contents of a workstation. Both of these areas are important, and it is crucial that an up-to-date list of the hardware and software is available and at hand. This requirement is taken care of in the hardware and software inventory.

In order for workstations to be represented in the NDS in the same way that users are, they must have an object associated with them in the same way that users do. These special objects contain all the information about the workstation. Some of the information stored in the object is essential and some is optional. In this chapter I look at these special objects and how they can be used to empower the needs of your organization.

NDS Considerations

If you have a lot of users and therefore user objects, you will probably have a lot of workstations and workstation objects. The placement of these objects is very important in order to obtain acceptable performance from your NDS. If your partitions are approaching the guideline recommendations of up to 5,000 objects per partition and you have several thousand workstations to import, then you may wish to consider repartitioning before these new objects are added, as shown in Figure 5-1.

> The creation of workstation objects could potentially double the number of objects in your NDS. You should give careful consideration to how to restructure your tree in preparation for these new objects.

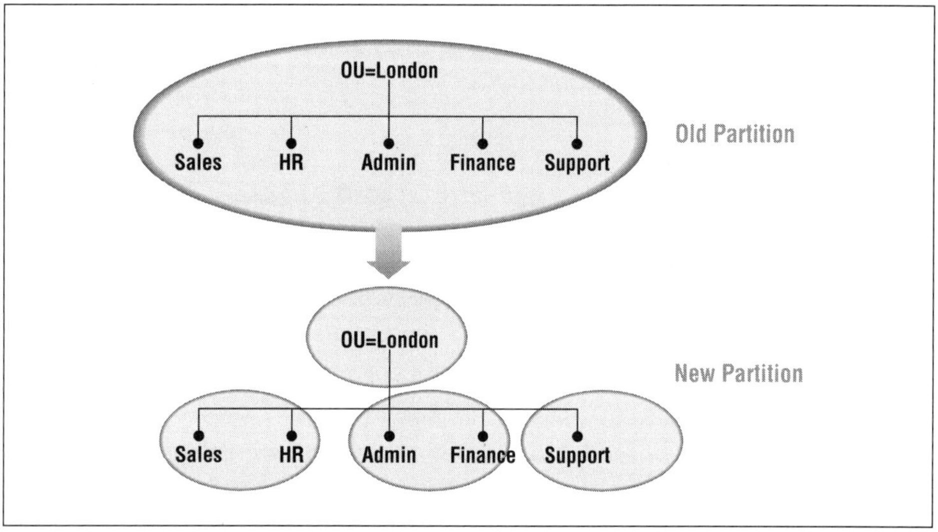

Figure 5-1. Repartitioning in preparation for new objects

A workstation object is not as frequently used or accessed by users as it is by the administrator. This means that their placement need not be close to the users, but organized in a way that is convenient to you. Figure 5-2 shows the workstation objects placed in a container of its own and in a partition that already has a few existing objects.

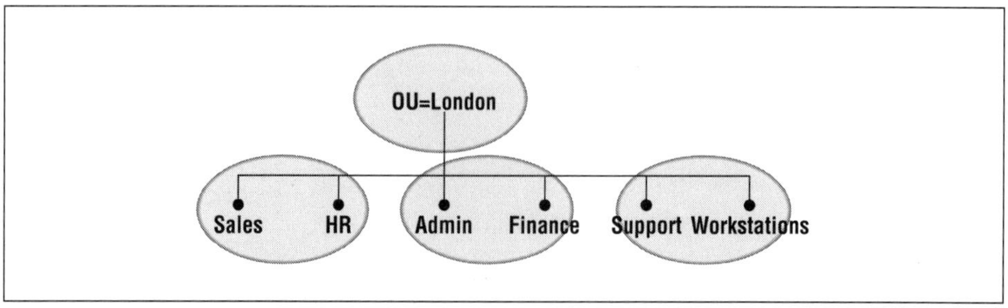

Figure 5-2. Workstation container placement

As with all ZENworks objects, the location of workstation objects in the NDS is important. It is crucial that they reside in a partition whose master replica is in the same geographical location as the workstations. The reason for this is simply performance, both from the point of view of accessibility of the object and in replication traffic on the WAN.

Workstation Objects

With the admission that workstations, like users, have needs, albeit in a slightly different sense, the workstation object becomes a significant factor in the planning and building of your network service. The objects can be associated with policies that dictate how the workstation appears to the user and how it can be secured from the user. The objects can be associated with applications, such that the application is visible only to certain workstations (rather than users). The workstation object is also important in the functioning of the Remote Management component of ZENworks. ZENworks requires these objects to exist for many desktop management components to work. You will need to eventually take a view on how to implement the workstation object in your organization.

Having therefore decided that workstation objects are a good thing, you embark on a project to create objects for all your workstations. Unfortunately, this process is complicated and tedious. The end result is worth the trouble, but you need to proceed carefully, testing the whole process until you have a plan that will work in your organization.

The Registration and Creation Process

Most objects can be created in the usual way, through the *NWADMIN* program by selecting the container and creating the object. This is not so with workstation objects, which have to be registered first before the creation process can begin. The registration is performed by enabling a policy in a policy package. The policy itself is explained in Chapter 4, *ZENworks Policy Packages*, but I will summarize it here as well.

The whole process begins with the workstation import policy in a user policy package. Selecting the workstation import policy and clicking the Details button will reveal several pages that need to be configured, as shown in Figure 5-3.

Workstation Location

This page allows you to specify where you wish the objects to be placed after they have been registered. The placement of these objects should be carefully considered. The workstation can be created in either the user's container, the same container as the workstation import policy, or a specific container. If you

How to Create Workstation Objects

1. Enable workstation object import policy for the users who are doing the registration.
2. Select where they should be created after registration.
3. Log in as one of the associated users.
4. Go to the user's parent container and import the workstation.

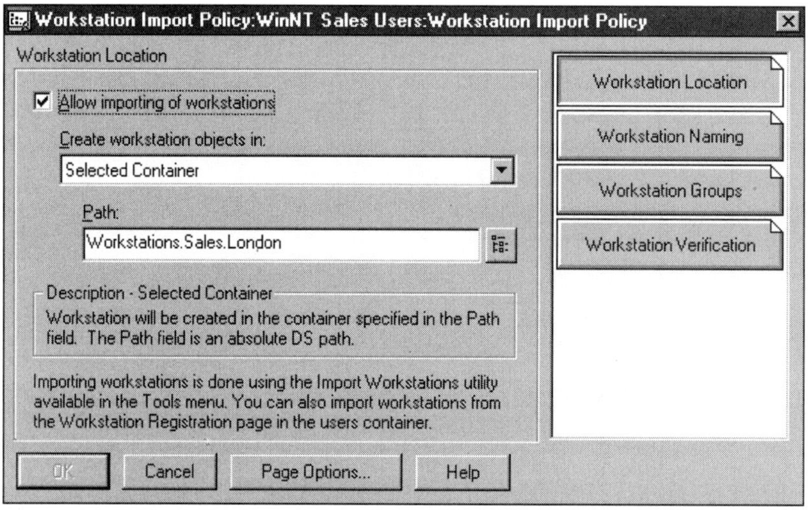

Figure 5-3. Workstation registration configuration

have decided on a special container for your objects, you will select the latter and indicate the container explicitly.

Workstation Naming

This setting is also important. Unlike users, who can be called just about anything, workstations have limitations on their names, because the name should represent a characteristic of the workstation. There is, however, a fair amount of flexibility in the name, which can be the computer name, network address, or an amalgamation of several components. Given that each object in a container must have a unique name, you would be well advised to choose a name which you are sure is unique. This could easily be the network address, except that you are unlikely to remember a workstation by its address. If you are sure that the computer name is unique, then it is certainly a suitable name.

If you are worried about duplication of names, append the network address to the workstation name. A name cannot exceed 64 characters in length.

Workstation Groups
: This setting allows you to group workstations geographically, departmentally, or by some other means. These groups have the same problems as user groups, so if you feel that grouping in this way has advantages, use it sparingly. It may be better to use containers to identify larger clusters of workstations and workstation groups to break them down into smaller sets.

Workstation Verification
: This setting specifies the time required to wait for the client to verify the workstation object creation after the initial registration process. This process allows the workstation to function as an "NDS user" because it cannot function normally until the object exists. The client in this case will not action any work that has been set for the workstation until it has verified that the object exists and is valid. The default value for this is 60 minutes, which seems reasonable, although if you plan to register all the workstations yourself, you may wish to reduce the time allowance.

When you have decided the best settings for your workstation registration and creation and have configured the policy, you may wish to test it first by associating the policy with a suitable user ID. This ID can be used to test the whole process before wholesale implementation of the policy. It is important to realize that when the user logs in, he will need to write to a specific area of the NDS schema created during the install process specifically for this task. If you opted not to give rights for workstation registration during the install process, you will have to go through this procedure at this stage. Remember, though, that if you grant these rights, it can be difficult to subsequently revoke them. It is probably better to use an Admin-equivalent ID that has the rights anyway than to grant the rights to all users without understanding what is involved. The rights granted in this case are quite specific and do not endanger the security of your NDS.

Having associated a user ID with the workstation import policy, you will have to grant rights for that user to write the workstation registration data to the schema. This step is performed using the *WSREG.EXE* program, which can be found in the *Win32* subdirectory of *sys\public*. Run the program, indicate the container that you wish to grant rights to, and you are ready for the next step. Next you will have to log into a workstation with the user ID associated in the previous step. During the login procedure, the user policy will be executed and will now also execute the workstation registration program, which will write the workstation information to the NDS. The workstation should now be registered in the user's parent container. Open this container, select the Workstation Registration page, and you should see the workstation registration in the window, as shown in

Figure 5-4. Select the workstation and click the Import button. The workstation will now be created in the location specified in the user policy.

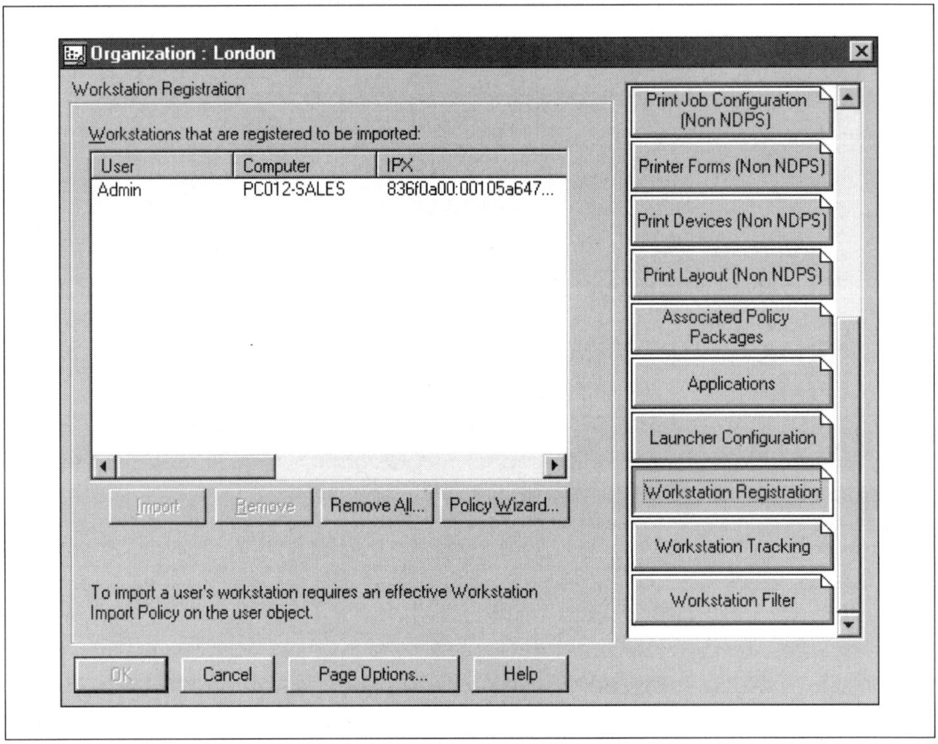

Figure 5-4. Workstation Registration data

The workstation objects can actually be created in two different ways. The first is the method already discussed, in which the workstation is selected in the container and imported manually. You are also able to select several workstations in the usual way with the Shift or Ctrl keys. The second method is through the *NWADMIN* program. From the Tools menu, select Import Workstations and you will be presented with a dialog box allowing you to select a container to read the registrations. There is also an Include Subcontainers checkbox, which allows you to perform this task on a large branch of the tree or even the whole NDS tree.

Having created this new object, the obvious next step is to look at the workstation object details. Open the workstation object and you will be presented with a screen similar to Figure 5-5. I discuss this series of pages in the next section.

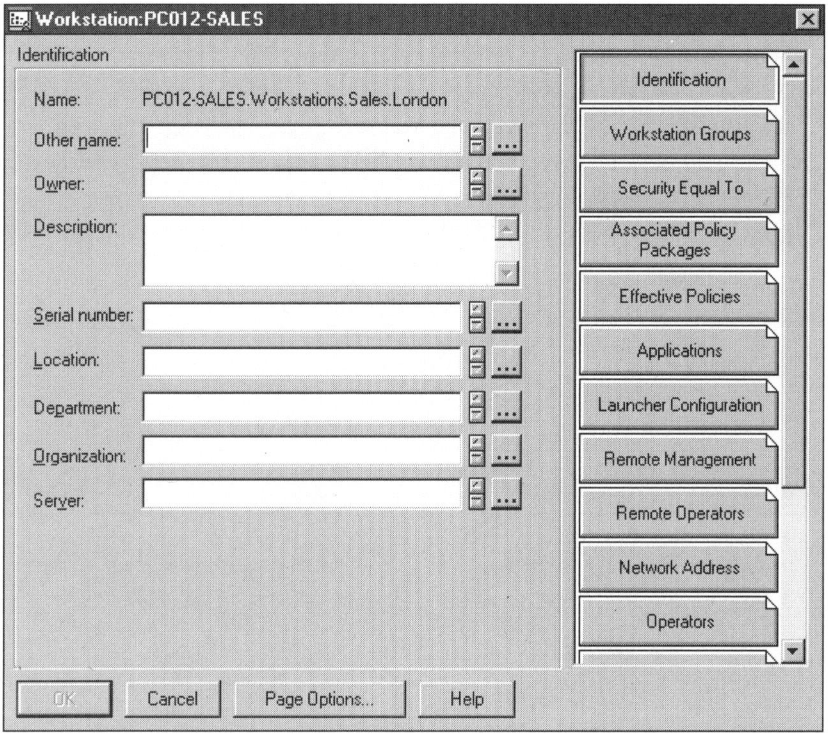

Figure 5-5. Workstation object details

Workstation Object Details

As with all objects, when they are opened there is a varying range of properties to be understood and configured. These properties are all represented as pages in the object in the usual way. None of the contents of the object are earth-shattering in significance, but the issues need to be discussed nonetheless.

Identification

This page contains numerous fields to enter details about the workstation, its owner, and its location. These details are important when you have a large number of workstations in your organization. There are also fields available for serial number and a description box that allows you to enter other information about the workstation, such as the hardware maintainer and the contact details.

Workstation Groups

Workstation groups are very useful for organizing workstations in a host of different ways. Because the workstation object creation process was initiated through a user policy package, this allows you to group the workstations in the same way as you have grouped the users. If you have a user policy package, for say, the Sales Department, you can specify that when the workstations are created, they are placed in a workstation group called Sales.

Workstations can be members of several groups. The Workstation Groups page allows you not only to view which groups the workstation is a member of, but also to specify other groups of which the workstation should be a member.

Security Equal To

All NDS objects have rights that can be assigned in a variety of ways. If you wish the workstation to have the same rights as another object, then that object can be indicated here. You may wish to assign the same rights to workstations that you do to users; if this is the case, indicate a reference user object in the window. The concept of rights is important if you are to regard the workstation as an entity with needs. If the workstation needs resources from the NDS or fileserver, they may need some rights to acquire them.

Associated Policy Packages and Effective Policies

In Chapter 4, I discussed the ZENworks policy packages. Some of these packages are associated with users and some with workstations. When a policy package is directly associated with a workstation, the relevant policies will appear in this window. The policy package will be shown only if the workstation is explicitly associated with the package. If the package is associated with the parent container or a workstation group, then the package contents will be shown in the effective policies page. There is also a mechanism to associate a policy package with the workstation and to view the details of the package.

Applications

Application objects are discussed in detail in Chapter 6, *The Novell Application Launcher*. These objects represent applications that the object knows how to run, install, and make visible to the user in a variety of ways. Generally speaking, a user can double-click an icon to run a program. These icons are frequently shortcuts to the real location of the executable program. The Novell Application Launcher places special NAL shortcuts to application objects, where they can be conveniently accessed. The locations of these special shortcuts are shown in Figure 5-6 and are listed as follows:

Force Run

The Force Run option executes the application automatically without giving the user a choice. To enable it, check the first column next to the application.

App Launcher

The Application Launcher is a special window in which you can display all the available applications for the workstation. If you wish the application to become visible in this window, check the second column.

Start Menu

The Application icon can also be placed in the Start menu on the workstation. If this is desirable for the application, check the third column.

Desktop

If you want the icon to be placed on the user's desktop, check the fourth column.

System Tray

The system tray is an area on the taskbar. If you wish the icon to be located there, check the fifth column.

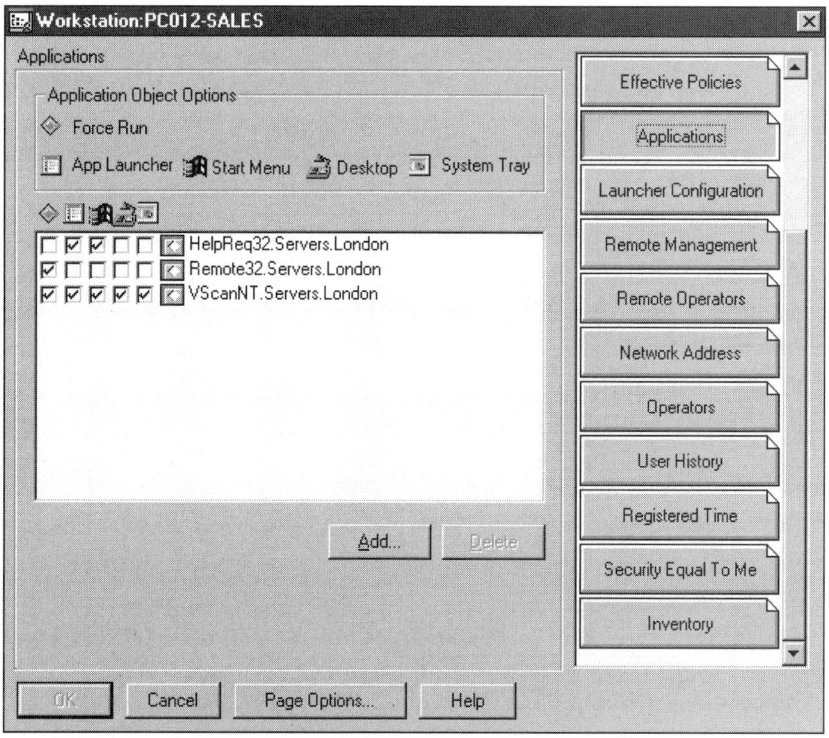

Figure 5-6. Workstation associated applications

Launcher Configuration

The Novell Application Launcher must be correctly configured in order for users and workstations to see and make use of application objects. This configuration can take place in a user object, a workstation object, or a container object. The configuration details for the Application Launcher are fully explained in Chapter 6. If you need to specifically modify the Application Launcher for a particular workstation, the details can be entered here.

Remote Management

Remote Management allows a Helpdesk operator to take control of a remote workstation in order to assist a user or perform remote diagnostics. This component is usually configured within a policy package as described in Chapter 4, but can also be configured on a per-workstation basis if a particular workstation has this requirement. The full details of the Remote Management utility are described in Chapter 8, *Remote Management*.

Remote Operators

The Remote Management function available to the Helpdesk operators is a useful and powerful tool, but it is not a privilege that should be granted to everyone. At the same time, it may not be desirable to grant full Admin rights to operators who wish to perform remote management. This page allows you to specify users who have rights to remotely manage the workstation. The ZENworks Remote Management feature is discussed in detail in Chapter 8.

Network Address

All workstations obviously must have a network address in order to communicate with the NetWare server. This address can either be an IPX address or an IP address. The address is displayed in this dialog box. If both protocols are installed, then both will be displayed.

Operators

If you wish to grant users the right to modify the contents of the workstation object, then add them to the list shown in this page.

User History

It is frequently useful to know which users have been using a particular workstation. If you wish to know to what extent users are sharing workstations, this page is a simple way of finding out. This information is visible through this page, although it is not really useful for audit purposes because there is very little other information such as when the user was using the workstation. The users listed in this page are added when the workstation registration program is run on the workstation.

Registered Time

The time stored in this field shows when the workstation registration program was last run on the workstation. The value here will be the workstation import time if the workstation registration program has never been run on the workstation.

Security Equal To Me

When an NDS object has been granted rights using the Security Equal To page and this object was used as the reference for it, then the objects inheriting this object's rights will be displayed on this page.

Inventory

If you wish to take advantage of ZENworks' ability to collect inventory on the workstation, then you need to enable it in the associated workstation policy package. Through the Inventory page in the workstation object, it is possible to view summary information about the workstation inventory. The issues of workstation inventory will be discussed later in this chapter.

The Inventory Server and Database Server

The inventory function is a very useful part of ZENworks, but as always, it requires a degree of planning and preparation before you embark. You must consider where to store the data and where the server-based data management programs are to run. The way this is accomplished will vary according to the number of workstations being inventoried and your network topology, but there are two server concepts that need to be considered:

The inventory server
: This server runs the Gatherer process, which accepts the data from the workstation and reorganizes it so that it can be stored in the database tables. The data is held in temporary files on the server that are picked up by the Storer process. This process takes the temporary files and sends them to the database server.

The database server
: The database server holds the inventory data in a file on the *sys* volume called *\public\zenworks\database\zeninv.db*. The database server runs the Sybase process that manages the data in the file.

In the simplest implementation, the inventory server and the database server may be the same machine, and indeed, that is probably the best solution for a LAN-based Netware installation with fewer than 3,000 workstations, just because it is simpler to implement and manage. If you have more workstations, you may consider multiple inventory servers and a single database server, as shown in Figure 5-7.

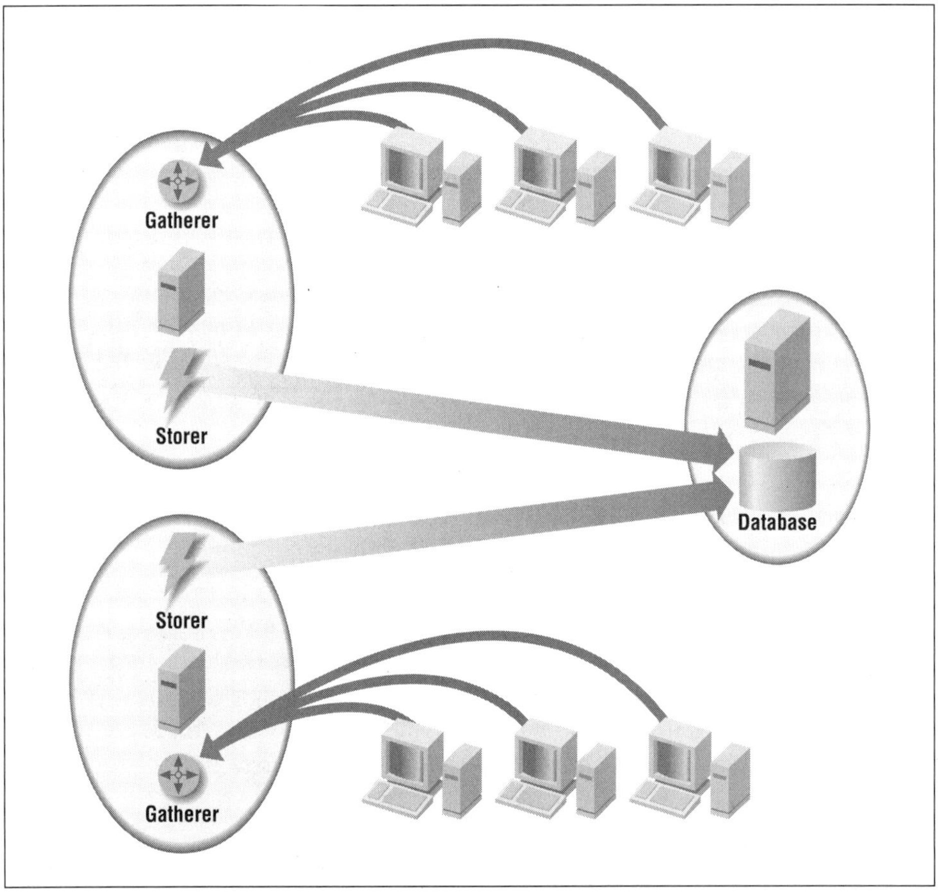

Figure 5-7. Multiple inventory servers and a single database server

If you have more than 10,000 workstations, you will not only need multiple inventory servers, but possibly more than one database server as well. The problem with this is that there is no mechanism for the databases to communicate with each other, so any reports will be on a per-database server basis. In this situation you will probably need to export the data from each server to a comma-separated value file and then import it into a spreadsheet.

> Plan to have an inventory server for each LAN of up to 3,000 workstations and a database server for every 10,000 workstations. If you have LANs connected via WANs, you may need to have a database server at each geographical location if the link is slow. Do not use inventory servers at the other end of WAN links or modem lines.

The inventory servers can become very busy if they receive and process data from thousands of workstations. You should consider providing a standalone server for this purpose; otherwise, functionality from that server may be greatly reduced.

The database server should also be considered carefully, particularly with regard to memory requirements. The server has a memory cache that uses a minimum of 16 MB of memory. This value should be increased 64 MB if you are storing data from 3,000 workstations. This size can be changed by closing all connections to the server, shutting down the Sybase server process, modifying the command that starts the process in the *sybase.ncf* file, and modify, the cache parameter from `-c 16M` to `-c 64M` or whatever value you are increasing to. It is also important to realize that a drastic increase in the cache size may require additional physical RAM on the server.

Workstation Inventory

Workstation inventory generally refers to hardware inventory, but includes an inventory of the installed software as well. The software inventory will be discussed later in this chapter. The workstation inventory can be enabled through a workstation policy package. The creation of policy packages, which contain a host of functions to enable, disable, and restrict the workstation, is covered in Chapter 4.

Once you have created one or more workstation objects, you can create and configure a policy package with which to associate them. If you wish to collect the workstation inventory, you will need to create a workstation object for the workstation, associate it with a workstation policy package, then enable and configure the workstation inventory, as shown in Figure 5-8.

The policy has three pages that need to be correctly configured in order for the inventory function to work:

Policy Schedule

The inventory can be scheduled to run at certain times or be triggered by events. You may not wish the work to be done during login, because it will only increase login time, which the users will invariably complain about. A

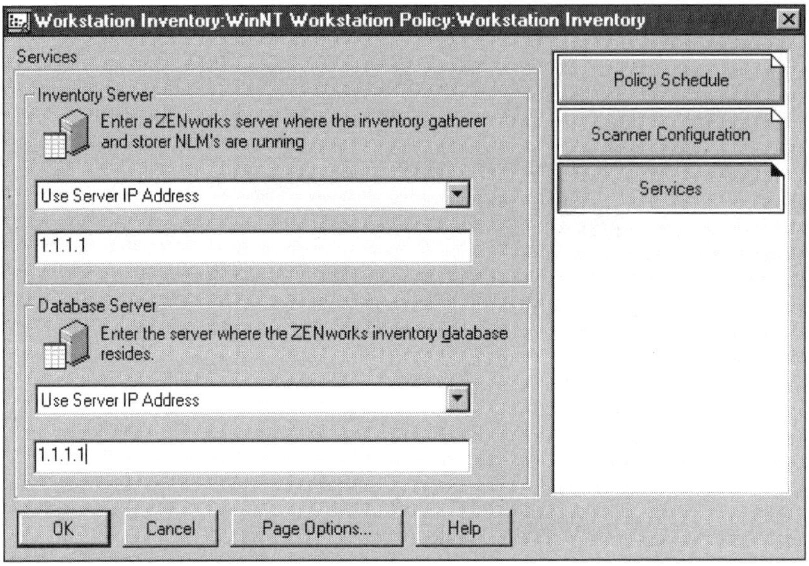

Figure 5-8. Workstation inventory configuration

better choice may be the middle of the night, or when the screensaver is active.

Scanner Configuration

In order for the scan to take place, you will need to indicate where the scanner program is located. There are different scanner programs for Windows NT/2000 (*NTSCAN32.EXE*) and Windows 95/98 (*WINSCAN.EXE*), which are provided by NetWare for the purpose (although there is no scanner available for Windows 3.1). You will also need to indicate the dictionary from which to obtain software package details for the identification of applications installed on the workstation. If you want the software scan to take place, you will need to enable it here as well. Click the Software Scan Policy button to indicate which packages should be detected.

Services

After the scan has taken place, you will need to indicate where the data should be sent and how it should be managed. The inventory server should have its address entered in the first field and the second should contain the address of the inventory database server. It may well be the case that the inventory server and the inventory database server are on the same physical machine.

When the workstation boots, it will log into the NDS, and the policies associated with the workstation will be executed, including the workstation inventory. In order to enable the workstation to run the programs associated with the scanner software, the workstation will need to be given the NetWare filesystem rights File Scan and Read to the *sys:public\zenworks* directory, shown in Figure 5-9. This is a clear example of a workstation being given specific rights separately to the user.

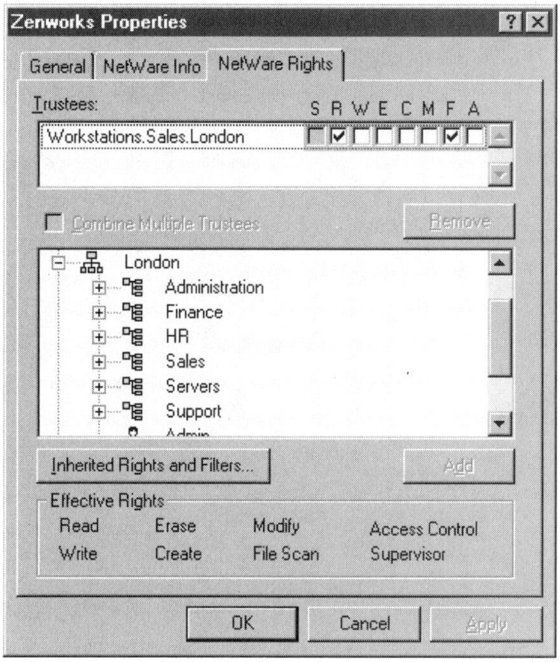

Figure 5-9. Assigning workstation object rights to NetWare volumes

After the rights have been granted, reboot the workstation and the inventory program will run, collecting the data and sending it to the database. This process may take a few minutes or a few seconds, according to the speed of the processor and what is being collected.

The inventory can be viewed by opening the workstation object and selecting the Inventory Page, as shown in Figure 5-10. This figure shows a summary of the data collected, including operating system information, hardware information, and network address data.

To view the full inventory for this workstation, click on the More Workstation Information button. This runs a Java application (which is a bit slow) to load a further information window. The window displays the inventory, as shown in Figure 5-11.

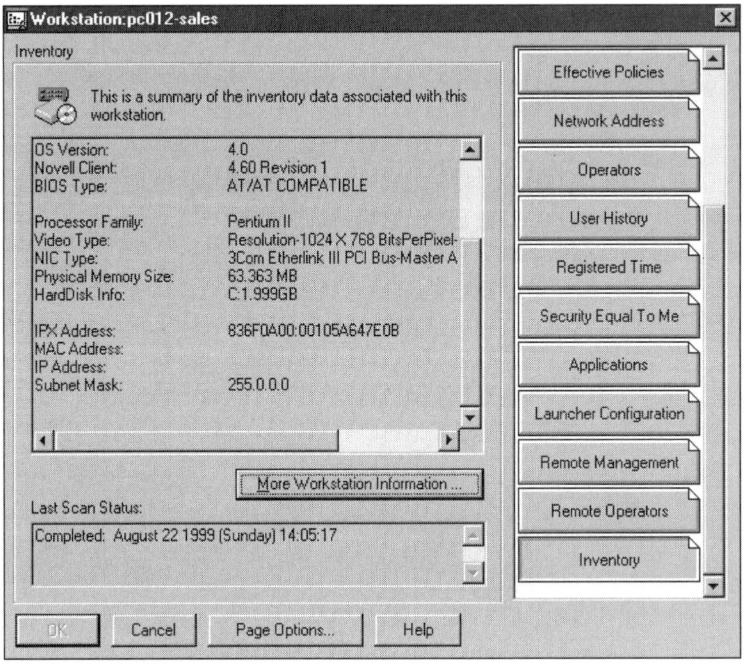

Figure 5-10. Inventory summary

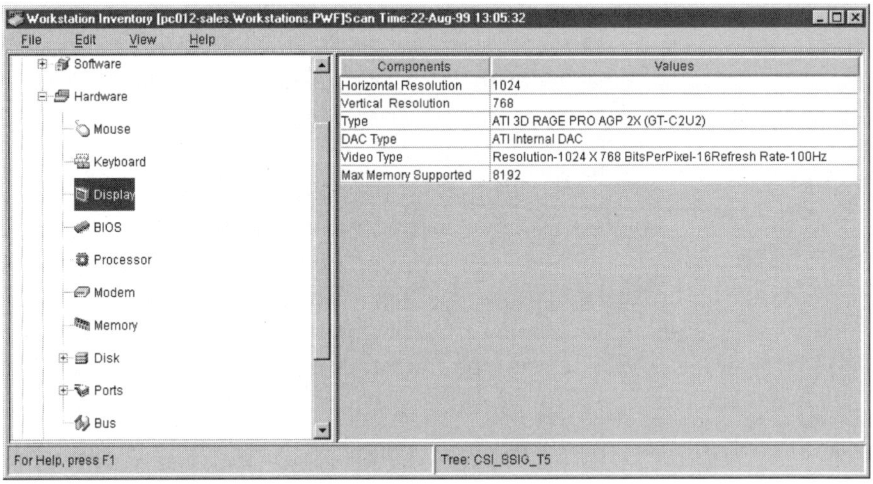

Figure 5-11. Full inventory

Software Inventory

The workstation software component is the real culprit when it comes to differences in workstation characteristics. When a workstation starts misbehaving it is sometimes the hardware at fault, but most often it is software. Each workstation is a dynamically changing system where the software components add and modify registry keys, change the contents of memory addresses, and process data. All these components contend for resources, and sometimes that means that it all goes wrong. When the user phones the Helpdesk and says, "My computer has crashed; what is wrong?" you need as much information about the workstation's software as possible. What has the IT department installed? What has the user installed? A software inventory can be immensely valuable in this situation. It is no less valuable for managing software licenses. No computer manager wants to be outside the law on computer software licenses, but not knowing what is going on in your organization is a serious problem. You must be in control of software licenses and going around once a year to check will not be good enough, even if you have the time and inclination to do it.

The ZENworks software inventory tool is not a sophisticated system, but it will allow you to obtain most of the critical information about what is installed on the remote system. The inventory can be collected as often as you like, but collecting too frequently will probably cause irritation of the user and unnecessary load on the network and inventory server. It is not possible to collect the data independently of the hardware inventory, so a complete inventory must be scheduled for an appropriate time or event.

To enable the software inventory for a set of workstations, not only must the Enable Software Inventory box be checked in the Scanner Configuration page on the workstation inventory policy, but you must also click the button marked Software Scan Policy, which will reveal a window similar to that shown in Figure 5-12. You will need to go through the list to define what should be searched for on the set of workstations covered by the workstation policy package.

To enable the software inventory you need only check the appropriate box in the Scanner Configuration page. The problem is that you will get no data unless you modify the Software Scan policy. This is because, by default, the policy has all the software packages unchecked and will therefore report nothing.

The most complex part of the software inventory process is the recognition mechanism. When is *winword.exe* Version 95 or Version 97? This is dealt with by recognizing key files of a particular size. The software inventory recognition

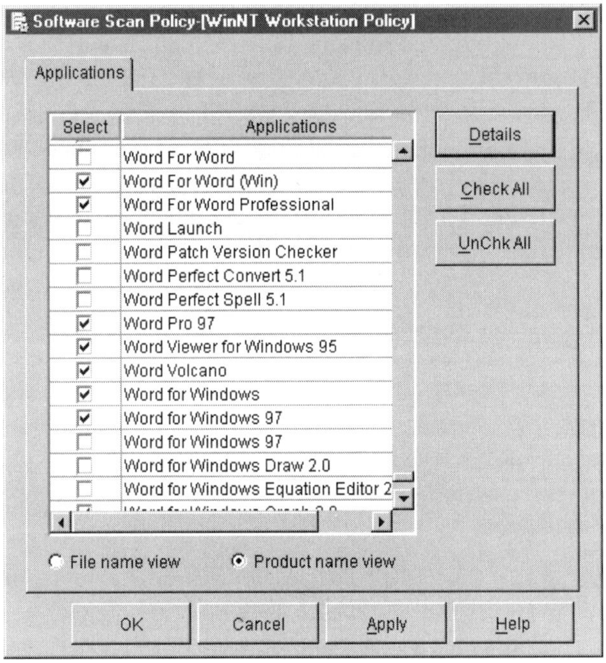

Figure 5-12. Software scan policy

configuration is held in *idappl.ini*, which can be found on the *sys* volume in the *public\zenworks* directory. A segment of this file is shown in Example 5-1.

Example 5-1. Software Inventory Configuration File

```
<I>,WINTUTOR.EXE,103088,Windows Tutorial application file,4.00.950
<I>,WINTUTOR.EXE,1848320,hpmouse,1.2
<I>,WINUP9.EXE,644214,Network Drivers For Windows - Winup9,9
<I>,WINVER.EXE,20752,VERSION REPORTER APPLET,4
<I>,WINVER.EXE,3632,Windows-version utility,4.00.1111
<I>,WINVER.EXE,3648,Windows-version utility,4.10.1998
<I>,WINWORD.EXE,1268224,Microsoft Word For Windows,2
<I>,WINWORD.EXE,1273024,Microsoft Word For Windows,2.00a
<I>,WINWORD.EXE,1277984,Microsoft Word For Windows,2.00b
<I>,WINWORD.EXE,1278240,Microsoft Word For Windows,2.00c
<I>,WINWORD.EXE,3482624,Microsoft Word {French Canadian},6.00a
<I>,WINWORD.EXE,3483136,Microsoft Word For Windows,6
<I>,WINWORD.EXE,3483648,Microsoft Word For Windows {Czech},6.0c
<I>,WINWORD.EXE,3490816,Microsoft Word {French Canadian},6.00c
<I>,WINWORD.EXE,3782144,Word for Windows,7.0a
<I>,WINWORD.EXE,3845120,Microsoft Word For Windows 95,7
<I>,WINWORD.EXE,5317904,WORD 97,97
<I>,WINWORD.EXE,5324560,Word for Windows 97,8
<I>,WINWORD.EXE,5327632,Word for Windows 97,8
<I>,WINWORD.EXE,5328896,Word for Windows® 97,8
```

Example 5-1. Software Inventory Configuration File (continued)

```
<I>,WINWORD.EXE,894848,Microsoft Word For Windows,1.1
<I>,WINWORD.EXE,899408,Microsoft Word For Windows,1.1a
<I>,WINWORKR.EXE,175575,Networker Client Pak For PC Desktops,3.1
<I>,WINWORKS.EXE,32384,PFS:WindowWorks,2.02
<I>,WINWORKS.EXE,38986,PFS:WindowWorks,1.1
<I>,WINZIP.EXE,145328,WinZip,4.1a
<I>,WINZIP32.EXE,717824,WinZip Executable,6.3 (32-b)
<I>,WINZIP32.EXE,866304,WINZIP,6.2
```

The example shows a comma-delimited file with five fields as follows:

- Internal start of line marker
- Executable or identifying filename
- File size in bytes
- Identifying application name
- Application version number

It is quite possible to add lines to this file; it is not recommended using a simple text editor, but you can add applications by using the editor discussed later in this chapter. It is downloadable from Novell at *http://www.novell.com/* with new applications added quite frequently.

If you wish to scan for particular programs, you will need to add these to the scan file. This is achieved by using the Software List Editor, as shown in Figure 5-13. The List Editor is invoked by selecting the workstation policy, which contains the inventory action from the NDS browser screen, and selecting Tools → Workstation Remote Management → Edit Software Inventory List.

To recognize all software, leave all of the items checked, but be aware that there is a time penalty for this. It is quite possible to have a useful check of what has been installed without having to tick every single box. If you wish to test for WordPerfect 5.1, then check for the executable but not for WordPerfect Spell or WordPerfect Convert. This means going through every entry in the list, but it may well be worthwhile because you will probably eliminate about 50% of the list as a result. Another way of speeding up the file scan is to limit the number of extensions being searched on the hard disk. If you find that after going through the list you are only actually searching for *.EXE* and *.COM* files, then edit the list at the bottom of the Software List Editor window to indicate that only these file types should be scanned.

If you wish to add programs to the list, click the New button and you will be given a dialog box allowing you to enter the programs details. This file will be appended to the bottom on the *ldappl.ini* file.

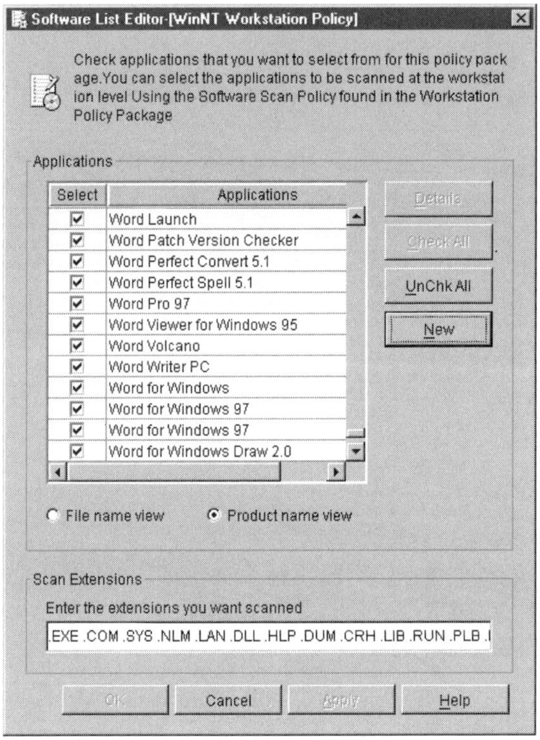

Figure 5-13. Software List Editor

Reporting

There is very little point in automatically collecting lots of inventory data unless you can extract it in some useful way. It is certainly possible to look at a particular workstation and its inventory, but suppose you wanted to look at trends in the data.

The ZENworks reporting function allows you to run a series of prepared reports on the data through the *NWADMIN* program. Before you can run these reports, you will need to install the Sybase ODBC driver on your workstation. This is done easily by running the ZENworks reporting tool that is automatically installed as an application object when the Full Pack was installed. Associate the application object with your user ID and run the object on your workstation. Through the 32-bit ODBC control panel, you will see the ZENworks inventory driver installed, as shown in Figure 5-14.

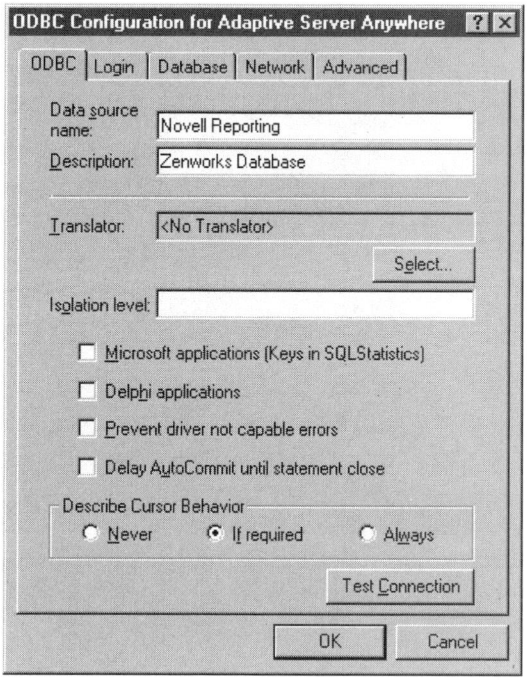

Figure 5-14. The Sybase ODBC driver

Load the *NWADMIN* program and from the Tools menu select ZENworks Reporting. This will load a Java program that will allow you to select which report to run, as shown in Figure 5-15. The program will send a query to the database, returning the data in a report style that can be either saved or printed. The reports are divided into four sections with several reports in each section: inventory lists, inventory reports, application distributions, and application launches.

Inventory Lists

Inventory lists are simple lists of workstations that have particular features, resources, or software. With some reports there is an opportunity to specify a search characteristic to restrict the list, or you can use the wildcard `%` character.

Workstation Scan Time

This report will return the date and time of the last inventory scan on every participating workstation. The report does not prompt you for any search restrictions.

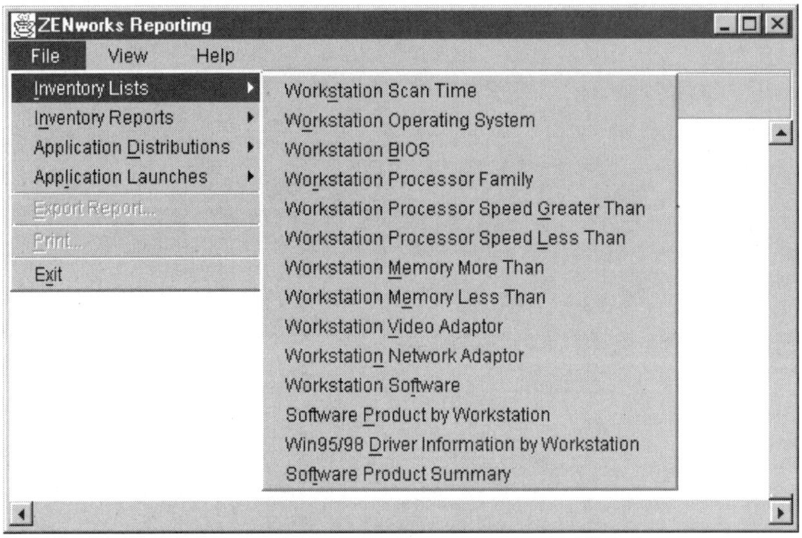

Figure 5-15. ZENworks Reporting tool

Workstation Operating System

When this report is selected you are prompted for the operating system type and the version. If you wish to perform a review of all workstation operating systems on your network, you can enter a wildcard in both fields or you can restrict the search. If you wish to find all the Windows 95 machines enter `95` in the operating system type and a `%` in the version number.

Workstation BIOS

A wildcard search in this report will return the revision date of the BIOS in each workstation.

Workstation Processor Family

This report will return a list of workstations and the type of processor in each. The search can either be a wildcard or the search can be restricted to a particular processor type.

Workstation Processor Speed Greater Than

This is a restricted search report that you report by processor speed. No wildcards are allowed and the value entered must be an integer. The report title implies that the report will return processors with a speed greater that the given value, but it actually returns those greater than or equal to.

Workstation Processor Speed Less Than

Very similar to the report Workstation Processor Speed Greater Than, but returns processors less than or equal to the given integer value.

Workstation Memory More Than
: This report returns a list of workstations with memory greater than or equal to a value specified in kilobytes.

Workstation Memory Less Than
: This report is similar to Workstation Memory More Than, but returns workstations with memory less than or equal to a specified value.

Workstation Video Adapter
: If you wish to find all the workstations and their video adapters, then a wildcard is allowed here. If you wish to restrict the list to all machines with S3 adapters then `S3` would be a valid search criterion.

Workstation Network Adapter
: This report returns the type of network interface card in each workstation; a wildcard search is allowed in the search criteria.

Workstation Software
: This report prompts you for a software product name and version number and returns a list of software installed on each workstation, by software name. Wildcards are allowed in this report.

Software Product by Workstation
: This report is similar to the Workstation software, but ordered by workstation name.

Win95/98 Driver Information by Workstation
: This report returns a list of drivers installed on each Windows 95/98 workstation and orders it by workstation name.

Software Product Summary
: This report will prompt you for a software product and version number or wildcards and return a product summary with all software installed, including version number and number of workstations having the software.

Inventory Reports

These reports are more comprehensive than the simple inventory lists because they combine the data returned in the simple lists. As they are clearly more complicated, they will obviously take longer to run. They include the following:

General Workstation
: This report prompts you for the workstation name and returns the operating system, processor, BIOS, video, memory, disk, and network card, and order it by workstation name.

Asset Management

If you wish to know the workstation name along with the model number, asset, or inventory number for each workstation, then enter the workstation name when prompted or supply a wildcard.

Hardware

This report produces a list of the hardware that you might consider to be the limiting factors on the workstation. The report lists the RAM, hard disk size, and processor for each workstation or for the range indicted by a wildcard.

Networking Information

If you wish to obtain information about the workstation's network hardware and address information, then this report supplies the network card, drive mappings, IP address, MAC address, and subnet mask for each workstation.

Application Distributions

This set of reports lists application information by distribution or installation of the application, as opposed to the launch or execution of the application. It includes the following:

Distribution Success or Failure by Application

This report prompts you for the application object and returns information regarding which applications were successfully distributed, including the user who performed the installation, workstation name, and date and time of the distribution. The failure report will return a list of application failures.

Distribution Success or Failure by User

If you wish to search for users who have had successful application distributions, this report prompts you for the user ID and returns all users who successfully received application distributions, including the workstation, application, and date and time of each distribution. The failure report will return a list of application distribution failures by users.

Distribution Success or Failure by Workstation

If some of your applications are associated with a workstation, then you may wish for a list of workstations to which applications were successfully distributed. To obtain the list of failures by workstation, run the failure report.

Application Launches

Application launch reports are very similar to the distribution reports above and provide reports on the actual usage of applications rather than the installation. In the same way you will be prompted for either an application object, a user object, or a workstation object to provide a report of either launch success or failure.

The inventory database

Those of us who have attempted hardware and software inventories over the years can be secure in the knowledge that it is a more difficult project that it appears. The purpose of having such a database is to retrieve data reports providing information for your own needs and for management, as shown earlier in Figure 5-15. The clear way forward is to design the database based on what information you wish to retrieve. It is difficult to envisage, however, what these reports will be. Fortunately there are a lot of organizations suffering from this very same problem and several big IT vendors have put their heads together to propose a database design to suit this complex requirement.

The Common Information Model

The Distributed Management Task Force is an industry-based organization that exists to develop the unification of management standards and initiatives for desktop, enterprise, and Internet environments. The task force is reviewing the Common Information Model (CIM), and a committee exists to contribute to the development of this important area. The committee is comprised of industry leaders who have an interest in the area. The task force has a large web site at *http://www.dmtf.org* with lots of information regarding the CIM database schema.

The model is divided into three layers:

Core Model Layer
: This layer includes information relating to all areas of systems management including:

    Managed system elements
    : This includes components such as hardware elements and logical elements of the managed computer system.

    Services
    : This area covers general information about services offered by the systems and how they are configured.

    Products
    : Products are mostly about general information such as the contractual obligations involved and where it was purchased.

Common Model Layer
: This layer defines information common to particular technologies and includes:

    Operating systems
    : Information regarding the type of operating system, version, and other relevant operating system-dependant information.

Applications

More detailed information about applications that run on the systems is held in this model.

Devices

Information on which devices are installed on the system and how they are configured.

Users

Information about users such as their names, username location, etc.

Networks

Network information, such as protocols.

Extension Model Layer

This layer is open and is left for more specific areas that cannot be included in the Core and Common models.

The CIM is an object-oriented model that is implemented in the Sybase relational database; each class or association has a corresponding table with the same name.

Querying the Database

The data can also be extracted from the database by accessing the tables through the ODBC driver and writing it to a spreadsheet through a tool such as Microsoft Query. There are a large number of tables in the database, some of which contain data and some of which contain associations between tables (see Figure 5-16).

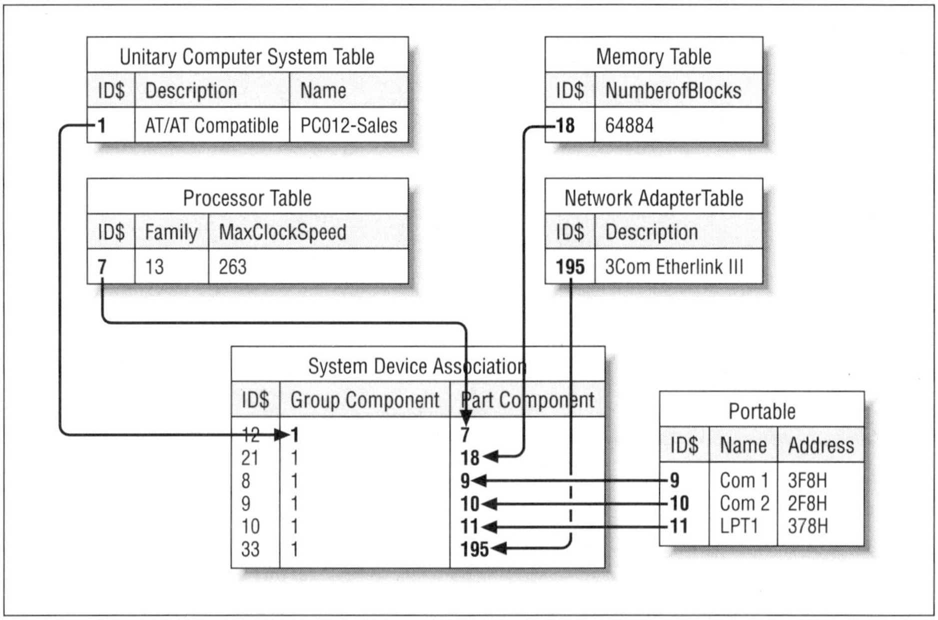

Figure 5-16. Associating components to systems

The association SystemDevice acts as a cross reference between the UnitarySystemComponent table and the other tables that identify the individual parts contained in the computer system. The part components and associated tables are linked through a table called UCSAssociation, as shown in Table 5-1.

Table 5-1. Components and Their Association Tables

FromClass	ToClass	Association	FromAttribute	ToAttribute
MWProcessor	UnitaryComputerSystem	SystemDevice	PartComponent	GroupComponent
MWDesktopMonitor	UnitaryComputerSystem	SystemDevice	PartComponent	GroupComponent
DesktopMonitor	UnitaryComputerSystem	SystemDevice	PartComponent	GroupComponent
ParallelPort	UnitaryComputerSystem	SystemDevice	PartComponent	GroupComponent
SerialPort	UnitaryComputerSystem	SystemDevice	PartComponent	GroupComponent
ConfigurationFile	MWLocalFileSystem	FileStorage	PartComponent	GroupComponent
MWSCSIController	UnitaryComputerSystem	SystemDevice	PartComponent	GroupComponent
MWKeyboard	UnitaryComputerSystem	SystemDevice	PartComponent	GroupComponent
MWPointingDevice	UnitaryComputerSystem	SystemDevice	PartComponent	GroupComponent
Bus	UnitaryComputerSystem	SystemDevice	PartComponent	GroupComponent
MWDiskDrive	UnitaryComputerSystem	SystemDevice	PartComponent	GroupComponent
CDROMDrive	UnitaryComputerSystem	SystemDevice	PartComponent	GroupComponent
Server	UnitaryComputerSystem	SystemComponent	PartComponent	GroupComponent
MWSlot	UnitaryComputerSystem	SystemPhysicalDevice	PartComponent	GroupComponent
BIOS	UnitaryComputerSystem	InstalledBIOS	PartComponent	GroupComponent
MonitorResolution	MWDesktopMonitor	MonitorSetting	Setting	Element
NTService	UnitaryComputerSystem	HostedService	Dependent	Antecedent
OperatingSystem	UnitaryComputerSystem	InstalledOS	PartComponent	GroupComponent

Table 5-1. Components and Their Association Tables (continued)

FromClass	ToClass	Association	FromAttribute	ToAttribute
OperatingSystemSetting	MWOperating-System	OSElement-Setting	Setting	Element
DOSOperatingSystem	UnitaryComputerSystem	InstalledOS	PartComponent	GroupComponent
DOSStyleMemorySetting	UnitaryComputerSystem	InstalledOS	PartComponent	GroupComponent
Extended-Memory-Setting	DOSOperating-System	DOSMemory-Element-Setting	Setting	Element
Expanded-Memory-Setting	DOSOperating-System	DOSMemory-Element-Setting	Setting	Element
MWOperating System	UnitaryComputerSystem	InstalledOS	PartComponent	GroupComponent
NetwareOperatingSystem	UnitaryComputerSystem	InstalledOS	PartComponent	GroupComponent
MWPhysicalMemory	UnitaryComputerSystem	SystemPhysicaldevice	PartComponent	GroupComponent
Memory	UnitaryComputerSystem	ComputerSystemMemory	PartComponent	GroupComponent
MWLocalFile-System	UnitaryComputerSystem	HostedFile-System	PartComponent	GroupComponent
MWRemote-FileSystem	UnitaryComputerSystem	HostedFile-System	PartComponent	GroupComponent
MWDiskette-Drive	UnitaryComputerSystem	SystemDevice	PartComponent	GroupComponent
CDROMDrive	UnitaryComputerSystem	SystemDevice	PartComponent	GroupComponent
IPProtocolEndpoint	UnitaryComputerSystem	HostedAccess Point	Dependent	Antecedent
IPXProtocolEndpoint	UnitaryComputerSystem	HostedAccess Point	Dependent	Antecedent
EthernetProtocolEndpoint	UnitaryComputerSystem	HostedAccess Point	Dependent	Antecedent
DNSName	UnitaryComputerSystem	Designates	Designation	Host
Environment-Variable-Setting	MWOperating-System	Environment Element-Setting	Setting	Element
Driver	UnitaryComputerSystem	Installed-Driver	PartComponent	GroupComponent
ShellDriver	UnitaryComputerSystem	Installed-Driver	PartComponent	GroupComponent

Table 5-1. Components and Their Association Tables (continued)

FromClass	ToClass	Association	FromAttribute	ToAttribute
Product	UnitaryComputerSystem	InstalledProduct	Product	ComputerSystem
InventoryScanner	UnitaryComputerSystem	InstalledProduct	Product	ComputerSystem
Y2KInfo	Product	Y2KCompliancy	Compliant	Product
LogicalFile	Product	ProductFile	InstalledFile	Product
ComponentID	UnitaryComputerSystem	ComponentSystem	PartComponent	GroupComponent
MWPCVideoController	UnitaryComputerSystem	SystemDevice	PartComponent	GroupComponent
VideoAdapter	UnitaryComputerSystem	SystemDevice	PartComponent	GroupComponent
MWCacheMemory	UnitaryComputerSystem	ComputerSystemMemory	PartComponent	GroupComponent
PhysicalComponent	UnitaryComputerSystem	SystemPhysicalDevice	PartComponent	GroupComponent
DMIEnabled	UnitaryComputerSytem	SystemDevice	PartComponent	GroupComponent
WsUser	UnitaryComputerSystem	WsUsedBy	WsUser	Computer
NetworkAdapter	UnitaryComputerSystem	SystemDevice	PartComponent	GroupComponent
IPNetwork	ipprotocolendpoint	InIPNetwork	GroupComponent	PartComponent
POTSModem	UnitaryComputerSystem	SystemDevice	PartComponent	GroupComponent

Table 5-1 allows you to link the components and parts to form an SQL query to extract data from the database in whichever form you wish. Even if you use a query tool, you will still need some knowledge of SQL to perform the table linkage, but if you are not an expert, you can always use a spreadsheet to tailor the data to a suitable form.

A Final Word

As with all of the work performed in preparation for your service delivery, planning and testing are paramount. In previous chapters I have suggested using a test tree, which reflects as far as possible a similar structure to your real NDS structure, to help in your planning exercise. There are areas in the workstation object creation exercise that are difficult to reverse, so it is important to have a clear understanding of what to do before proceeding in your live NDS tree. You should also be clear about where exactly to place the workstation objects in your NDS. For a small organization, the location of these objects in the NDS will have little effect, but for a large NDS spanned by WAN links, careful consideration should be given to this decision.

The structure of the NDS is a topic you should not ignore. Make sure that your NDS performance is not compromised by inappropriate object placement. If you plan to use inventory it may be possible to use existing server infrastructure to accommodate this function, but if you have a lot of workstations and plan to collect frequently, you may wish to buy new hardware to handle the data.

6

The Novell Application Launcher

Modern 32-bit Windows applications are one of the great new inventions of the last decade. Users have more power and access to information than they could have even imagined ten years ago. These applications are in great demand not only by the users, but also by management, who see advantages to business through a potential increase in the amount and quality of work being performed by the organization. The problem comes when the application stops working for inexplicable reasons or when the user has fiddled with and broken it. The work required to ensure that applications are installed and continue to work properly can potentially be very large. It is important to grasp the need to make these applications available in a controlled and consistent way. Windows 3.x programs are easier to repair compared to complex 32-bit applications, but nonetheless should also be managed where possible.

Most system administrators are operating system specialists. They can install, tune, patch, and generally create a perfect installation. The problem with users is they aren't interested in operating systems. They want applications, and applications can make a mess of what was a perfectly installed operating system. When the user calls to say, "The application doesn't work any more," what do you do? Well, the only thing you can do is to fiddle with the application, which sometimes works, but more often you use the CD-ROM to reinstall from scratch. What other option is there? The other option is to use the Novell Application Launcher to manage the application.

The Novell Application Launcher (NAL) is a major component of ZENworks. It performs remote desktop application management on Windows NT/2000, Windows 95/98, and Windows 3.x by providing a special link to an application executable that is not stored on the local workstation but in the NDS. NAL performs tailored application installations on the remote desktop that can enable the user to reinstall. It can also self heal by checking the installation each time it is run. There is a great deal more to the Application Launcher, but these two functions alone can save you a huge amount of time because you don't have to visit the workstation to install or fix an application.

NAL Overview

The Novell Application Launcher consists of several important components that link together to form a working system. The following list describes the major NAL components:

The Application Launcher frontend
: The Application Launcher has an agent running on the workstation, which performs the work contained in the application object. There are two styles to choose from: one is a simple window that can also be used as a shell, and the other that integrates into the Windows95/98 or Windows NT/Windows 2000 explorer shell. The frontend presents an application object to the user in a similar way that a shortcut does, so the user does not directly run an executable, but runs whatever is dictated in the associated application object.

The snAppShot tool
: This useful tool allows you to discover what occurs on the workstation during the installation of an application. This will include particular settings that you require to make the application work in your environment. The snAppShot tool creates an application installation base on your server of exactly what you wish to deliver to your users.

The application object
: This object is created by you from the application installation base created by the snAppShot tool. All of the installation components are visible in the object from the GUI *Nwadmin* program.

How the Application Launcher Works

Being a client-server system, the NAL has two main components: the application object that is the server component and the NAL agent, which runs on the client PC. The client component integrates into the desktop and displays the application objects as if they were shortcuts. The user clicks on the shortcut and the program executes in the way dictated by the object. The application object can contain other information about the application, such as how to install or reconfigure itself, as shown in Figure 6-1. This has distinct advantages over a normal shortcut in that the application not only becomes dynamically available to the desktop, but the installation can be managed also.

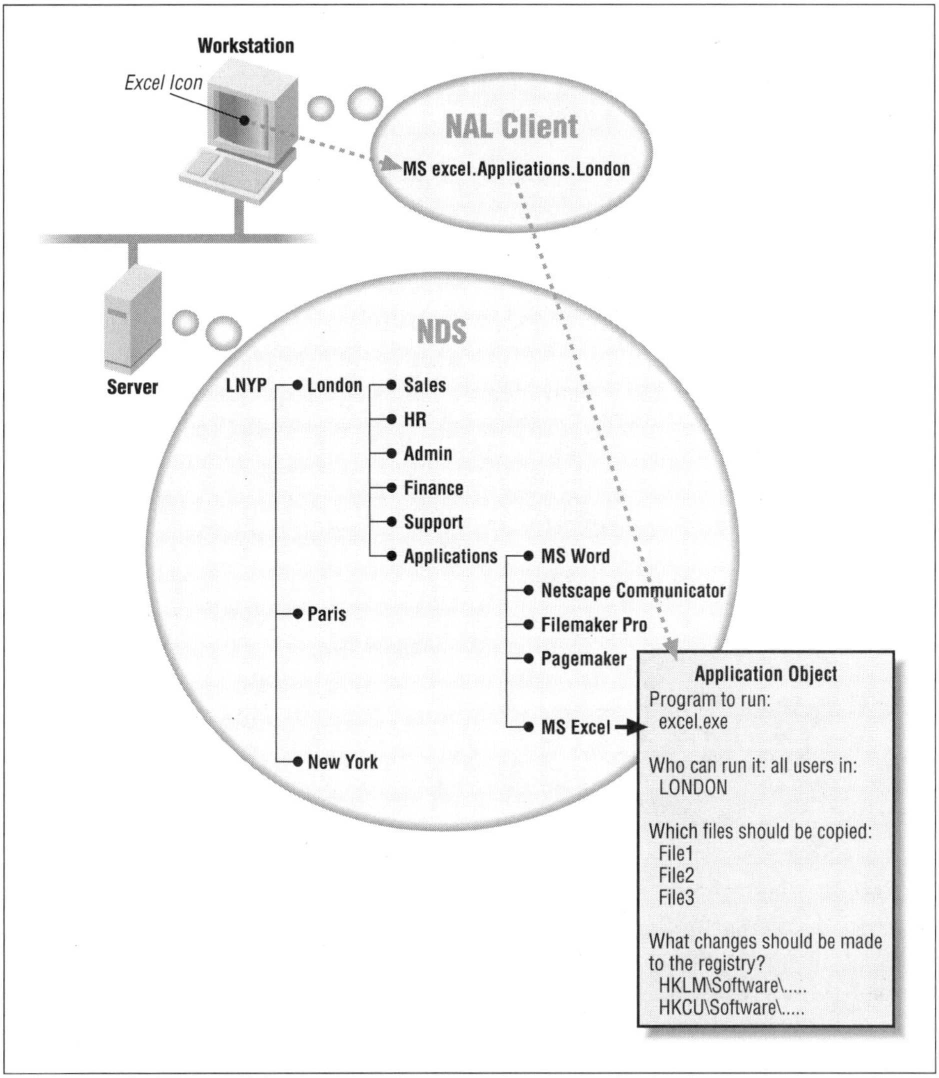

Figure 6-1. How the Application Launcher works

The application object presents itself as an icon on the workstation in the same way a Microsoft shortcut or a Windows 3.x program does. The difference is that this icon does not directly reference an executable in the usual way, but instead references an object in the NDS. When the user runs the application by clicking on it, the NAL opens the application object and obeys the instructions contained within. This can include copying files to the local hard disk and modifying or creating registry keys. These sorts of action are quite difficult to contend with normally under Windows NT/2000, because these areas may be protected from user intervention. Traditionally, this problem could only be overcome by giving the user more rights to the system than you would normally be prepared to do. The NAL does this on behalf of the user because rights are assigned to the application Launcher instead of the user. The application object has a vast range of configuration and environment settings that can be used to ensure that the application runs the way you wish. There are NAL clients available for Windows 95/98, Windows NT/2000, and Windows 3.x (which has less functionality).

NDS Considerations

Application objects can affect NDS performance if they are not placed correctly. It is not the object in itself that can cause this but the association with users and workstations. It is generally a bad idea to associate an application with a user or workstation that spans a WAN link. Always try to situate the application close to the users and workstations in their geographical locations, as shown in Figure 6-2.

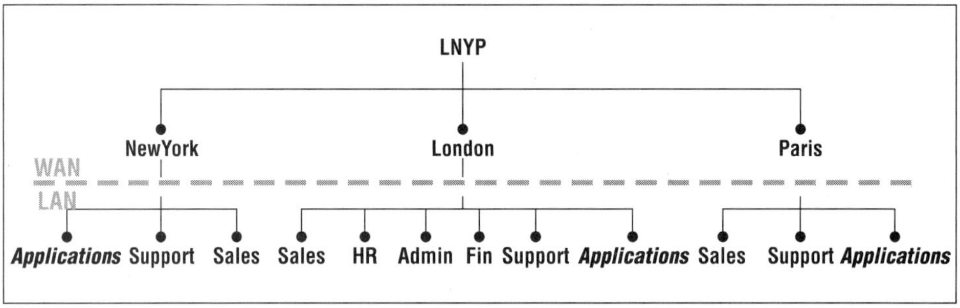

Figure 6-2. Application object placement

Be careful to place applications close to their associated objects. If your organization is geographically diverse, duplicate the object and place it near the users or workstations on each remote location.

Placing the object in this way does not mean a multiple installation of the application. It is quite possible to install in one location and copy the application and the object to another, or to simply partition and replicate the application container. Because there is potential danger of making changes to one object in the tree and failing to make similar changes to a duplicated object, you should consider implementing change control procedures here to ensure object consistency.

The Application Install Process

In the days of DOS, when you installed an application, you knew exactly what was going on. The files were put into a directory, you put the directory in the path, and presto, it worked. When Windows appeared on the scene, something strange started to happen. Files were still being copied into the directory, but now, certain changes were made to the Windows directory. Files were being copied there also, and *.ini* files were being modified. For the most part, it was clear enough what was going on and you could find the files and the *.ini* file changes. With Windows 95/98 and Windows NT/2000, it is much more complicated. You have no idea what is going on because all these changes and more are still happening, and now you have the registry to deal with as well.

The key to installing large numbers of workstations is consistency. It is certainly true that the installation should be correct, but where it isn't correct (which can easily happen), it should be consistently incorrect. This gives you a clear way forward to make a global correction. Hand configuring applications will invariably involve differences between them. This is potentially a direct route to chaos. In an ideal word it is desirable to have all your workstations exactly the same. In the real world, this is difficult to achieve because of hardware differences, but where it can be achieved, as in the case of applications, it should be done.

The NAL User Interface

The Novell Application Launcher is a component that runs on the workstation when the user logs in. This component checks the user objects to see if there are any application objects associated with them. It will then read the value of application inheritance level and work back up through the tree checking for container-associated applications until the inheritance level is reached. Application inheritance is discussed later in this chapter in "Launcher Configuration." These objects will then be displayed on the workstation for the user.

The Application Launcher comes in two flavors: The Application Launcher Window and the Application Explorer. There are pros and cons to using one or the other and it is really a matter of requirements and choice as to which you should use. Table 6-1 lists the platforms and features supported by the two interfaces.

Table 6-1. NAL Window and Explorer Features

Platform or Function	NAL Explorer	NAL Window
Windows 3.x	No	Yes
Windows 95/98	Yes	Yes
Windows NT 4	Yes	Yes

Table 6-1. NAL Window and Explorer Features (continued)

Platform or Function	NAL Explorer	NAL Window
Windows 2000	Yes	Yes
Replace shell	No	Yes
Enhance shell	Yes	No
Show local applications	No	Yes
Show personal folders	Yes	Yes
Force run	Yes	Yes
Icons in Launcher	Yes	Yes
Icons in Start menu	Yes	No
Icons in desktop	Yes	No
Icons in system tray	Yes	No

The essential difference is that the Application Explorer will integrate into the Explorer interface under Windows NT/2000 and Windows 95/98, as shown in Figure 6-3. From this you can see the Application folder in the Start menu that is a distinct menu item from the Program menu. The menu opens out in the usual way to display application objects in the way you have defined in the NDS. The windows scattered across the screen represent the applications folder, with each screen opened up in a new window. If you wish to use this interface, you will need to run the *Nalexpld.exe* program from the *sys/public* volume.

The NAL Explorer is also integrated into Windows NT/2000 or 95/98 Explorer, as shown in Figure 6-4. The applications are visible within the Explorer tree only if the Application Explorer folder is placed on the desktop in the Launcher Configuration.

The Application Launcher Window places all the applications in a single window that is Windows 3.x Program Manager style and can also be used as a shell, as shown in Figure 6-5. In this view, it is clear that none of the information is shown in the Start menu but contained in a single window, which has been maximized to view the contents.

Under Windows NT/2000, the Application Launcher (NAL Explorer or NAL Window) has two components. The first is the user component that runs in the user space on the workstation, and the second is the NAL service that runs as a service in the system space. The user space has the same privileges as the user currently logged in and the system space has full privileges on the operating system. When a user logs in to the secure NT workstations with user privileges and runs an application, a large number of components may need to be copied to the workstation into areas where the user does not have rights. This problem is dealt with by the NAL service, and because it is running with system privileges, it performs this

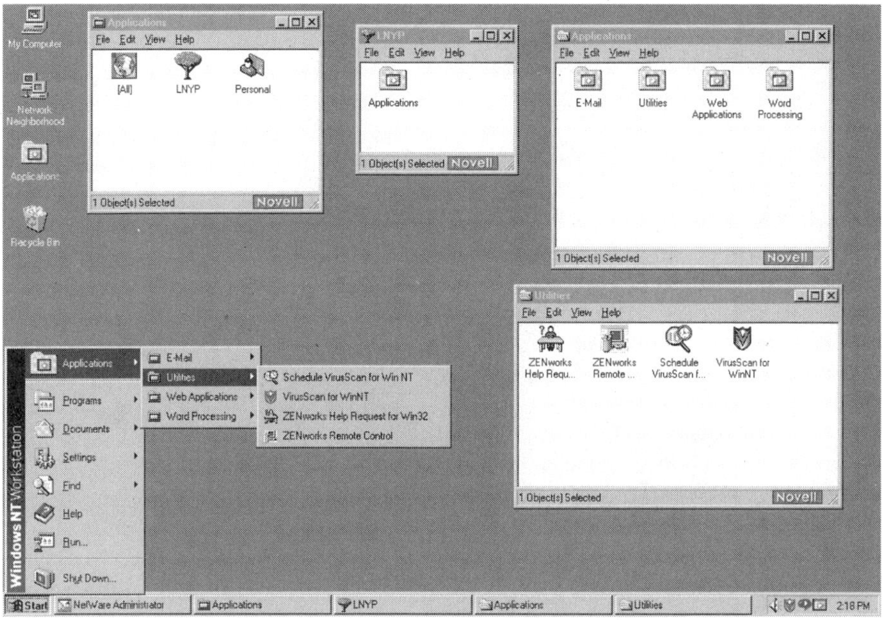

Figure 6-3. The NAL Explorer

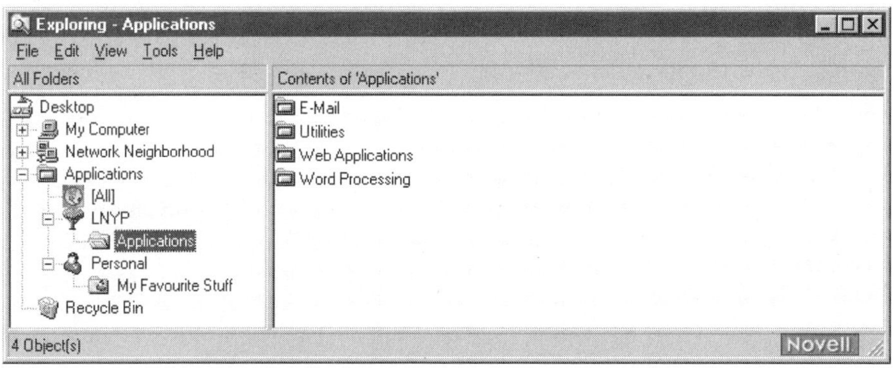

Figure 6-4. Integration into the Explorer

work on behalf of the user. This useful feature allows you to lockdown the workstation to prevent users from fiddling in inappropriate areas and yet perform installations in a controlled way.

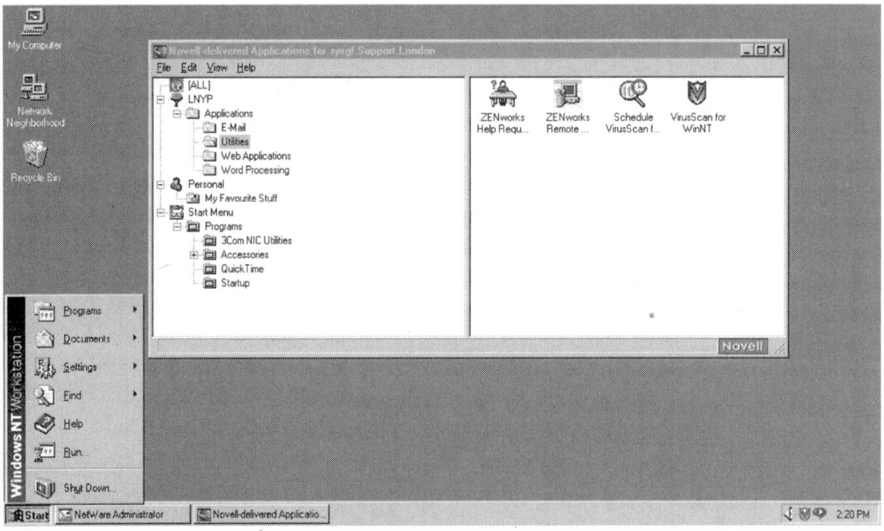

Figure 6-5. The NAL window

The snAppShot Tool

When an application is installed on a workstation, all sorts of changes can be made to that workstation of which you may be unaware. These changes can be files installed in various places on the workstation hard disk or changes to the registry. The application vendor rarely supplies information about what changes are made to the system and if they do, the information is difficult to find. The snAppShot tool is used to help with the awkward task of finding out what happens during the installation. The discovery process is performed by analyzing the system before the install and again after the install, and then subtracting the two to find the differences. These differences are stored in a template file, which can then be used to create an application object or simply viewed for your own information.

Before you run the tool in earnest, you will need to decide where to put all the files and settings that are discovered. This is an important decision because all the application details are stored in the application object, except for the files themselves. When a user runs the application for the first time, these files will have to be copied to the user's workstation. The best location for these files is probably a network drive, mounted on the user's workstation. If you have a lot of servers in one geographical location, you may wish to use a UNC path that will allow all the install files to be stored on a single server. The downside to this is that this server will be a single point of failure. It is probably not a good idea to provide a UNC path to a server on the other side of a WAN link for this purpose. It is better to set up a source path server for each geographical location.

Quick Method for Snapshotting Your PC

1. Use a base operating system with no applications installed.
2. Do the before snapshot using the Custom option.
3. Give the application a name and the object a name.
4. Give a path to store the application files—preferably a network volume.
5. Get it to check file, INI, and registry changes on the local hard disk.
6. Install the application.
7. Run it once and get it working the way you like it.
8. Finish the snapshot.

When you use a tool such as snAppShot to detect changes in the system, it will only do so effectively when the system is as basic as possible. The best system on which to perform a snapshot application installation is an operating system with no other applications already installed. Generally, a fully configured operating system with the NetWare client installed along with any relevant service packs is all that is required. This is an excellent representative system, which is much more likely to detect a system change, such as a new DLL file, than one with applications already installed, including DLL files which you would prefer to detect.

When you first run the tool, you are asked how you would like to run it. The options are shown in Figure 6-6 and are as follows:

Standard
: This option uses default factory settings to perform the snapshot.

Custom
: This option gives you the most flexibility when configuring the snAppShot tool and is the option that I almost exclusively use. When you have specified the options you wish to set, you can save them where they can be used to perform the express option.

Express
: This option will load the default settings that you will have saved earlier and proceed with the snapshot by creating the directory showing you the settings and starting the before snapshot. The after snapshot will be performed automatically and the template file created.

In order to fully explain the snAppShot tool, I will go through the custom option step by step. After the initial screen, you will be prompted for a settings file that has the default preferred settings, such as the template location directory. Unless

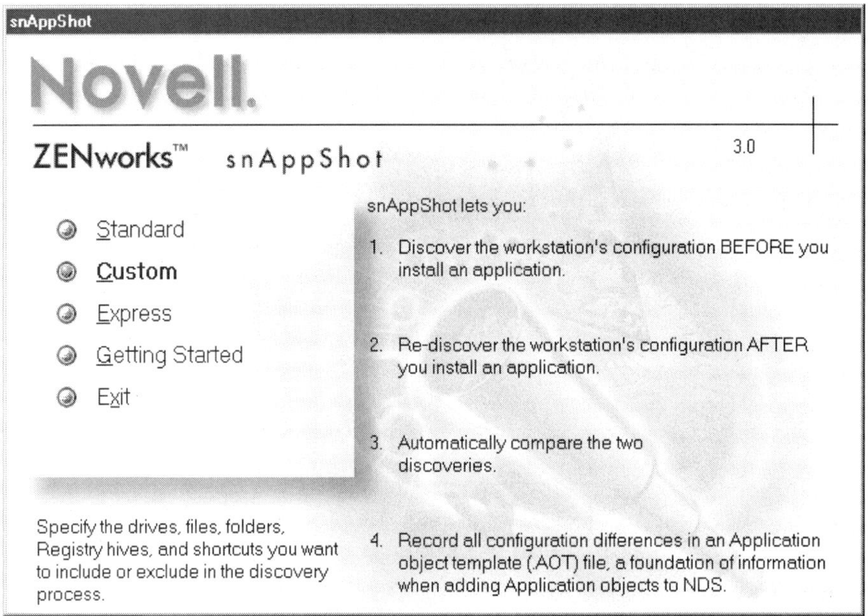

Figure 6-6. snAppShot options screen

you have previously saved your preferred settings, you should select the snAppShot default settings. You will then need to enter the name of the application object and the caption name of the application to be seen by the user. Both of these can easily be changed later if need be. The next screen asks you to enter the location to store the template file and any files that have subsequently been installed on the workstation during the application install. You are then prompted to select where the snapshot will check for changes, as shown in Figure 6-7.

You will probably wish snAppShot to detect changes in all the available areas unless you are so familiar with the application that you know it only makes changes to certain parts of the system. If you wish to check only parts of the system, click the Customize button to select which components to ignore. This allows you to select files and folders to ignore, text files to include, and registry hives to exclude. In general you can accept the defaults offered and continue straight on to the next screen, which asks you to select which drives on the local machine to be scanned. Usually this is only the main system drive (drive *C:* for instance), but you may wish to include other drives as well. It is sometimes beneficial to scan the user's home directory, which will probably be mounted on the same drive letter for every user, so you can detect what should go to that drive by scanning your own home directory. This is useful especially if you plan to manage some files in that location. Having selected the drives to be scanned, you have finished

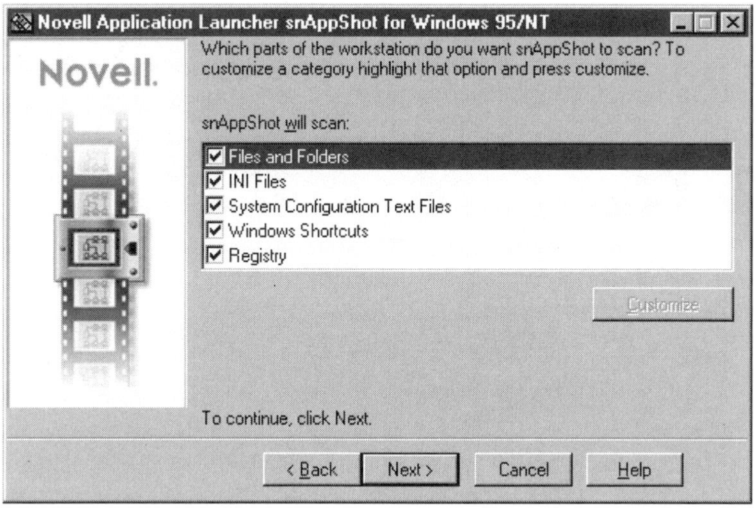

Figure 6-7. Parts of the workstation to be checked by snAppShot

configuring the before snapshot and are ready to perform the scan. This process will take a few minutes, depending upon how much is on the hard disk to begin with and how fast the machine is. When it is complete, you are invited to install the application. The Run Application Install button is there for convenience and allows you to browse around for the setup program, but it is not necessary to use this feature if you don't wish to. You can minimize the snapshot and install the application in the usual way.

Install the application and configure it to run in the way you wish. When you are finished with this process you are ready to perform the next step. You will be prompted to configure how you want to deal with files and folders, INI entries, and registry entries, as shown in Figure 6-8.

These criteria will be used to define the default behavior of these entries when the application object is created. The following options are available for file and folder entries:

Copy Always
: Setting this option will copy the file or folder regardless of whether it exists on the workstation already or whether it is older than the existing file.

Copy if exists
: If the file or folder already exists on the workstation, then always copy the file. If the file doesn't exist, do not copy it.

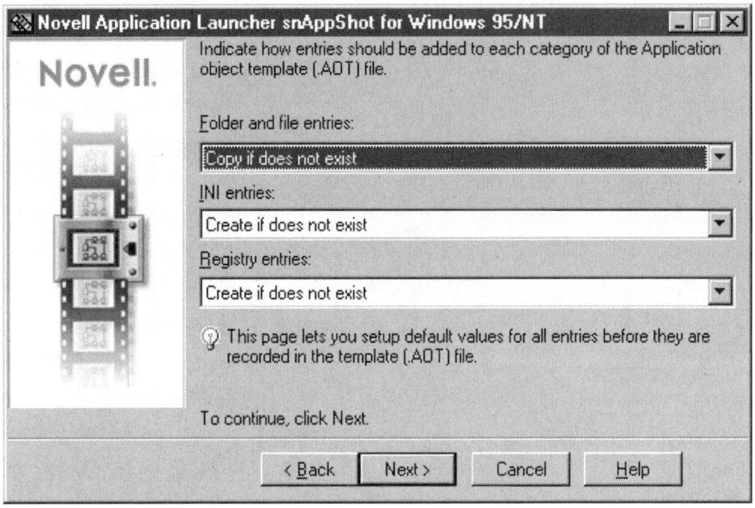

Figure 6-8. Default value criteria

Copy if does not exist
: If the file or folder doesn't already exist on the workstation, copy the file.

Copy if newer
: The file or folder will be copied if the existing file is older than the one waiting to be copied. If the file does not exist it will be copied.

Copy if newer and exists
: Similar to "Copy if newer" but will only be copied if the file already exists.

Request confirmation
: If the file exists, then the user will be prompted to decide whether to replace it.

Copy if newer version
: If the file is of a type that supports file versions, then it will only be copied if the version is newer.

Copy if different
: This will allow the copy to take place if the file date or file size is different.

Some programs use INI files that need to be managed also. These files are divided into sections and each line in the section is separately managed. The default criteria of what to do with these entries needs to be set as follows:

Create Always
: If the item exists in the INI file, then replace it every time.

Create if does not exist
: If the item doesn't exist in the INI file, then insert it; otherwise, leave the value as it was.

Create if exists
: Overwrite the value for the item each time, but if it doesn't exist, don't insert it.

Create or add to existing section
: This will add the item to the section even if it is already present.

Many modern programs use the registry to store their settings. These items also need to be managed as follows:

Create Always
: This option will update the registry value or key regardless of whether it exists on the workstation already.

Create if does not exist
: If the value exists on the workstation, it will not be updated, but it will be created if it doesn't already exist.

Create if exists
: The value will always be updated if it exists, but will be left alone if it doesn't.

If you have not used the snAppShot tool before, then a safe option is the "Create if does not exist" option for all three of these sections. This setting allows the default installation to be "nice" to the workstation when it is installed, by not overwriting parts of the system which may be better left alone. These choices can be changed later by editing the application object, but it is convenient to set a default behavior at this time. The next screen prompts you for the applications install path. If you have installed an application on the hard disk, then enter its path here. This item will be used later to define a special variable, also called a macro, which can be used to indicate the Install path rather than the Explicit path. The next screen allows you to define new macros that can be used later to provide specific entries. I shall discuss macros in more detail later in this chapter. In the window, you will see the TARGET_PATH variable defined if you indicated the directory into which the application was installed. If you wish to insert one of these macros to replace a string, enter it in this list and the string will be substituted. If you are installing an email program and you wish your email user ID to be replaced with the variable *%LOGIN_NAME%*, then when the user installs the program, this macro is substituted for his own user ID. If the installed application has a mail-to address set to *GFOSTER@LNYP.ORG*, then substitute *GFOSTER* for *%LOGIN_NAME%*, so that all occurrences of *GFOSTER* will be substituted. When the application is installed by the user at a later stage, the macro will insert his user ID instead, thus configuring the mail-to address correctly. Macros can be inserted later within the application object, so don't worry if you forget to add something.

All prompts having being dealt with, the after snapshot is performed for you, followed by the differences, which are recorded in the template file. You may find this process a bit arduous, but the tool is extremely useful and some perseverance in learning to use it is well worthwhile.

After the process is finished, you will find a series of files located in the install directory, including *1.fil*, *2.fil*, etc., another file called *filedef.txt*, and two more files called *<application_name>.aot* and *<application_name>.axt*. The *.fil* files are copies of the new files found to be present after the installation. They have all been renamed to have filenames with eight characters or less and a three-character extension. This is done in case the Install directory on the server does not support long filenames. The *filedef.txt* file is a list of the files installed on the workstation during the install and what they have been renamed to. The file with the extension *.aot* is the application object template file. This file contains a list of all the changes made on the workstation. This is a binary file that can be used to create an application object. The file with the *.axt* extension is a text version of the template file that can be edited or viewed.

The snAppShot tool is very useful for finding out what has happened during application installations. It is also a simple way of finding out what has happened when you perform a simple task. Suppose you wanted to find out what happens when the screen resolution is changed. Snapshot the PC, change the screen resolution, then complete the snapshot. Have a look in the *.axt* file and all the changes will be visible. If you have a lot of workstations that are essentially the same but have some minor differences, you can use snAppShot to trap the changes made between your base workstation image and the target workstation. You will be able to use this information to make consistent changes to machines with similar hardware by making an install-only application object.

Application Objects

Application objects store lots of information about applications such as the file to be executed, the icon associated, the working directory, and what files and settings are required to install it. These settings are collected from the snAppShot tool and inserted into the application object. Application objects can be quite simple, with just an executable and an icon. They can also just install some components and not run an application at all. They are very useful objects and you will use them a lot. What we will do in this section is go over this complicated object a page at a time and discuss what it does, how it works, and what issues are associated with it.

Quick Method for Creating Application Objects

1. Create an application template using snAppShot to capture what has happen during the install.
2. Create an application using the template created in step 1.
3. Change the application executable on the Identification page to run the correct program.
4. Change the application icon to one which matches the application's icon.
5. Add the operating system to be delivered to from the system requirements page. Unless this requirement is set correctly the application will not be available.
6. Associate the application with yourself, so that you can test it.
7. Refresh the Application Launcher client to make the application visible.
8. The application should install and run.

The Creation Process

The application object can be created in three different ways, each of which has its uses. The following list describes each of the three ways, as shown in Figure 6-9:

Create a simple application object (no .aot/.axt file)
: This will create an application object that is an empty shell containing no executable or any settings. If you need to create an object from scratch without any help from a template file, then select this option. All the fields in the object will be empty.

Create an application object with an .aot/.axt file
: If you have created a template via the snAppShot tool and wish to make an application object from it, then select this option. You will need to indicate the path to the *.aot* file. After the file has been read, the object will be created with all the configuration settings captured from the application installation.

Duplicate an existing application object
: There are times when you will need to duplicate an existing Application object. This happens more frequently than you may imagine, mostly when you have installed a piece of software which has several executable programs associated with it. An example of this is Microsoft Office, in which a complete suite of software is supplied from a single install. To create an application object for each of Word, Excel, and PowerPoint, you would not install each of

the programs separately, because there is a lot of shared code between the different programs. The best way to install Microsoft Office and to have three application objects (one for each program) available is to install Microsoft Office and capture the settings into an object called Word, which runs *winword.exe*; then you will need to duplicate the object and call it Excel, which runs *excel.exe* and performs the same actions for the other members of the Office suite. If the user has never run Office before, running any of the three application objects will install the whole Office suite correctly.

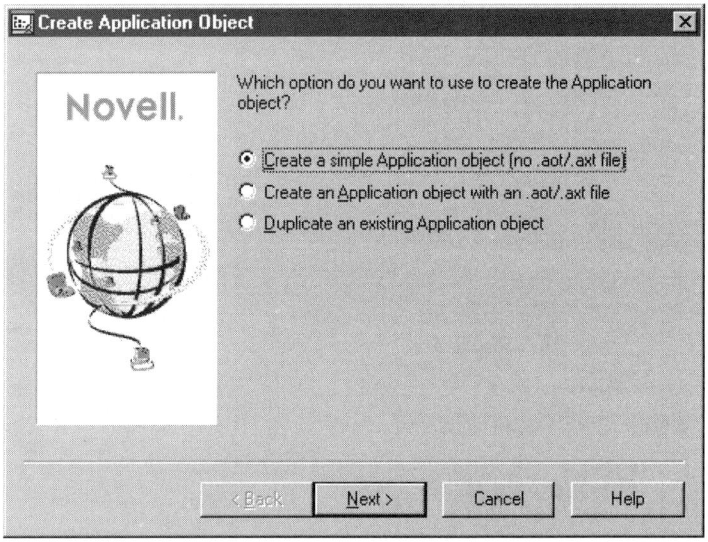

Figure 6-9. Creating application objects

Having created an application object, I will now proceed to investigate the contents of the object page by page. It is worth getting to know this object intimately if you wish to use the Application Launcher.

Identification

The Identification page shown in Figure 6-10 contains general application configuration information including the icon title, which is what the user will see as text next to the icon. The path to the executable is also defined here. Some tasks will require an executable to be run and some will not. If you wish the application object to just install something but not run anything, just select the Install Only button. Install Only applications are very useful for providing a range of functions that you may find useful for either forcing a default state or for tidying up the system. For instance, if you wanted a particular file to be updated on the workstation's hard disk each time the user logs in, you could use an application object that simply copies the file into place, forcing it to run at login. You could also use this function to tidy up a web browser's local cache so that the next user will have an empty cache when he uses the browser. Install-only objects are very useful for performing maintenance on workstations when the work involves the addition or removal of files or registry settings.

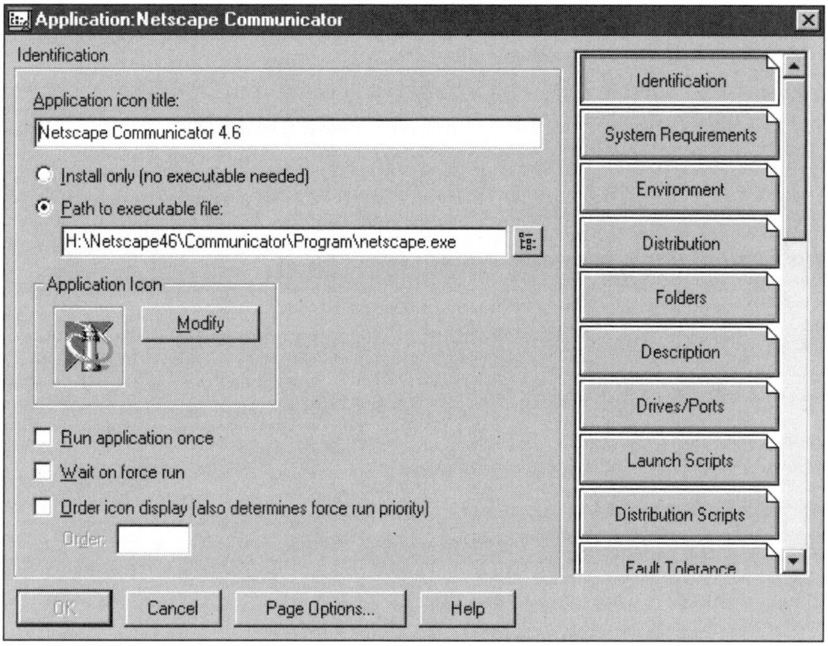

Figure 6-10. The Identification page

Application icon title

The name given to the application object and what the user sees could well be different. The object name itself is something that the user rarely sees and so its name serves a useful purpose only to you. The *icon title* is the caption the user sees and is defined in this field. The title can be as long as you like, but if you are using the NAL frontend, you may find long application titles don't appear completely in the window if you make the name too long. Changing the vertical icon spacing via the Display control panel on the workstation is one way of improving the visibility of the icon names. The NAL Explorer in the Start menu will show long item names without difficulty.

Path to executable and application icon

If you wish the object to launch an executable program, then the path to it can be indicated here. The path can either have a drive letter or can be a UNC pathname. If the application object is designed to simply perform an installation and you do not wish it to execute anything, then check the "Install only" box.

The application icon will be the same as the object icon in the NDS unless specified. If you have indicated an executable in the path, then that file will be opened and the list of icons made available to be selected. It is certainly desirable to associate the correct icon that is normally associated with an application to make the application more identifiable. If it is an install-only application object, there will not be an executable program from which to extract an icon, in which case you may choose an icon from a *.EXE*, *.DLL*, or *.ICO* file. This is simply done by using the Browse button to find an appropriate file which contains a suitable icon.

Run application once, force run, and icon order

There are several options listed later in this chapter about the icons that should appear to the user. If you wish the object to be available to the user but to run only once, then check the "Run application once" box. After the application has finished, the object won't be visible. If you change the version number in the object distribution page, then the icon will reappear in the user's work area again.

> Run-once applications will run once for the user, if it is associated with the user, or once for the workstation if associated with a workstation.

If you have chosen the "Wait on force run" option, which is explained later under "Associations," the application will not run until its turn. This is useful and sometimes essential when several applications have to be run automatically for the user. The order of application execution is ordained by the "Order icon display" option. The icon order allows the applications to be listed in the Application Launcher window or Start menu by indicating an integer value from 0 to 999, where zero is the highest priority. If no value is given for icon priority, then they will be ordered alphabetically. In general there is very little to go wrong here, because force run applications are there to tidy up or to launch programs. If you have a particular reason to run an application object first or last, then there is a mechanism to allow this through this function. For instance, if you launch *notepad* to display the message of the day, you may wish to ensure that it is run last so that the window is not obscured from the user by another window. In this case, it would be appropriate to assign a priority of 999 to make sure it runs last and to assign higher priorities to the other force run applications.

System Requirements

Most organizations have applications that should only be visible to certain workstations or certain users. This awkward requirement is easily taken care of by using user or workstation association as outlined later in "Associations." In many cases, the visibility criteria of the application is either dynamic or even more awkward, because the workstation may be slightly different in some way (such as having differing amounts of memory) and hard disk size. If an application object is designed to install a particular application on the hard disk, there is very little point in starting unless the workstation has sufficient space on the disk to accommodate all the files. There are physical restrictions for many applications and this page is designed to help you contend with these complex requirements.

The upper window of the System Requirements page lists all of the dependencies or filters to be used to make the object visible and when you select a previously defined dependency, the lower window lists the properties of that dependency. The available filters are described here and are shown in Figure 6-11.

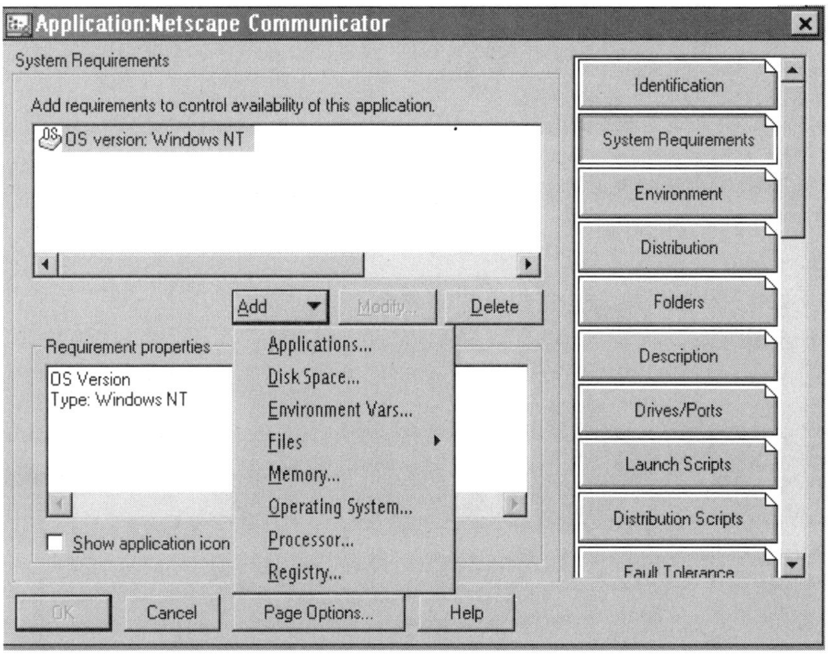

Figure 6-11. The System Requirements page

Application dependencies

If you wish the application to be available only when another application has already been installed, then the dependent application object can be selected. It may also be the case that the application should only be visible if another application hasn't been installed. These requirements can be defined through this page and any number of these application dependencies can be applied. The application dependency is very useful when you have conflicting applications requiring you to disallow the user to run an application if another is installed.

Disk space

There is very little point in beginning to install an application if there is not sufficient disk space to accommodate all the files. This check is frequently performed on your behalf when you install an application, because the setup process performs the check. As the NAL install process does not run Setup, you will need to make this check for yourself. There are several options available here, including all drives from *A:* to *Z:*, and also known variables such as "Windows System Drive." These variables can be useful if your workstations have the operating system installed to different drives.

Environment variables

If you wish to make applications available only to machines with variables set to particular values or variables not set to particular values, this can be indicated here also. This option is useful if you make regular use of environment variables to identify your machine types or implementation versions. If you use an environment variable to identify the revision of your workstation image, you can use it to restrict image-dependant applications. Make the old application object visible to the old image and the new application visible to the new image. The dependant application will roll out with the image.

File existence, version, and date

These file filters are quite straightforward and provide a great deal of flexibility for using files as a test for application visibility. In all cases, the file and location must be supplied where the only difference between them is the type of test on the file. In the first case, an indication whether the file should exist or not exist should be given. The second case is a test for the file version in which the test can be equal to, less than, greater than, less than or equal to, or greater than or equal to. In the third case, a test for the file's modification date is used as a filter to determine if the test can be on, before, after, on or before, or on or after.

Memory

If you don't have enough RAM, then you can't run the program. This filter will allow you to restrict an application to be visible only when there is sufficient RAM to run the program. Having said that, it is also possible to make an object invisible to machines with too much RAM. The available operators are equal to, less than, greater than, less than or equal to, and greater that or equal to. The amount of RAM must be given in MB.

Operating system

The operating system filter is quite important if you have a mixed workstation environment. You certainly wouldn't want Word 97 to be visible on a Windows 3.1 workstation. The application object should really be visible only to the operating system on which it was installed. It is also quite possible for an installation to be different under Windows NT and Windows 95. The operating system can be specified in the filter as either Windows 3.x, Windows 95/98, or Windows NT/ 2000. It is also possible to specify the actual version of the operating system. In the case of Windows 2000 you should use Windows NT Version 5 to target applications to this operating system only.

Processor

If you wish to limit the visibility of the application object by the workstation's processor, then this is where it is done. Available operators are equal to, less than, greater than, less than or equal to, and greater that or equal to, and selectable processors are 386, 486, Pentium, Pentium Pro, Pentium II, and Pentium III. If you have applications that are very CPU intensive it may be a good idea to allow them to run only on suitably high-spec workstations.

Registry

The application object can also be limited in visibility via a registry key. In this case you will need to indicate the key, the value to be tested, and whether you are testing for existence of the key or value or the nonexistence. You can also test for the actual data contained in the value that can be entered. The filter data can be entered by browsing the registry of the workstation currently in use.

Show Application icon even if criteria are not met

If you wish users to actually see the icons that have been filtered out, but not be able to use them, then check this box. The application object will appear grayed out to the user. The user is able to select the icon and discover what the requirements are for it. It may be that the workstation simply hasn't enough disk space to install it, a case that the user could easily rectify.

Environment

Applications that require a specific environment in order to function properly can be configured through this page, as shown in Figure 6-12. This may simply be extra parameters on the command line or a change to the working directory. If you have troublesome 16-bit applications, then you may need to configure how the Windows On Windows (WOW) session is handled.

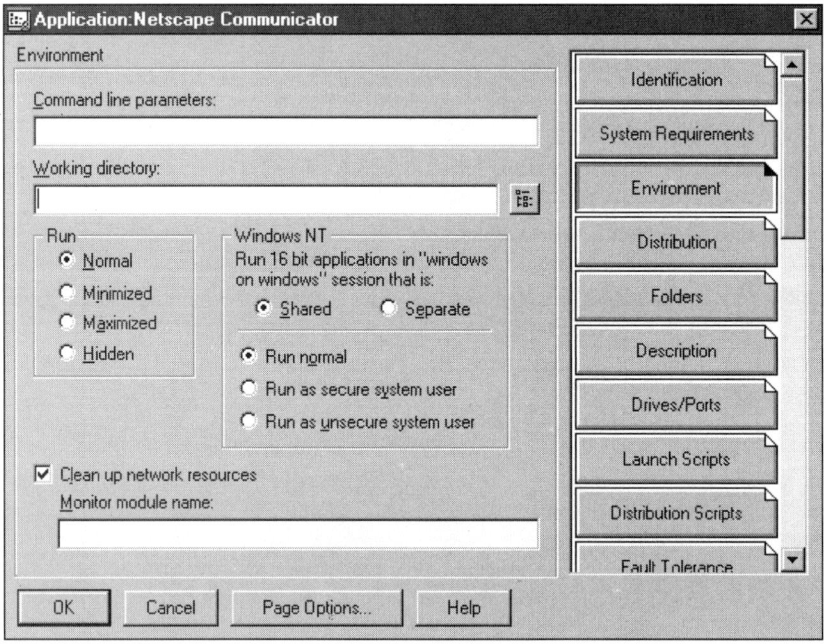

Figure 6-12. The Environment page

Command line and working directory

Extra values placed on the command line are frequently a requirement of an application. Some applications can behave quite differently depending on the parameters supplied on the command line. It is usually a good idea to check the shortcuts placed in the Start menu after installation and make a note of how the application is run in order to correctly configure this field. The working directory is also given in the shortcut and this field can be filled here. The working directory can be a useful way of forcing an application to save files in a particular place, but in general should be set to the directory path where the executable resides.

Run normal, minimized, maximized, or hidden

Most of your applications will run in a normal window. In some cases this size may be the maximum size if the application normally runs that way. Occasionally you may wish the application to be maximized for the user and, even more occasionally, run the program minimized. The Hidden option is quite useful if you wish a program to run without the user being aware of it. If you have an application that is forced on the user during login, it may be desirable to hide the interface from the user so that the results will not cause confusion.

Windows NT Windows on Windows

Under Windows NT/2000, 16-bit applications can sometimes behave badly. This section allows you to configure how WOW should handle these applications. If possible, it is always better to allow a separate WOW session for each application, depending on how much RAM you have available on the workstation. The WOW component of Windows NT/2000 is a virtual DOS machine in which each session emulates a separate PC Windows session. This is essential for programs that were written to have exclusive control of the computer. Sometimes the 16-bit program needs to communicate with another 16-bit program through Object Linking and Embedding (OLE) or Dynamic Data Exchange (DDE). In this case you should configure the application to share the WOW session so that the applications run on the same virtual machine.

Windows NT run

Most applications run on a Windows NT/2000 workstation without requiring any more rights than the user normally has. This means that the application is granted the same rights as the user when it runs. To make the application run in this way, you should have the application in Run Normal mode, as shown in Figure 6-12. You may occasionally require an application to run with higher privileges for some reason, and this can be achieved by running the application as a system. There are two options here. The first and most desirable is to run as a secure system user. This option allows the application to run without the user being able to see the user interface. The user will not know that the application is running unless he goes to the task manager. A good example of a secure system user is the case where you wish to grant or revoke NTFS permissions to a file on a NT workstation. The rights can be set using the *cacls* program, but the user may not have the rights required to change them. Running the *cacls* command as a secure system user will allow the rights to be changed without giving rights to the user. You may wish to run this command as a force run and also hide it so that the user doesn't know what is happening.

The second option is to run as an unsecure system user. This option makes the application run with system privileges as in the previous option, but allows the user to gain access to the user interface. This will effectively give the user full system privileges through this application so it should only be used with care. If you created an application object that ran *regedit* or *regedt32* and allowed it to run as an insecure system user, then the user would be able to do whatever he liked with the registry on any NT workstation. This is clearly a risk to the security of the workstation, but there may be times when you find this useful. It is tempting to use the unsecure system user function as a way of running badly behaved programs which require a higher level of file system access. There may be problems with making use of this function in this way; the application may not gain access to the user's HKEY_CURRENT_USER icon the way you might expect, because the application is running as a system. The unsecure system user function is more suited for running more simplified applications such as a registry editor.

Clean up network resources

It is possible to map a drive automatically when an application is launched in the Launch Scripts page. This is an extremely convenient way of ensuring that the right resources are available for the application to run properly. If you do connect network resources through an application object, such as a drive mapping through launch or distribution scripts, then it is likely that you will want to disconnect them when finished. This can be done by checking the "Clean up network resources" box. It is possible to disconnect a drive mapping in the after launch script, but if you launched a second application that uses the same drive, you may find that by closing the first application, the mapping is removed before the second application is finished. It is better to allow the "Clean up network resources" function to do the drive disconnection for you.

Monitor module name

The process of cleaning up network resources is triggered by the user closing the application. Some applications use a shell program to start the application but will actually run a different program module shortly afterwards and close the first program down. It is therefore possible that you wish a different executable or module to be the trigger for the resource cleanup, otherwise the resource will be removed before the program has actually been terminated. In this case, indicate the module to be monitored here.

Distribution

The page shown in Figure 6-13 is designed to allow you to define general characteristics for application distribution. If you wish the application to be completely reinstalled each time it is run, the Distribute Always option on this page will allow you to do this, because it globally affects the whole application. If you wish only the registry component to be reinstalled each time and not the files, the Distribute Always option on the registry page should be used instead.

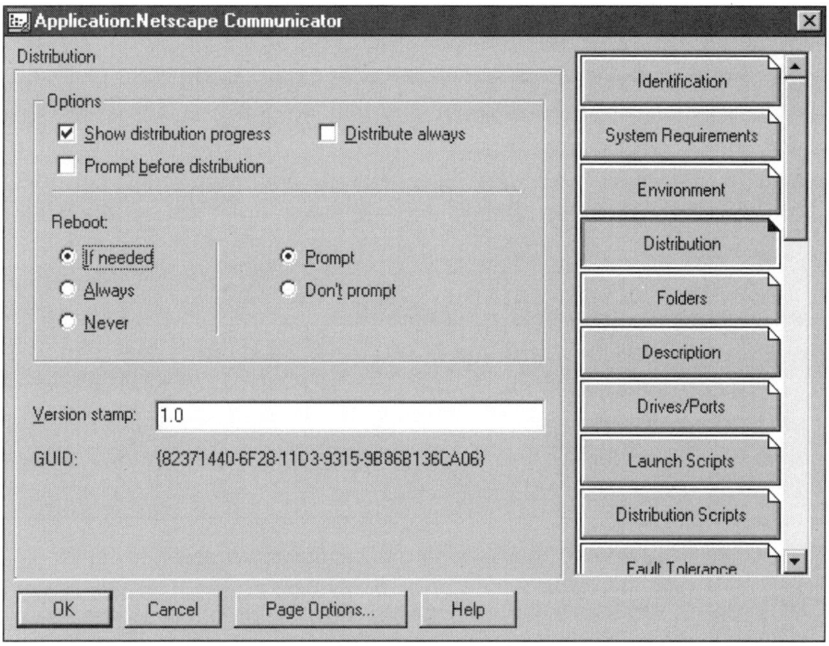

Figure 6-13. The Distribution page

Show distribution progress and prompting

When a user clicks on an application object that has not been installed on the workstation, a progress bar can be displayed that shows how far the install has gone. If the application is very small and makes little or no modification to the workstation, there is little point in showing the progress, as the user will not see it for long enough to make any difference. If the distribution is large, then it is probably a good idea to have it displayed as it gives the user a feel for what is going on and how long it is going to take.

If you wish to give users the option to install the application or to postpone it, then you can check the "Prompt before distribution" box. The text entered in the Description Property page is displayed along with the prompt, which can give useful information to the user about what he is about to install.

Distribute Always

If you wish to distribute the whole application every time the user clicks the object, then check the Distribute Always box. This setting is global for the whole application and may seriously impair the performance of the application during initial launch. When an application is distributed, the Application Launcher will carry out the instructions defined in the object. This means that if all your files, INI settings, and registry keys are set to "Create if does not exist," the distribution will carry out those instructions, resulting in very little work done. If you select Distribute Always under these circumstances, you will find that the user will wait for the application to distribute, with very little actually occurring on the workstation, because the settings and files already exist and may indeed have the wrong values. If you really wish the entire application to be completely reinstalled each time, then check the Distribute Always option, but make sure that the settings that you want overwritten, the whole application if necessary are set to Create Always. In most cases it is not the entire application that needs to be reset to a default state, but certain configuration files and registry keys. These individual settings can be set to Distribute Always and Create Always on a case-by-case basis through the Application Files, INI Settings, and Registry Settings pages that are detailed later.

> Don't expect the Distribute Always options to reinstall the application every time simply on its own. If you have set the all the application files to "Create if does not exist," then the Distribute Always will just check for the existence of the files each time the application is launched, but not replace them. If you wish the application to be reinstalled each time, then set the files to Create Always and do the same for registry keys and INI settings.

> If you set the application to reinstall completely each time, you will seriously affect the launch time if there are a lot of files and settings in the object. There may also be serious consequences for network performance if a lot of users are launching applications at the same time. You could plan to reinstall the main application components overnight using the Pre-Install function which is discussed later.

Reboot

Applications will frequently need the workstation to reboot in order to start devices or services or to register fonts. If this is the case for a particular application, you can define how this should occur. In some cases it is difficult to plan when a reboot should occur because an application may need to replace an already open Dynamic Link Library (DLL) on the workstation. In this case, a reboot needs to occur so that the file can be replaced and be planned for with the If needed option. It is probably a good idea to prompt the user before the reboot as there may be open applications and user files on the workstation. If the application is installing a resource that you know will need a reboot, and which may cause instability of the workstation as a result of not doing so, then check the Reboot Always box.

GUID

Each application object has a number called a Global Unique IDentifier (GUID) that is generated when the application object is created. This number is used to identify the application object and to handle the application distribution. When a user launches an application, the Application Launcher checks the workstation's HKEY_LOCAL_MACHINE for the GUID to see if it has been distributed before. When the application is distributed, the GUID is stamped into the registry at the location HKEY_LOCAL_MACHINE\Software\NetWare\NAL/1.0\Distribute\<tree_name>\<GUID>. The Application Launcher can therefore take care of an application that has never been run on a workstation.

When settings or files are identified as items to be tracked on a per-user basis, the key is stamped into the user's HKEY_CURRENT_USER in a similar location. This allows the Application Launcher to manage application components for each user. Where an application has been run on a workstation by one user, the next user's personal settings are distributed to him when he launches the application.

There may be cases where you wish an application's GUID to be shared by other applications. If you install a suite of software such as Microsoft Office on a workstation, you will need an application object for each of the applications in the software suite. Each of the three components (Word, Excel, and PowerPoint) will have separate application objects that are duplicates of one another because there is no distinction made between installing each of the components. When the installation of Microsoft Office is performed, you get everything in the suite. It is very difficult to determine which parts of the installation are for Word and which parts are for Excel because of the amount of shared code involved. If you create an application object from the whole Microsoft Office installation, you can define which executable to run from the object, for instance, *winword.exe.* To make an application object for Excel, you simply create a new object by copying the Word object, then changing the executable from *Winword.exe* to *Excel.exe,* and similarly for PowerPoint. This will give you three identical objects where the only difference is the executable being run from it. The problem here is that all three application objects have different GUIDs but their install content is exactly the same. This means that the user has to put up with the distribution occurring for all three objects even though the installation is the same. This problem is solved through the Sync Distribution GUIDs option. This function can be found through *NWADMIN* program by selecting all the objects to be synced, then Tools → Application Launcher Tools → Sync Distribution GUIDs. This will set the GUIDs in all the selected applications to be the same value.

Version stamp

Use the version stamp to manage different releases of your implementation. If you install an application and configure the object for the user, it will be distributed normally. If you subsequently wish to make a change to that distribution, either because there is a problem with your implementation or perhaps a patch to be dealt with, you will need to ensure that a new distribution occurs. This can be accomplished either by changing the GUID or incrementing the version number. Any change to the version number will have the same effect as changing the GUID of the application. This version number need not bear any relation to the version of the software; it is simply there for managing your implementations.

Folders

Folders are used to collect applications into sensible groups. Windows 3.1 uses program groups for this and Windows 95/98 and Windows NT/2000 use folders in the Start menu. ZENworks is no exception and folders are even more flexible because they are not tied to the workstation, but are stored centrally in the NDS. ZENworks has a special object available called the *folder object*, which will be discussed later in this chapter. When the application is installed into a folder object, it will be visible in this page, as shown in Figure 6-14.

Description

If you wish to provide the users with a more complete description of the application, then you can do so through the Description page, as shown in Figure 6-15. The user will see the description when they right-click on the application object and select Properties.

Drives/Ports

Some applications may need drives to be mapped to particular resources before the application will run successfully. An example of this may be a program that has data on one or more CD-ROMs. If the CDs are mounted somewhere on the network, they can be mapped to the appropriate drive so that the program that uses the CD-ROM can get the data stored there.

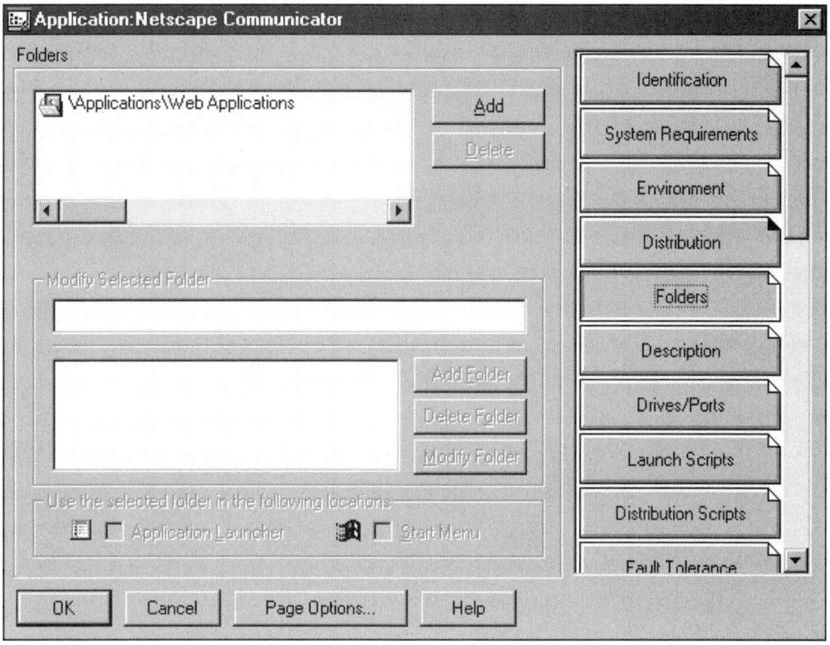

Figure 6-14. The Folders page

You may also wish to capture a printer for a particular application. This mapping can be performed here, as shown in Figure 6-16. The drive and printer mappings are made before the application is actually executed so that all required resources are present when the application runs. The drive and printer mappings will remain on the workstation unless you check the Clean Up Network Resources option on the Environment property page.

If the drive is already mapped to the correct volume, the mapping will be retained. In this case, the "Clean up network resources" option will not remove the drive because the object did not connect it. If the drive letter is already in use, the mapping will not be made and the application will not be executed. If several applications are using the mapping and you terminate the first application (which made the original mapping), the mapping will be retained because the Clean Up Network Resources option will not be queued until the last application using the mapping has finished.

Launch and Distribution Scripts

Launch Scripts and Distribution Scripts perform very similar functions and are therefore dealt with together in this section. The scripting in this case is the

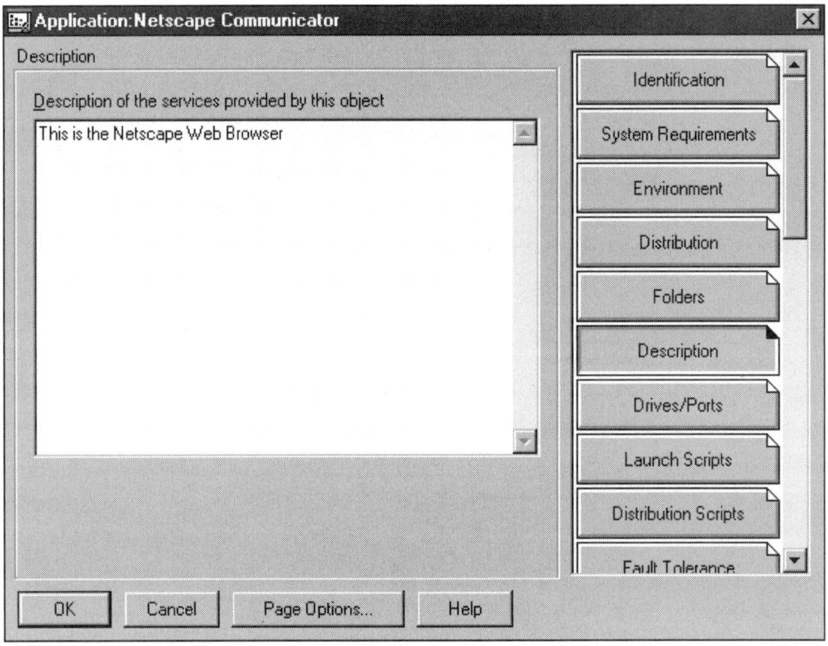

Figure 6-15. The Description page

language used for writing login scripts. A description of this language is in the Help page, which includes a list of login script functions that are not supported in the application object.

The real difference between Launch Scripts, shown in Figure 6-17, and Distribution Scripts, shown in Figure 6-18, is when they are run. The Distribution Scripts are run before or after the application is installed or distributed by the application Launcher. The Launch Scripts are run before and after the program is run. If a user clicks on a program that has not yet been installed, and you have configured scripts for distribution and launch, the scripts will run in the following order:

1. User clicks on the program icon.
2. The Application Launcher determines the application is new to the workstation.
3. The before Distribution Script is run on the workstation.
4. Application is distributed to the workstation.
5. The after Distribution Script is run on the workstation.
6. The before Launch Script is run.
7. Application is launched and the user makes use of the application.
8. The after Launch Script is run when the user finishes with the application.

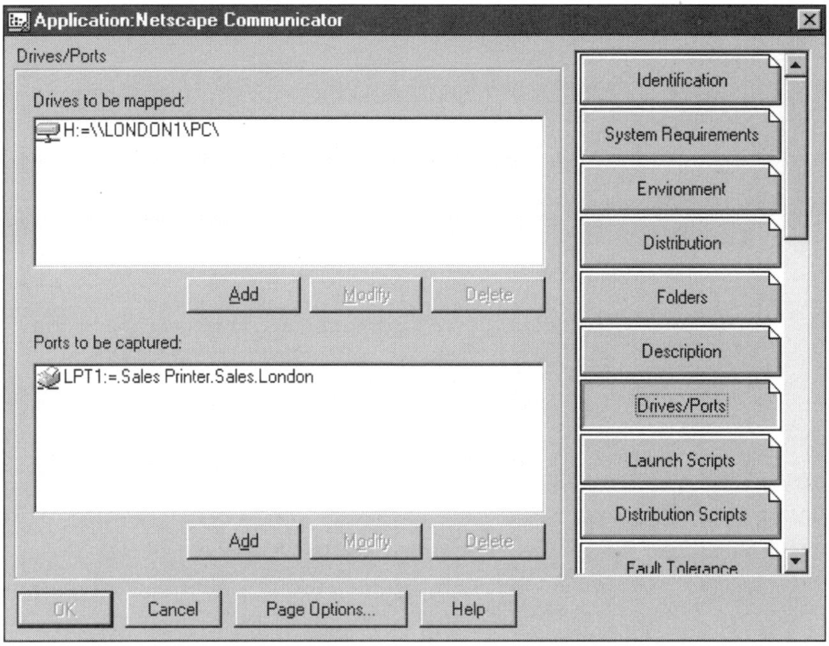

Figure 6-16. The Drives and Ports page

Fault Tolerance

The delivery of applications through a distributed mechanism such as the Application Launcher inevitably promotes caution when considering the questions, "What happens when the server goes down?" and, "I have three servers on my network, so how do I spread the application load over the servers equally?" These are important questions when you rely on servers to hold applications and other resources needed to make the whole system work.

When you have given consideration to ensuring that your NDS is protected through the partitioning and replication process, you will also need to consider what to do about server-centric functions. These function fall into two categories: those that can be become less server-centric and those that can't. The latter category includes the provision of home directory space, where the user's files will literally disappear if the server goes down. This issue is difficult to resolve easily, but a partial solution may be to acquire the most resilient servers possible. Applications also fall into the latter category because they launch from a particular server and if the server fails, there are no applications. This is a problem that can become less server-centric through the use of the failover mechanism provided on the Fault Tolerance page.

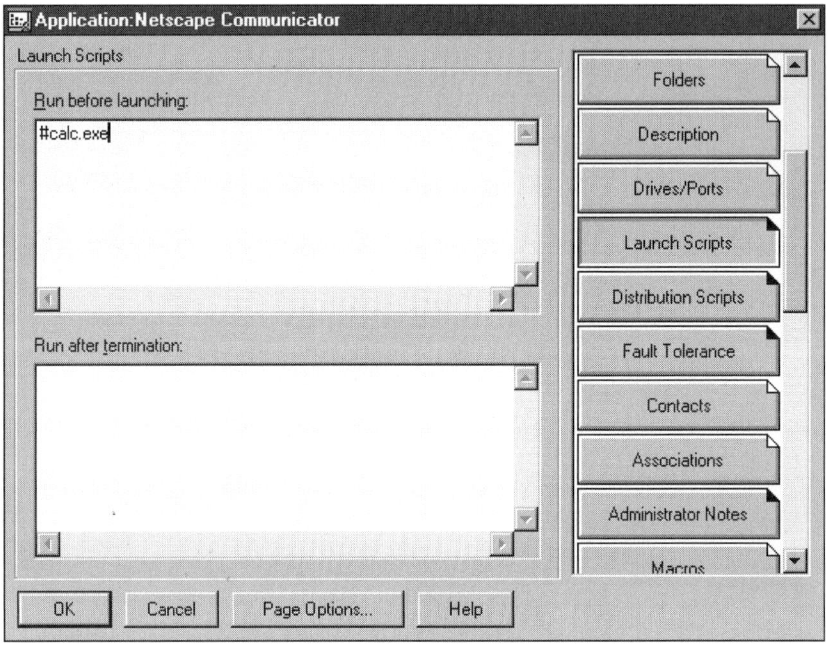

Figure 6-17. The Launch Scripts page

> If you decide to install a new server to provide fault tolerance for when the main application server fails, you might as well use it for load balancing as well. It may not even work when you actually need to fall back on it because it will be so rarely used (hopefully never) that it may develop a hardware fault without your knowledge. If you have to fall back from two load-balanced servers to a single server, you are no worse off.

If you have a lot of users accessing applications from the network, you will inevitably wish to consider adding an additional server to spread the application load, as well as providing fault tolerance. There is little point in having a server doing nothing but wait until another server has failed when you can just as easily load-balance the applications over both servers and provide better service. It is possible to load-balance over both servers by dividing your users geographically in some way, but this page will allow you to achieve a better balance in a simpler way. The Load Balance function will allow you to balance applications by providing an application object for each server and randomly selecting which should be used when the application is launched, as shown in Figure 6-19.

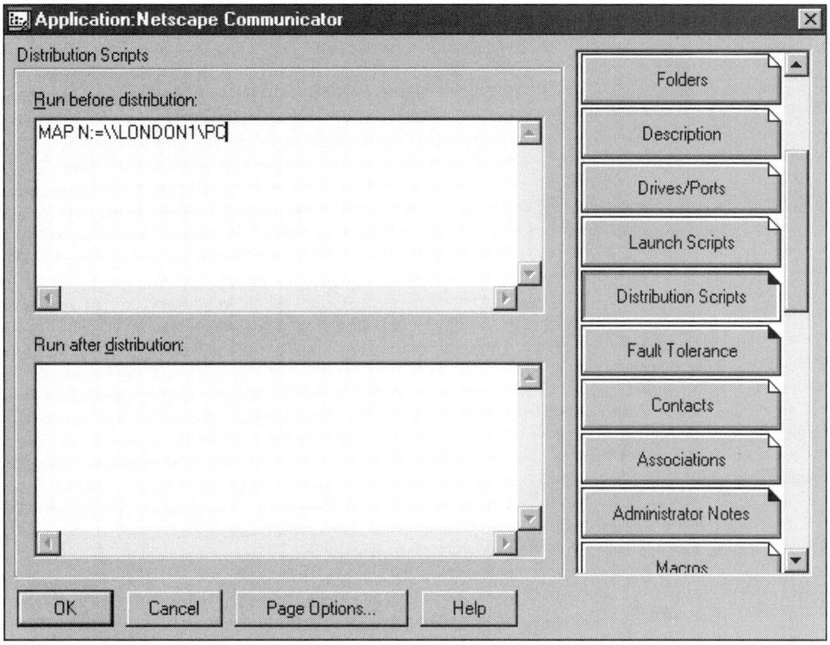

Figure 6-18. The Distribution Scripts page

Load balancing

If you wish to load-balance an application, you will need to prepare an application object for each of the servers that will share the load for this application. The reason for this is that any files to be copied to the local workstation will have to come from the server that is up, or the distribution will fail. To do this you can either use a different UNC pathname within each application object, or use a drive letter and connect to the appropriate server through a launch script. The primary application object is used to display the application object to the user and any one of the objects will be randomly selected to supply the service. When both Load Balance and Fault Tolerance are implemented, the load balance list will be tested first, followed by the fault tolerance list.

Fault Tolerance

To use the Fault Tolerance option (Figure 6-19), you will need to create an application object for each server from which the service is to be supplied. When an application is launched, one of the application objects is selected at random from the list of load-balanced applications. If the application object fails to launch, another one is selected. This process continues until there is a successful launch, or the list is exhausted.

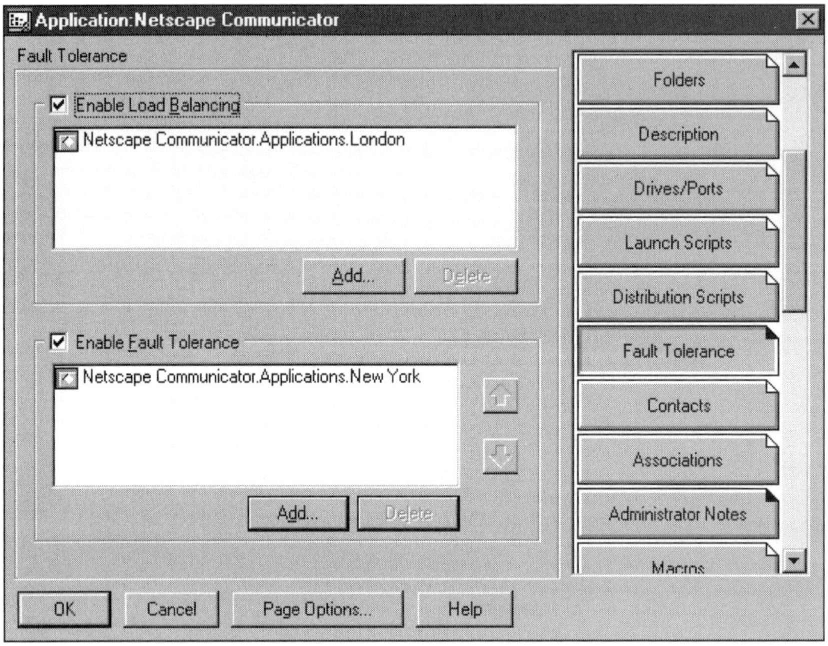

Figure 6-19. The Fault Tolerance page

Contacts

The Contacts page is used to display the IT support representative of whom to contact if the user needs some help with that application. When the user right-clicks on the icon and selects Properties, the contact information for the support person can be seen. It is possible to add as many support contacts as you wish within the window shown in Figure 6-20.

Associations

The Associations page, shown in Figure 6-21, is used to determine who can see the application object. By default the object is not associated with anyone and in order to make it visible, you will need to indicate who will be using it. Initially it is a good idea to make it visible only to yourself so that it can be tested. It is also a good idea to emulate what the users' rights are in this case so that a proper test can be made. I have discussed who can use applications as if it were only users who can do so, but there may also be workstations that should be associated with the application. If you have a single workstation with a scanner attached, you may wish to make the software available to all users, but only when they log in to that workstation. The solution to this is to associate the application with the workstation rather than the user.

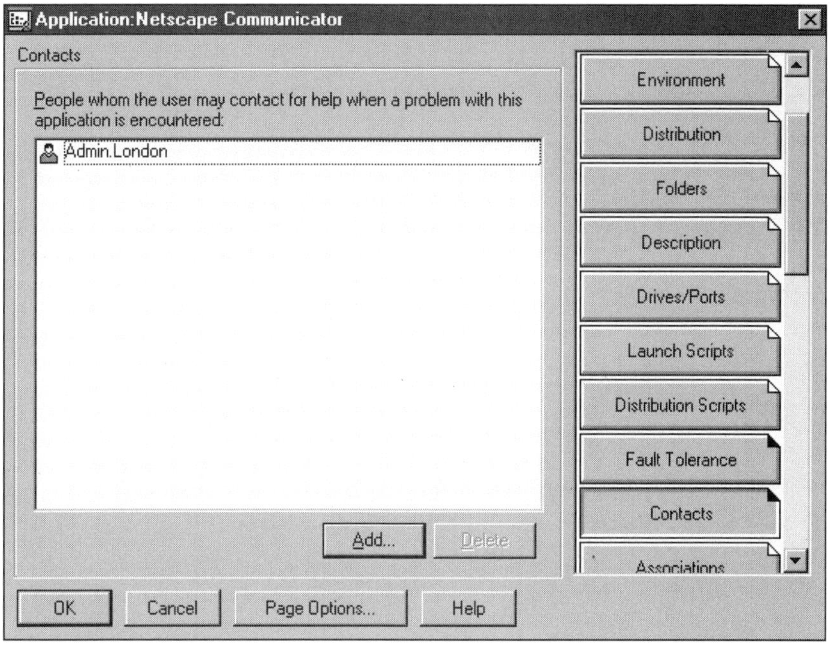

Figure 6-20. The Contacts page

It is also possible to associate containers with workstations, users, or both. Workstation groups and user groups are also valid objects to associate with the application. If a user is associated with an application on a workstation that also has the application associated, the application will only appear once.

Having made the association, you will need to decide how it is to be presented to the user. You will probably want to make the application as visible as possible, but if you have a lot of applications, putting them all on the desktop may not be a good idea. The Associations page allows you to specify not only who sees the application, but also where they see it. The following options are available for where the object can be placed:

Force Run
: Force Run executes the application automatically without giving the user or workstation a choice. To enable it, check the first column next to the user or workstation in the window. If you wish to force the application, but only once, then check the "Run application" once option on the Identification page.

App Launcher
: The Application Launcher is a special window in which you can display all the available applications for the workstation or user. If you wish the application to become visible in this window, place a check in the second column.

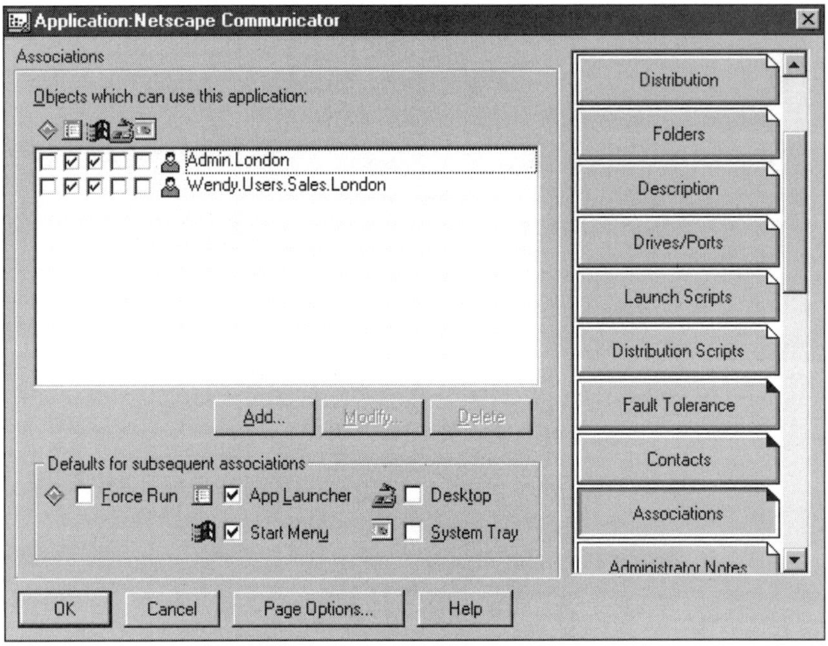

Figure 6-21. The Associations page

Start Menu
The Application icon can also be placed in the Start menu on the workstation. If this is desirable for the application, check the third column. This option will be available only if you use the Application Explorer option rather than the Application Launcher option, as discussed earlier in this chapter.

Desktop
If you wish the icon to be placed on the user's desktop, check the fourth column. It is probably not a good idea to force too many items on the desktop as it will soon become cluttered. The desktop is a good place for important applications such as virus checkers.

System Tray
The system tray is an area on the taskbar. If you wish the icon to be located there, check the fifth column. The space available in the system tray is even more limited than the desktop, and to some extent less visible. This area is really for special system applications or functions.

Administrator Notes

This page is designed for you to keep whatever information about the application you wish, but is very useful for documenting the installation details and what changes you have made to configure it for your environment. This is particularly the case when the role of managing your network is shared among several people, an example of which is shown in Figure 6-22. Change control is a vital part of any successful installation but is frequently underused. Aside from any unwillingness on the part of system administrators to take the time to make such notes, any amount of extra work or inconvenience required to make them do so can lead to the failure of the change control system. All the configuration details relating to applications are held in the object and this page is an ideal and convenient location for it.

When you install an application and make changes to the object to ensure appropriate delivery in your environment, you may think that you will remember what you did. The reality is that you probably will not remember. If there is more than one person installing applications, it is very helpful to make notes about what you have done so that it can be supported when you are not around.

Macros

Macros are used by the Application Launcher to insert text in place of a variable. In a sense, it may not be a macro in the way you understand it, such as a set of instructions like a program, but a variable substitution mechanism. These macros can be very useful for inserting either already defined variables or others which can be entered through the Macros page, as shown in Figure 6-23.

Macros can be used to substitute strings in the following areas:

- Path to executable (Identification page)
- Command line (Environment page)
- Working directory (Environment page)
- Mapping path (Drives/Ports page)
- Capture port path (Drives/Ports page)
- Registry setting key, name, string value (Registry page)
- INI settings: group, name, value (INI Settings page)
- Application files: source and target directory (Application Files page)
- Text files: find and add string (Text Files page)
- Icons and shortcuts: all locations (Icons/Shortcuts page)

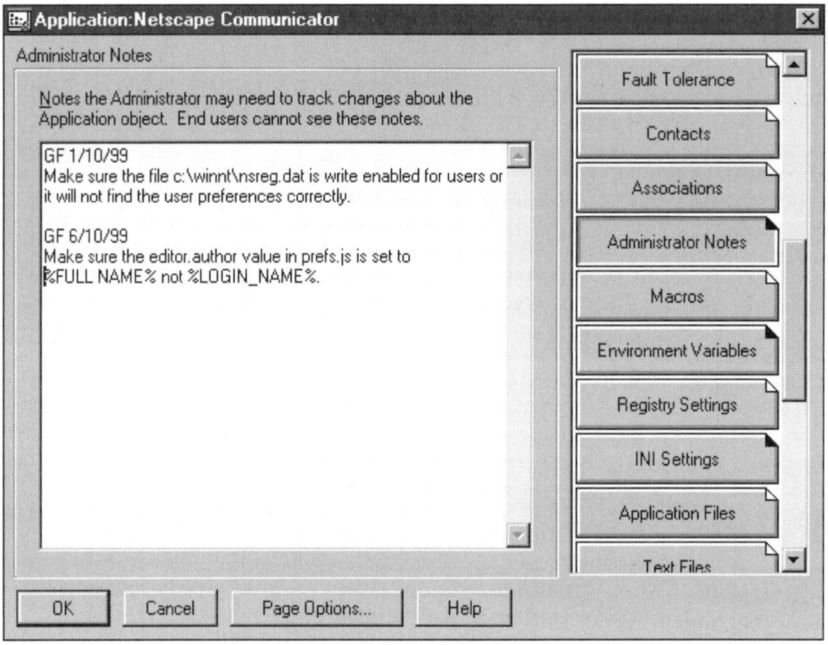

Figure 6-22. The Administrator Notes page

Several types of macros are available in this page as listed in the following sections in order of execution preference.

Application object macros

An application object macro is a variable that can be used only in the Application object where it is defined. Any macro defined in an application object is not defined with the same value in another object unless you specifically set it to that value. The two common macros seen here are:

%SOURCE_PATH%
: Location of source files to copy to the workstation and the location of the *.AOT* and *.AXT* template files.

%TARGET_PATH%
: Defines the target directory where the files are to be copied to the workstation.

Both of these examples are generated from the snAppShot tool, although others can be defined through the tool as well. The source and target paths can be either paths using drive letters or UNC pathnames. One of the clear advantages of using a variable for the path is when you decide to change either of the locations for some reason. If there are a lot of files to be copied, the definition of *%SOURCE_PATH%* will greatly simplify a change of location for the source location.

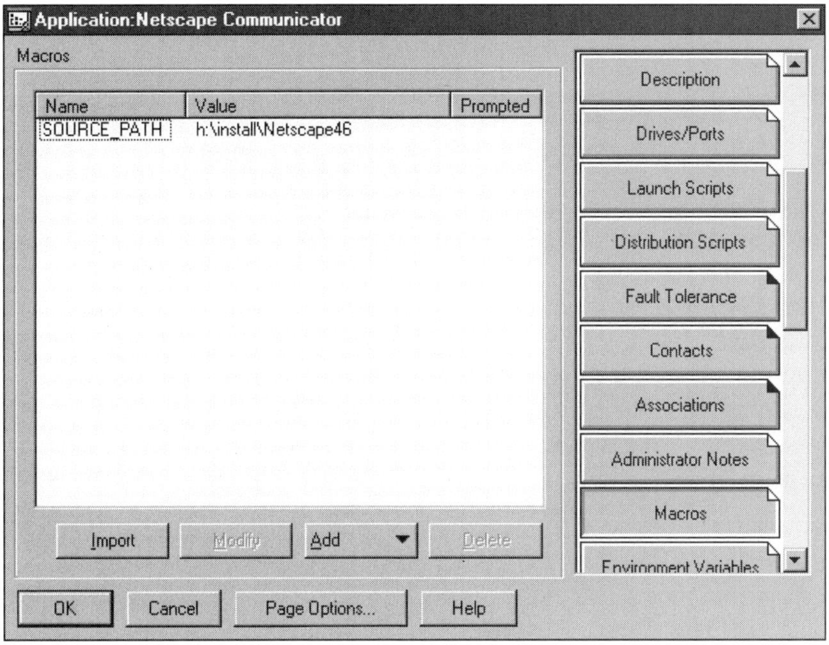

Figure 6-23. The Macros page

Windows macros

Under Windows 3.x, Windows 95/98, and Windows NT/2000, variables are used to define where particular parts of the operating system are to be found. If you install the operating system on a workstation's hard disk drive *C:*, then the *%*WINDISK%* variable will be set to `C:`. This variable is very useful if you have workstations that have Windows installed on different drives, as the Windows directory can be referenced as *%*WINDISK%\Windows*.

The following macros or variables are available under Windows 3.x, Windows 95/98, and Windows NT/2000 for redirecting application files that expect Windows directories to be in a particular location:

*%*WinDir%*
: This is the Windows directory, which is usually set to *C:\WINDOWS* or *C:\WINNT*. This variable is ideal for use where the target directory for a particular file is the Windows top-level directory.

*%*WinSysDir%*
: This is the Windows System directory; it is usually set to *C:\WINDOWS\SYSTEM* or *C:\WINNT\SYSTEM32*. It is used in the case where a file needs to be copied or referenced to the System directory.

*%*WinDisk%*

This variable should contain the drive letter for the Windows directory, usually set to *C:*, but may be another drive on some workstations.

*%*WinSysDisk%*

Similar to *%*WinDisk%*, but contains the drive letter for the Windows System directory, typically *C:* but again it could be another drive.

*%*WinSys16Dir%*

The installation of the `WIN32` add-in under Windows 3.x determined that a distinction between 32-bit system components and 16-bit system components should be made. This distinction is also present under Windows 95/98 and Windows NT/2000, where most system components are stored in the *system32* directory and 16-bit components in the *system* directory. In this case the Windows *system32* directory is referred to by *%*WinSysDir%* and the 16-bit system directory by *%*WinSys16Dir%*. Typically under Windows NT/2000 the 16-bit system directory will be *C:\WINNT\SYSTEM* and under Windows 95/98 will be *C:\WINDOWS\SYSTEM*.

*%*TempDir%*

Applications frequently need an area of scratch space where they can store temporary files. Under Windows 95/98 this temporary directory will usually be *C:\WINDOWS\TEMP* and under Windows NT/2000 will be *C:\TEMP*.

The following variables are available on Windows 95/98 and NT only. These macros or variables are defined under the registry key HKEY_CURRENT_USER\SOFTWARE\MICROSOFT\WINDOWS\CURRENTVERSION\EXPLORER\Shell folders.

*%*AppData%*

This variable is used only by Windows NT/2000 as a common area for storing application data. It is mostly used by Microsoft applications such as Internet Explorer. The typical path stored in this variable will be *C:\WINNT\PROFILES\<USER>\APPLICATION DATA*.

*%*WinDesktop%*

The Windows desktop items personal to each user are stored in each user's profile. Under Windows 95/98 this will be *C:\WINDOWS\DESKTOP* and under Windows NT/2000 it will be *C:\WINNT\PROFILES\<USER>\DESKTOP*.

*%*Desktop%*

This variable is confusingly similar to the *%*WinDesktop%* variable. The difference is that the *%*Desktop%* variable defines the location of the desktop files. The variable is usually set to *C:\WINDOWS\DESKTOP* under Windows 95/98 or *C:\WINNT\PROFILES\<USER>\DESKTOP* under Windows NT/2000.

*%*CommonWinDesktop%*

This is a Windows NT/2000-only setting which points to the common desktop directory, usually *C:\WINNT\PROFILES\ALL USERS\DESKTOP.*

*%*CommonDesktop%*

This Windows NT/2000-only variable defines the directory that contains files and folders that appear on the desktop for all users, usually *C:\WINNT\PROFILES\ALL USERS\DESKTOP*, but can also be set to a location on the fileserver.

*%*Favorites%*

This variable defines the location of the user's favorite items and is usually set to *C:\WINDOWS\FAVORITES* under Windows 95/98 and under Windows NT/2000 to *C:\WINNT\PROFILES\<USER>\FAVORITES.*

*%*Fonts%*

The fonts stored on the system are located in a directory defined by this variable, usually *C:\WINDOWS\FONTS* under Windows 95/98 and *C:\WINNT\FONTS* under Windows NT/2000.

*%*NetHood%*

Objects that appear in the Network Neighborhood are stored in the location defined by this variable, usually *C:\WINDOWS\NETHOOD* under Windows 95/98 and *C:\WINNT\PROFILES\<USER>\NETHOOD* under Windows NT/2000.

*%*PrintHood%*

This variable is only used under Windows NT/2000 and defines the location for printer links, usually *C:\WINNT\PROFILES\<USER>\PRINTHOOD.*

*%*Personal%*

The Personal directory defined by this variable is a location where a user's documents can be stored. This variable is usually set to *C:\WINNT\PROFILES\<USER>\PERSONAL* under Windows NT/2000. When the user's documents are stored in the roaming profile in this way, it can make the login and logout time very slow if the user has a lot of documents stored there. It can be set to a network or local volume also, such as *F:\DOCUMENTS.*

*%*Programs%*

This variable points to the directory that contains the user's program groups, usually *C:\WINDOWS\START MENU\PROGRAMS* under Windows 95/98 and *C:\WINNT\PROFILES\<USER>\START MENU\PROGRAMS* under Windows NT/2000.

*%*CommonPrograms%*

This variable points to the directory that contains the directories and objects for the Common Program groups that appear on the Start menu for all users, usually *C:\WINNT\PROFILES\ALL USERS\START MENU\PROGRAMS.*

*%*Recent%*

The user's recently used files are stored in a directory defined by this variable, usually *C:\WINDOWS\RECENT* under Windows 95/98 and under Windows NT/2000 *C:\WINNT\PROFILES\<USER>\RECENT.*

*%*SendTo%*

Items found in the Send To menu are objects located in the directory defined by this variable, usually *C:\WINDOWS\SENTO* under Windows 95/98 and under Windows NT/2000 *C:\WINNT\PROFILES\USER\SENDTO*.

*%*StartMenu%*

Objects to appear in the Start menu are located in the directory defined by this variable, usually set to *C:\WINDOWS\START MENU* under Windows 95/98 and *C:\WINNT\PROFILES\ADMINISTRATOR\START MENU* under Windows NT/2000.

*%*CommonStartMenu%*

Items for the Common component of the Start menu under Windows NT/2000 are located in this directory, usually *C:\WINNT\PROFILES\ALL USERS\START MENU.*

*%*Startup%*

The user's Startup program group is defined by this variable, usually *C:\WINDOWS\START MENU\PROGRAMS\STARTUP* under Windows 95/98 and *C:\WINNT\PROFILES\<USER>\START MENU\PROGRAMS\STARTUP* under Windows NT/2000.

*%*CommonStartup%*

Under Windows NT/2000 the Common startup folder is defined by this variable, usually *C:\WINNT\PROFILES\ALL USERS\START MENU\PROGRAMS\STARTUP.*

*%*Templates%*

Document templates are stored in the location defined by this variable, usually *C:\WINDOWS\SHELLNEW* under Windows 95/98 and under Windows NT/2000 *C:\WINNT\SHELLNEW.*

*%*TempDir%*

This variable defines the temporary directory, usually *C:\WINDOWS\TEMP* under Windows 95/98 and *C:\TEMP* under Windows NT/2000.

Login script variables

The NetWare operating system's login script language has a host of variables defined that are not only very useful in login scripts but can also be used as macros in this page. Not all of the variables are available, so beware. The following is a list of variables that can be used as macros:

COMPUTER_NAMEDAY
: This variable contains the name of the computer with the day of the month appended to it.

FILESERVER
: Name of the NetWare fileserver to which the user is connected.

FULL_NAME
: The user's full name as entered in the user object.

HOUR24
: The hour of the day in 24-hour format.

HOUR
: The hour of the day in 12-hour format.

LAST_NAME
: The surname of the current user as entered in the user object.

LOGIN_NAME
: The user's username that he uses to log in to the NDS.

MINUTE
: Current minute of the hour.

MONTH
: Current month number of the current year in two-digit format.

NDAY_OF_WEEK
: Current day of the week where Sunday = 1.

NETWORK
: The IPX network number to which the workstation is attached.

OS_VERSION
: This variable contains the operating system version which under Windows 3.x will be the DOS version and under Windows 95/98 will be the Windows version.

OS
: This variable is set to the operating system type, which is set to WIN95, WIN98, WINNT, or MSDOS under Windows 3.x.

PLATFORM
: This variable defines the workstation platform such as W95, W98, WNT, and WIN for Windows 3.x.

PHYSICAL_STATION
: This variable contains the Media Access Control (MAC) address of the workstation.

REQUESTER_CONTEXT
The NDS context of the user running the application.

SECOND
Current second of the current minute.

SHORT_YEAR
This variable contains the short-year number, such as 99 rather than 1999.

Environment Variables

Many applications use environment variables as a mechanism for locating resources on the workstation. Under DOS, these settings were provided through the *autoexec.bat* file or when the user issued a *set* command at the command prompt. Under Windows 95/98 and Windows NT/2000, users need to restart the system after setting a system-level environment variable so that it is registered correctly. The Application Launcher can set an environment variable on behalf of the user before the application launches through the page shown in Figure 6-24. The Environment Variables page is available to Windows 95/98 and Windows NT/2000.

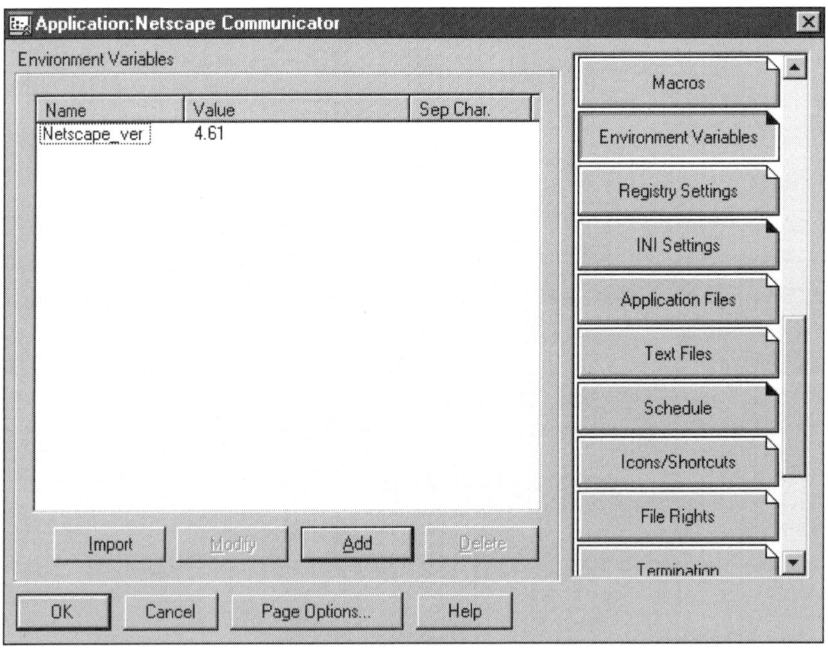

Figure 6-24. The Environment Variables page

The page allows you to add a variable or, if the variable already exists, either overwrite the value contained in the variable or append to it using a separator character. The Append function is particularly useful if you wish to modify the PATH environment variable using a "`;`" separator.

Registry Settings

The need for an efficient central store of settings, both for the operating system and for applications, became apparent during the life of Windows 3. Under this system, all settings were stored in text files with the extension *.ini*. The Windows 3 *.ini* file had the advantage that you could edit the files very easily, but they were very slow and were also scattered around the system in a way that made it hard to find the relevant file. There was no official mechanism to allow for the storage of user-specific settings in *.ini* files. When there were user-specific settings, they were global for all users on a workstation and a particular setting made by a user would affect all users of that workstation.

Under Windows 95/98 and Windows NT/2000, all compliant 32-bit programs store their settings in a database called the registry. This database has an extra feature in that user-specific settings can actually be specific to the user provided the user identifies himself at the login dialog box. This important new feature provides excellent flexibility for the user and headaches for the system administrators. How do you ensure that the essential settings for the user are actually supplied to him? The answer used to be that when you designed your system, you made sure that the component of the registry for the default user was perfect, so that when he logged in for the first time, he got an HKEY_CURRENT_USER that met all the requirements. This was not a perfect solution because it took no account of what happened if you didn't get it perfect and it also took no account of future upgrades to the system. It is certainly true that you should get the default user registry as perfect as you can, but you must have a mechanism for making additions or alterations to it as well.

> Supplying the appropriate HKEY_CURRENT_USER settings to the user when he first logs in is a real headache. The Track Distribution Per User function will allow you to define areas that need to be supplied on a per-user basis. It is generally good practice to define all settings in HKEY_CURRENT_USER to be tracked on a per-user basis.

The main components of the registry you need to worry about are HKEY_CURRENT_USER and HKEY_LOCAL_MACHINE, which are shown in Figure 6-25. In either case you have several options on how to deal with the subkey:

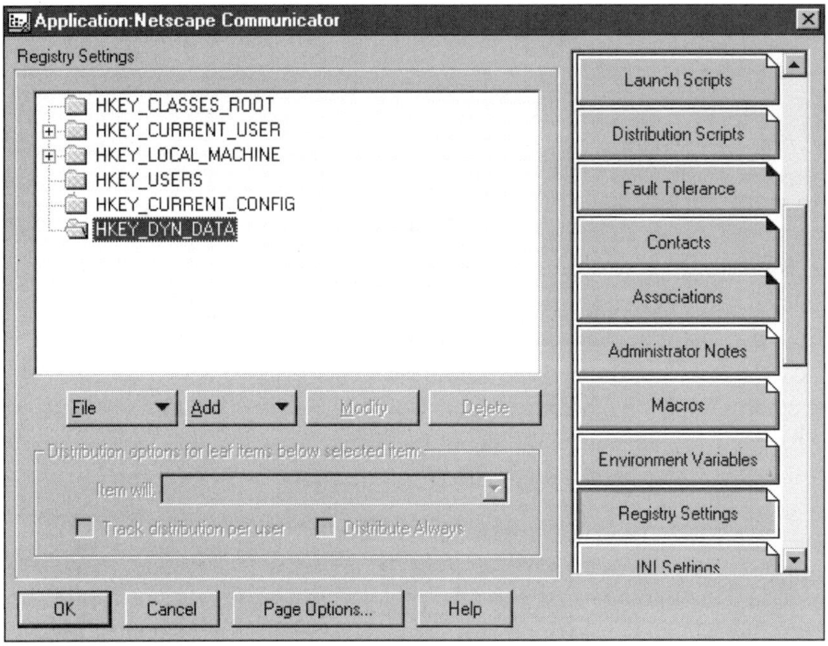

Figure 6-25. The Registry Settings page

Create Always
: Creates the value in the registry even if it exists there already, thereby potentially overwriting the existing value.

Create if does not exist
: Creates the value only if it does not currently exist in the registry. If there is a setting already present, it will leave it unchanged.

Create if exists
: Changes a value only if it currently exists in the registry.

Delete
: Removes the registry key and everything below.

The HKEY_LOCAL_MACHINE component contains data and settings specific to the workstation that need to be inserted into the registry in order for the application to work correctly. In most cases, when the key does not actually exist, it can be inserted without difficulty by using the "Create if does not exist" option. Where the key already exists, you will need to decide what the effect will be if the values and keys are overwritten or not. In general when you install a new piece of software, it will create keys in HKEY_LOCAL_MACHINE that will not affect any existing keys. When you install Netscape Communicator, a key will be created under HKEY_

LOCAL_MACHINE\Software\Netscape. This key will be unique if you haven't installed Netscape before, so you should be able to set all the keys under HKEY_LOCAL_MACHINE\Sofware\Netscape to "Create if does not exist." When the user runs the software for the first time, the applications' GUID will be stamped into the HKEY_LOCAL_MACHINE\Sofware\NetWare\NAL component of the registry, thereby identifying that the workstation-specific components have been completed and no more distribution is required. If you are upgrading a piece of software, you may have more trouble if the keys that exist have inappropriate values for the new software. In this case you will need to identify these keys and set them to Create Always so that the value is overwritten in the registry.

The HKEY_CURRENT_USER component has similar issues as those for HKEY_LOCAL_MACHINE. The additional problem occurs in the case where you are using roaming profiles. When the first user on a workstation runs the software and the components are installed on the workstation, some components will need to be carefully managed. The first user's HKEY_CURRENT_USER is mounted in the registry and will have the correct settings installed for the software. When the user logs out, his HKEY_CURRENT_USER is dismounted from HKEY_USERS. If another user decides to use the same workstation and the same application distributed for the previous user, then the application will work okay, except that the HKEY_CURRENT_USER component will not be inserted. The reason for this is that NAL will think that the application has been distributed and that no more work is required. The way out of this problem is to ensure that any settings that need to be distributed for the user have "Track distribution per user" enabled for those components. This will be the case for all components in HKEY_CURRENT_USER. When NAL encounters a "Track distribution per user" setting, it will check whether the user has the GUID for the application stamped into HKEY_CURRENT_USER\Software\NetWare\NAL. If the GUID is not found, the user will receive the settings before the application is launched.

The Distribute Always function is also available on the Registry Settings page. This feature is similar to that on the Distribution page, except in that case the feature is global. The Distribute Always function on this page is for when you wish a particular value to be checked every time the application is launched. If you have the "Create if does not exist" feature applied to the key, the distribution will perform that function. The case-by-case Distribute Always feature is much more useful when you use it with the Create Always function. In this case, the key will be forced onto the workstation or user each time the application is launched.

INI Settings

The INI file was historically used to store application settings under Windows 3.x, and if you are distributing the application to that operating system, you will certainly need to manage those files. If you plan to use the application on Windows

NT/2000 or Windows 95/98, you will also need to manage the files. Modern 32-bit programs should really use the registry to store their settings, but in reality, INI files are still widely used.

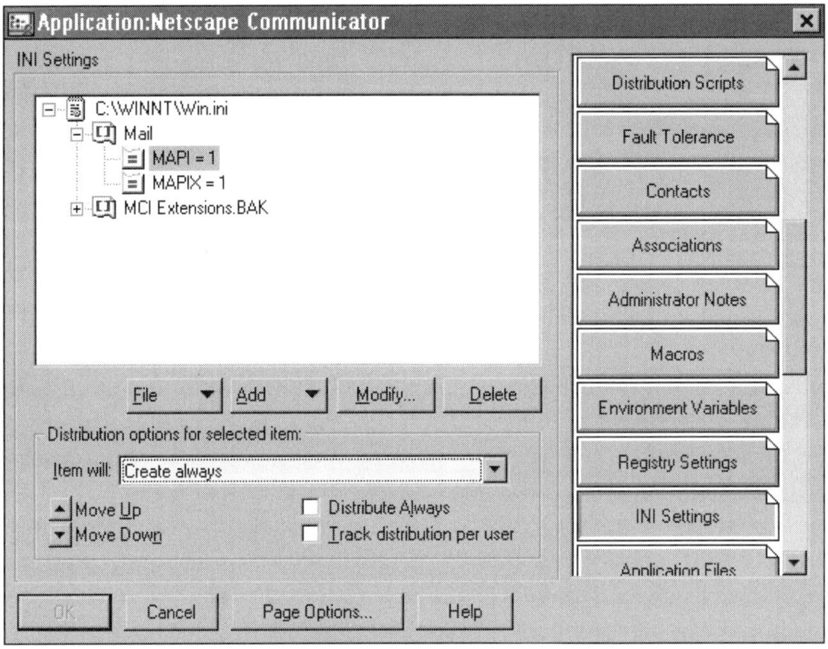

Figure 6-26. The INI Settings page

INI files are composed of sections, usually shown in square brackets [ ], and keys with values as shown in Figure 6-26. Each of these values and sections can be modified in the following way:

Create Always
: Creates the value in the INI file even if it already exists there, thus potentially overwriting the existing value.

Create if does not exist
: Creates the value only if it does not currently exist in the INI file. If there is a setting already present, it will leave it unchanged.

Create if exists
: Changes a value only if it currently exists in the INI file.

Create or add to existing section
: Adds the key and value to the section in addition to same key, which already exists. This setting is useful when adding several `DEVICE =` keys into a *SYSTEM.INI* file.

Create or append to existing value

If the key and value do not exist they will be inserted; otherwise, the value will be appended to the existing value.

Delete

Removes the INI file key or section.

Delete or remove from existing value

When a key has multiple values you may wish to remove one of the values, but not the whole key. When the key only has one value it will remove the key as well.

Some INI files are designed to be specific to the user. If you get users sharing workstations, it may be best to store the file in the user's home directory so that it will be available each time and configurable with user-specific settings. This has similar issues to those discussed earlier in "Registry Settings." In this case, when a user first accesses the software and the INI file is distributed to his home directory, any subsequent user will also need the file and its contents distributed to them. To ensure this happens, enable the "Track distribution per user" feature for all the keys in the INI file.

The Distribute Always function is available on this page to manage keys and values on a case by case basis. The Distribute Always feature is also available on the Distribution page, except in that case, the function affects the application globally. If you wish a particular value to be checked for correctness every time the application is launched you may wish to set it to Distribute Always. If the setting is told to "Create if does not exist," the distribution mechanism will probably create it the first time and then needlessly check it for existence each subsequent time. The Distribute Always feature on this page is much more useful when you use it in conjunction with the Create Always function, where the setting will be forced to the workstation or user each time the application is launched.

Application Files

All applications have files, and in the simplest case this may be a single executable. If all applications were composed of a single executable, life would be much simpler for system administrators. The reality of the situation is that software packages usually have lots of files and they are not placed in a single location, but scattered all over the place. If you install an application to the local hard disk, you will probably find files in the install directory, the Windows directory, and in the Windows system directory. If you install the application to a network volume, there will probably be files installed onto the local workstation as well as in the users' home directories. The application page, shown in Figure 6-27, helps to manage these files so that the application will run correctly within the environment you have created for it.

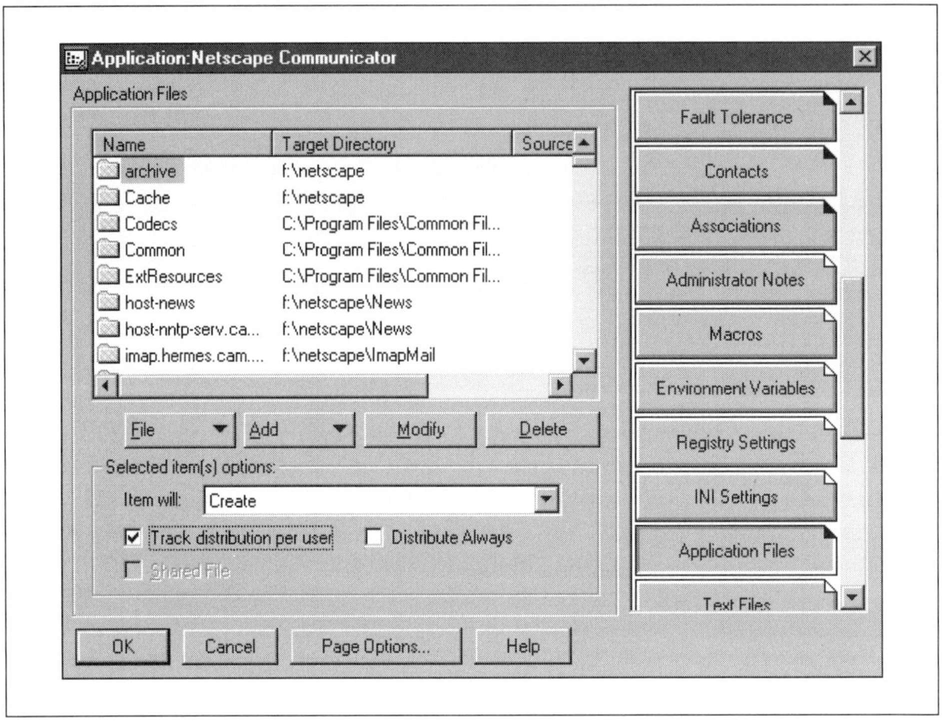

Figure 6-27. The Application Files page

Application files need to be installed into the appropriate locations for the application to find them where it expects. Application files are not usually modified by users, so the worst that can happen to them is that they will be deleted. The safest option with application files is to copy them if they don't exist, but there are other options that may be relevant for certain files:

Copy Always
: Copies the file even if it exists there already, thereby potentially overwriting the existing file.

Copy if exists
: Copies a file only if it currently exists on the workstation.

Copy if does not exist
: Copies the file only if it does not currently exist on the workstation. If the file is already present it will leave it unchanged.

Copy if newer
: Copies the file only if the date and time are newer or if the file does not currently exist on the workstation.

Copy if newer and exists
: Copies the file only if the date and time are newer than the existing file. If the file does not currently exist on the workstation, the file will not be copied.

Copy if newer version

Copies the file only if the file version is newer than the existing file or if the file does not currently exist on the workstation. Version information is available in *.DLL* and *.EXE* files and does not apply to all file types.

Copy if different

Copies the file if the date, time, or size is different on the same named file on the workstation. This is similar to "Copy if newer," but combines file size as well.

Request confirmation

The file copy process will occur only if the user gives permission.

Delete

Removes the file from the workstation unless it is marked as a shared file.

If your users share workstations, you may wish to ensure that certain files are present in the users' home directories. If a user wishes to save web site information in his Netscape Bookmark file, you will need to ensure that the file is present on the user's home directory so that if he uses a different workstation, this personal file will be available to him. To do this you will need to indicate where the file is to be placed and enable the "Track distribution per user" feature. This will ensure that each user who uses the workstation will have the correct files in place when the application launches.

When you install an application, certain files are copied into place that are also used by other applications. Suppose you had an application X that installed *VBRUN300.DLL* onto the workstation and an application Y that also installed this *.DLL* file. The *.DLL* file in this case will be shared by both applications and should be flagged as a shared file. If you subsequently decide to withdraw application X and delete all the files from the workstation, the shared file will not be deleted and application Y will continue to function.

The Application Files page hosts the Distribute Always function in the same way as the Registry Settings and INI Settings pages and is available to manage files on a case-by-case basis. The Distribute Always feature is also available on the Distribution page, except that in that case the function affects all the settings in the Application object. If you wish a particular file to be checked every time the application is launched, set it to Distribute Always. The Distribute Always feature on this page is useful when used in conjunction with the Copy Always function. The file will be forced to the workstation or user home directory each time the application is launched.

Text Files

Other files on the workstation also need to be managed. These are files such as *AUTOEXEC.BAT* and other similar batch files, or *CONFIG.SYS*. Text files are more difficult to manage because, unlike INI files, they are unstructured. With modern operating systems, these configuration text files do not need so much management as under DOS and Windows 3.x. Applications still make frequent use of text files to store configuration information. Application developers frequently have good reason to do this if they are providing the application on more than one platform. An example of this is the JavaScript file *PREFS.JS*, shown in Figure 6-28, which is used by Netscape to store configuration data. If a file such as this is not correctly configured, the user will be prompted to enter the correct configuration information. This may not be desirable if you wish your users to accept correct and standardized settings. An incorrectly configured file will only generate more calls to your Helpdesk. It is much better to manage the file in some way.

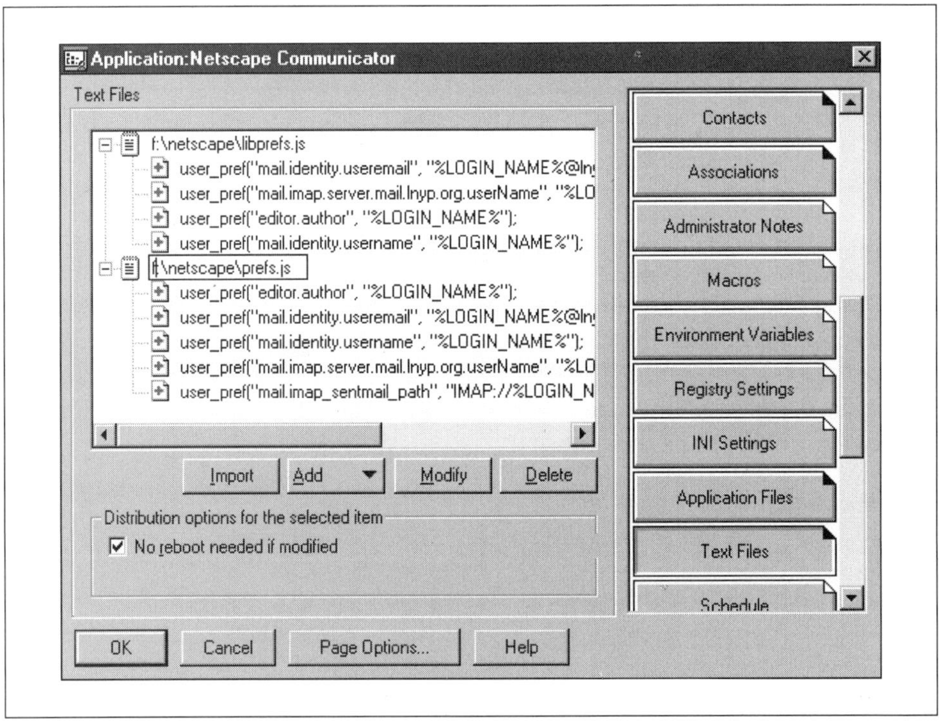

Figure 6-28. The Text File page

To manage a text file you will need to indicate the full path and the filename and then indicate what you wish to do to modify the file as follows:

Add text to the file

This setting will allow you to insert a line of text either at the beginning of the text file or a line at the end of the text file.

Delete text from the file

This option will allow you to remove a string of text or an entire line of text from the text file.

Find and replace text in the file

This option will allow you to either replace one string in the file with another or a complete line of text with another complete line.

Schedule

Generally speaking, most of your applications will be available to certain users or certain workstations. There are cases where the application needs to be run at a particular time. If you wish to schedule a virus scan to take place at certain times, you can arrange this to happen when it is convenient or most appropriate.

Applications are generally visible to the user at all times, but there may be some applications that should be visible only during certain hours, as shown in Figure 6-29. If you wish the application to actually run at that time, check the "Force run" box in the Associations page. This will cause the application to appear at the scheduled time and to execute as soon as it appears.

The following options are available to specify the visibility of the application:

Range of days

This option will allow you to specify either a range of dates or specific days of the week to have the application available. There is also a mechanism to specify a time range to make the application available.

Specified days

This option allows you to enter specific dates during which the application is to be visible. You are also able to set what time range the application is available in the defined day. There is a maximum of 350 entries allowed in this field.

Icon/Shortcuts

Icons and shortcuts are used under Windows 3.x, Windows 95/98, and Windows NT/2000 in various ways. Under Windows 3.x, program items and programs groups form the essential configuration of the Program Manager. Under Windows 95/98 and Windows NT/2000, shortcuts are used to provide the environment under which an application is to be launched. All of these functions are available within the Icons/Shortcuts page, shown in Figure 6-30, allowing you the flexibility of placing any one of these functions where you wish and to configure it how you wish.

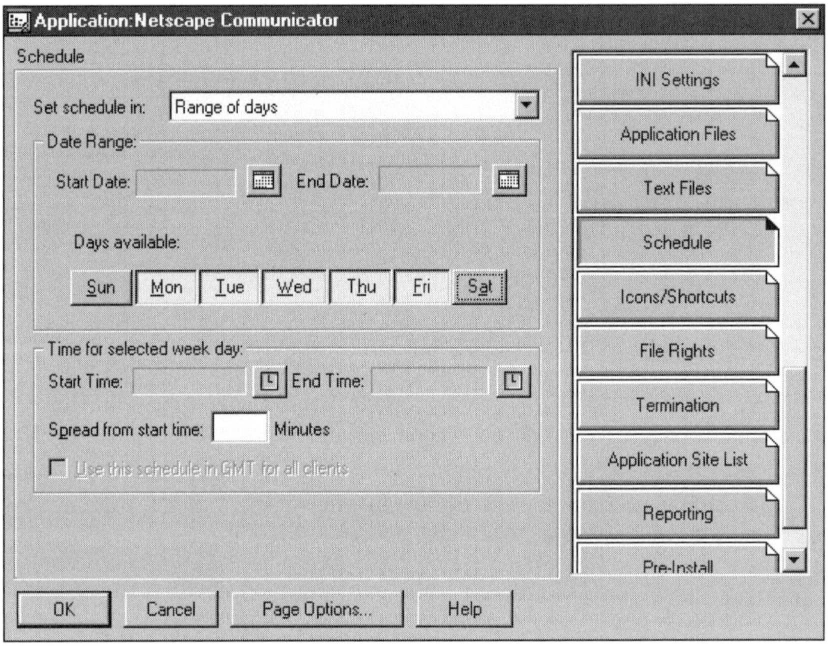

Figure 6-29. The Schedule page

Under Windows NT/2000 and Windows 95/98, shortcuts form the basis for the management of applications in the Start menu. The Application Launcher can be configured to insert these shortcuts in a way that allows some control of this system, if you feel that this is the best way of delivering them in your environment. The Novell Application Explorer will probably be a much better system for managing your desktop and Start menu than inserting shortcuts into every desktop. Under Windows NT/2000, the Start menu is divided into an All Users section, which is the lower half, and a Personal section, which is the upper half. The Shortcut page will allow you to add items to these menus and to delete them as well. If you have an item to be added to the Personal section of the Start menu for each user, then you are able to configure the shortcut and its location, but you should also enable the "Track distribution per user" option as well so that every user who uses the workstation will be have the shortcuts appear.

The Distribute Always function is also available in this page, allowing you to be able to force the shortcuts or program files to the user each time he logs in. To make the shortcut reset to a default state each time the user logs in, set the Distribute Always feature to ensure correctness, if you require it.

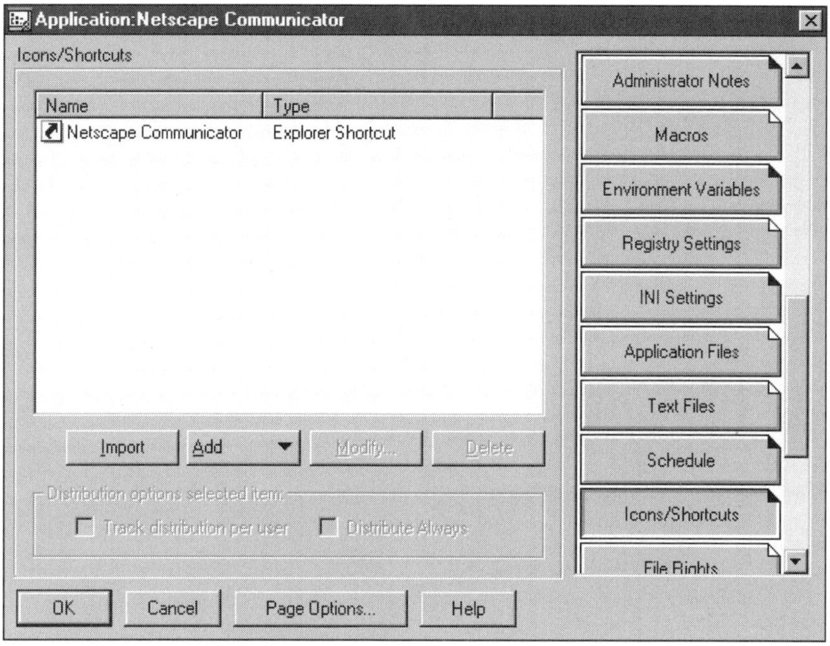

Figure 6-30. The Icons/Shortcuts page

File Rights

Some applications require that rights to the NetWare filesystem are granted before they will function properly. There may be desirable or undesirable reasons for this, but you have essentially no choice in some situations. If you have an application that needs special filesystem rights, you can either define them by default, so that users get the rights when they log in, or you can grant them rights dynamically and subsequently revoke them when the application has terminated, as shown in Figure 6-31. It is not possible to modify Windows NT/2000 NTFS filesystem rights within the application object, but this functionality is being planned in a future revision. If you wish to modify NTFS rights, the only way at the moment is to use the *cacls* command to make the modification and run it as a secure system user. This solution isn't ideal, but will work for you if you are really stuck!

Termination

If you have decided to make an application available only during a defined time interval, you will need to decide what to do if a user is still using the application during the unavailable time period. Clearly you will need to take some action or the user may simply keep the application open and only use the availability period

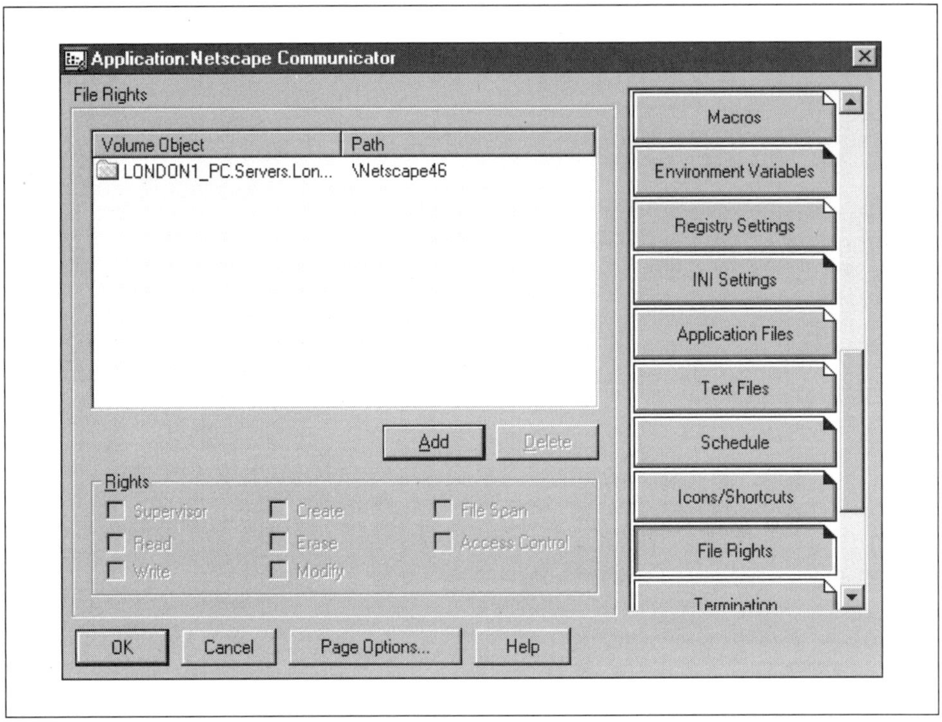

Figure 6-31. The File Rights page

as an opportunity to actually launch it. This essentially means that you will have to force a termination of the application in some way. There may be other reasons for determining when a termination should occur, such as a disassociation from the user or a change in system requirements. If you decide to perform some maintenance on an object and schedule a shutdown of the service, you may wish to terminate the service in a controlled way. Some applications behave unpredictably when forced to close. It is a good idea to test the results of such a forced closure on your application carefully.

The Termination page, as shown in Figure 6-32, allows you to control how to terminate the application in the following ways:

None
: Allow the user to continue using the application indefinitely.

Send message to close application
: This method places the onus on the user to close the application by prompting him to close the application. The message to the user is configurable and you are able to send a prompt to the user at specified intervals.

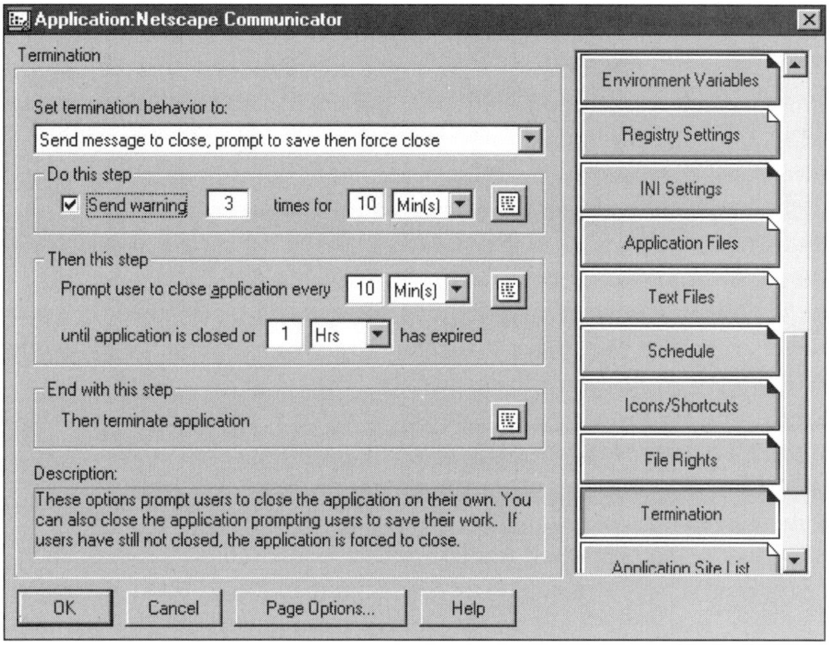

Figure 6-32. The Termination page

Send message to close then prompt to save data
: This method allows you to send a certain number of warnings before prompting the user to close the application.

Send message to close, prompt to save then force close
: This method guarantees that a closure will occur, but in the nicest possible way. If you really wish the user to terminate the application, you will need to consider some kind of forced closure.

Send message to close then force close with an explanation
: This mechanism is similar to the previous method, but skips the "prompt to save" step. If the application doesn't have a normal save function, such as a web browser, then this is a better choice.

> If you have a policy of having applications available only at certain times or with certain conditions, you will need to decide how you wish to enforce it or you may as well not bother to impose the restriction at all.

Application Site List

If you have a geographically diverse organization, you will probably have given due attention to the placement of an application's files so that not only is the application launched from the local server, but the files to be downloaded are also located locally. This is certainly easy, and should be done. A more complex issue of performance is related to the NDS object itself, which may contain just a few items of information concerning the application, such as the executable, or it may contain a very large number of registry keys. In the latter case, if you are logged into the NDS and physically located in New York, but the object is actually located in a partition that is only in London, then there may be performance issues over the time taken to read the object. It is certainly possible to replicate the partition to New York. If the partition is large, it may be desirable to actually make a copy of the objects so that they are present in the local office partition, but not causing a high-replication load. This is also a good idea and should be considered as it is an easy step to take to ensure performance. The problem is if you have users who travel about from one site to another. If they are based in Paris and travel to London, they will be authenticated from an object in Paris and may pick an application object from the NDS partition in Paris rather than the partition in London. This can lead to poor application performance; there can be a great deal of critical data to be read from the application object in order for it to run as you wish. The Application Site List page allows to you link application objects such that the local object in the local replica will be referenced rather than the remote object.

To use the tool you will need to chain together the application objects that need to be targeted. Select the application object in New York and then select the application object in Paris to link them together, as shown in Figure 6-33. When users travel to Paris, they will reference the application object in Paris rather than in New York.

When a user from New York logs in to a workstation in Paris, the nearest server, *Paris1*, responds to the login request. The user is authenticated to his user object in New York and is connected. When the user who is associated with the application object in New York clicks on the object, the Application Launcher realizes that he is in Paris and uses the Paris object as a reference for how to run and install the application, as shown in Figure 6-34.

Reporting

This page is used to collect information about an application, such as who has succeeded or failed to launch it. The data can be either stored in a comma-delimited file or can be sent to the inventory database via SNMP traps.

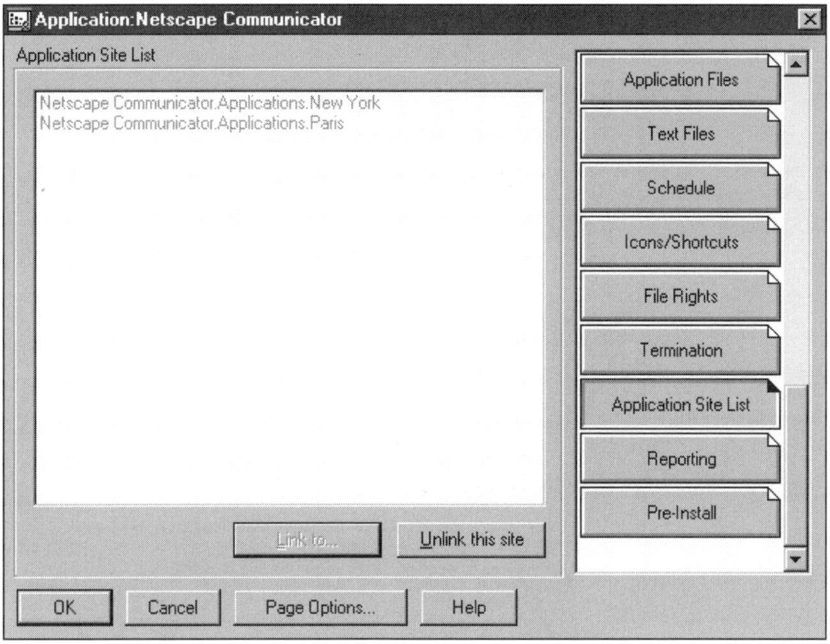

Figure 6-33. The Application Site List page

The configuration shown in Figure 6-35 shows the data being logged to a file with Launch Failure, Distribution Failure, and Hidden Icon Filtering reported to the file.

Pre-Install

Most applications have two components that need to be taken care of. The first is the component for the user and the second is the component, for the workstation. For the most part, the larger of these is the workstation component which in some cases is quite small and other cases quite large. This can be a real problem, not only for the users when they have to wait for all the files and registry keys to be installed, but also because it can cause the network to get very busy during the day. The problem is greatly assisted by installing the major components during the night when the user is not present and the network is lightly loaded.

The Pre-Install page allows you to configure the application so that the workstation component installation is performed out of hours. You schedule the distribution to take place after hours according to the schedule defined on the page, as shown in Figure 6-36. The Pre-Install will perform the entire distribution process including: file copying, modifying text files, INI files, and HKEY_LOCAL_MACHINE registry settings. The user-specific settings that are flagged "Track distribution per

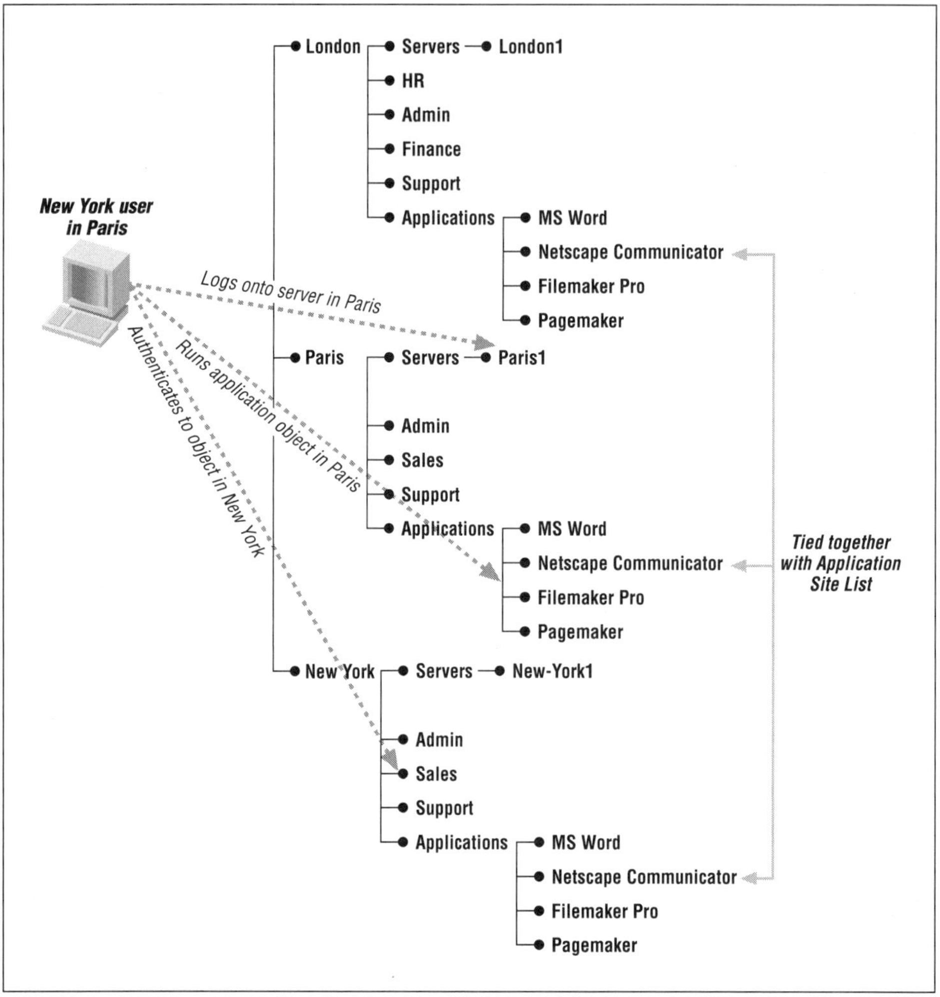

Figure 6-34. Connecting to the closest application

user" will not be performed by this Lights Out distribution. When a user logs in to the workstation the next day and runs the application, the user-specific settings will be installed. It is important that all user-specific settings are correctly flagged "Track distribution per user" or macro settings will resolve incorrectly when the distribution runs. If the workstation is shutdown or powered off during the distribution, the application distribution will be treated as incomplete.

Software Metering

The Software Metering page will only be present in the application object if the Software Metering component has been installed on the server. This page is discussed fully in Chapter 7, *Application Metering*.

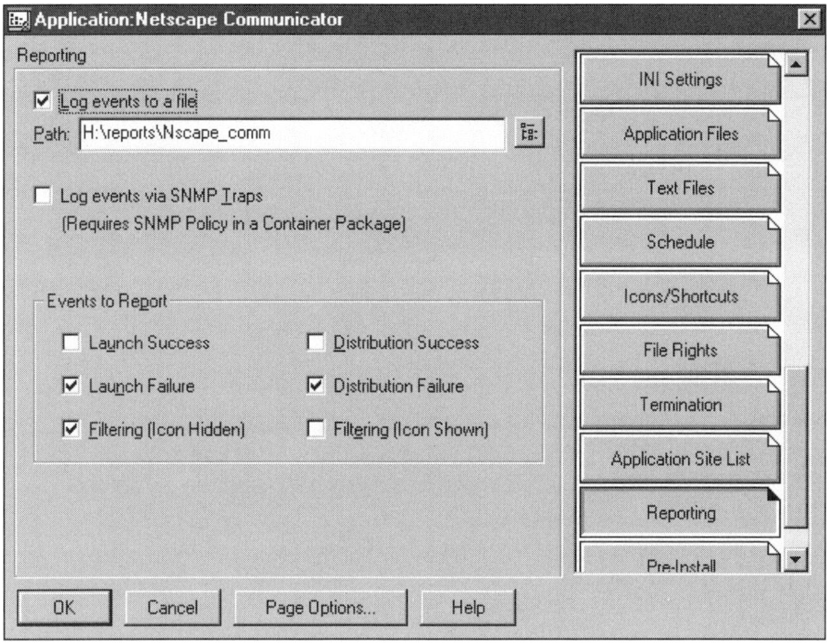

Figure 6-35. The Reporting page

Making Applications Work

The default configuration state of an application will not usually be acceptable immediately following installation. This will be true for applications installed and captured using snAppShot, even if you have been careful during the process. The installation allows you to rough out the app; it is up to you to make it work.

When you create an application object, one of the first things to be done is to define the executable for the program. When there is more than one executable, you may need to get the application working for the first, then try the second, and so on. For instance, if you installed Microsoft Office, the first executable to be checked will be *winword.exe*. Get this working the way you want, change it to *excel.exe*, and tailor it to the correct configuration state. Finally, configure *powerpnt.exe* and the whole suite is working. Next, you should duplicate the object with one for each program, set the executable, and appropriate icon, and display the application title. This will leave you with three objects, with one for each application. The final step is to sync the distribution GUIDs, associate with the users who are going to use it, and all is ready. You may wish to duplicate the objects in other parts of the tree as well for performance reasons. At this stage you should configure the Application Site List page as well if you have mobile users.

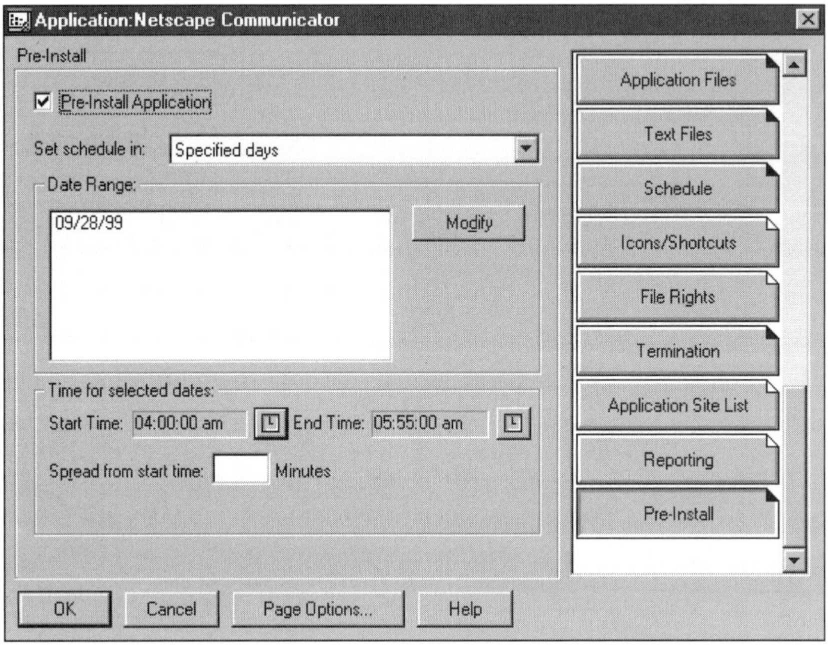

Figure 6-36. The Pre-Install page

The Identification page is an important page but, depending on the application, there may be a host of complex issues waiting for you. Some of the issues about coping with mobile users have been discussed already, but the issues are really no different for stationary users. These days a lot of IT departments use a single image of their favorite operating system and replicate it around the organization. There are a variety of ways of doing this. One way is to use a program such as *ghost* to save the disk image to a single file, and then replicate that image to all workstations. The advantage here is that not only can you very quickly roll out a standard image to all PCs, but you also have an excellent mechanism for fixing a workstation should it go wrong. The workstation can have an image reinstalled and if there is still a problem, it is probably a hardware fault. This is a simple and fast mechanism for these complex operating systems to be "fixed" and returned to service. The problem is that if the users store files on the hard disk or have their own applications stored locally, the whole process of reinstalling the workstation becomes a much more complicated and time-consuming task. It is better to store the users' files and settings on a network volume where they will not be deleted by a reinstallation and where the files will be backed up. This makes users effectively mobile in that it does not matter which workstation is being used because their files and settings will still be available to them.

The "Track distribution per user" issue has been discussed to some extent already, but as a matter of course you should apply this to all keys within HKEY_CURRENT_USER and to some of the files as well if they are being copied to the users home directory. There may also be keys that you consider too important to allow the user to have their own setting. In this case as well as "Track distribution per user," you should also use Distribute Always and set the registry key, file, or other setting to Create Always.

Launcher Configuration

In order for the Application Launcher to operate effectively and efficiently and to be displayed the way you want, you will need to make some changes as to how it is configured by default. These settings are configured either through a container object, a user object, or a workstation object. The details are configurable in the Launcher Configuration page in either of these objects, as shown in Figure 6-37.

Application Launcher configuration settings need to be applied to every user and workstation object in your tree. The good news is you don't actually have to edit each object and apply these settings, because they can be inherited from the parent object. These parent objects can also inherit from their parents and so on until you get to the highest container in your tree. There may be cases where the configuration will be slightly different for certain parts of you tree, but most of it can easily be inherited from the parent objects.

When the Application Launcher initializes itself, one of its tasks is to search the tree for configuration settings. This process starts with the object to which it has authenticated, which will be either a user object or a workstation object and work up the inheritance tree. The Application Launcher will continue up the tree searching for custom settings until it reaches a container object that has been designated as the "top" of the inheritance tree. If it finds custom configurations in any of the objects along the way, those configurations are applied. If it doesn't find any custom configurations, the configuration, which is set in the top container object, will be applied.

The top of the inheritance tree should be set to the lowest possible container, which encompasses a targeted group of users. In the tree shown in Figure 6-38, the top of the tree will be defined as the London container, the New York container, and the Paris container. This will prevent the Application Launcher from trying to find applications in other parts of the tree. The setting is made in the Launcher configuration in each of the three containers, which will be the top of each application tree. The following sections describe other settings in the tree.

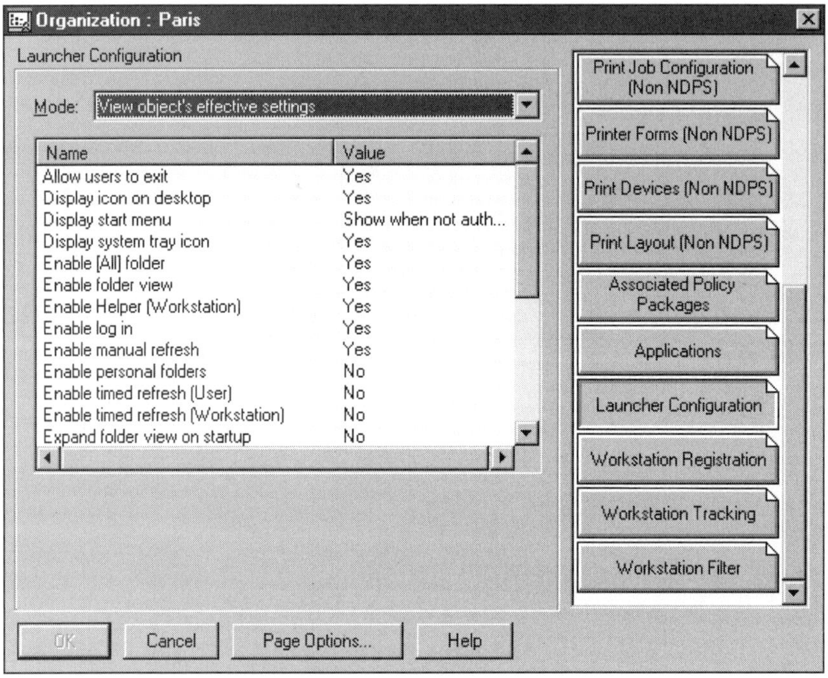

Figure 6-37. The Launcher Configuration page

User Settings

Allow users to exit

Under the assumption that most of your applications will be managed by the Application Launcher, allowing the users to exit the Launcher on purpose or otherwise essentially removes the applications from them. If this option is set to Yes, which it is by default, users can exit the Application Launcher or Explorer at will.

Enable [All] folder

The All folder is used to display all the application objects visible to the workstation in a single window. If you have a lot of application objects this may seem very confusing to users. The default setting for this is yes, so if you do not wish to see it, set it to no.

Enable manual refresh

If you add an application to the available list, it will not be visible to users until either they log in again or refresh the Application Launcher. A refresh can be either automatic, which I will discuss later, or manual. The manual refresh is relatively harmless and can easily be left to the default, which is yes.

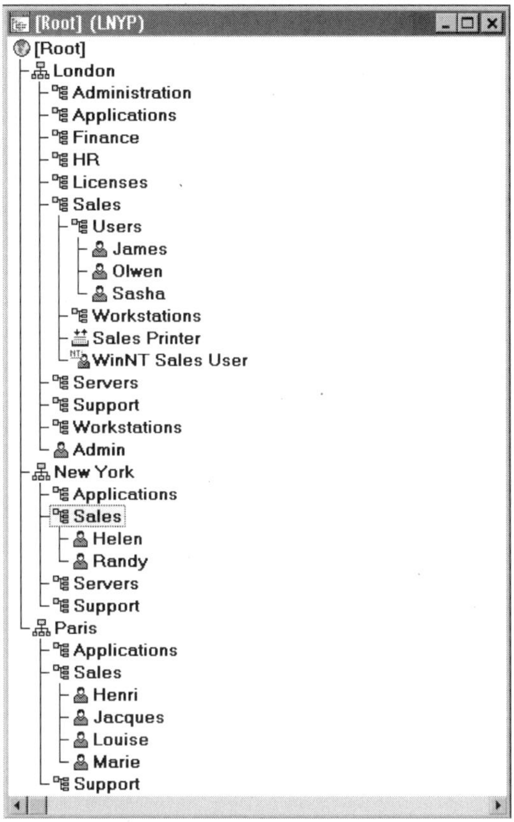

Figure 6-38. Application inheritance

Enable personal folders

Personal folders are designed to allow users to copy their own favorite application objects into. It will not allow users to put in objects with which they have not been associated. Personal folders are not enabled by default, so if you wish to have this function available to users, set it to yes.

Enable timed refresh

Timed refresh allows the Application Launcher to recheck the available applications in the tree. The time between scans is defined by the refresh frequency, explained later. If the scan time is quite long for collecting this information, this option will cause irritation for sure. If your users log in and out regularly then there is no need to change the default setting, which is no. If they stay logged in all the time, then you may need to enable it.

Read group objects for applications

It is possible to associate an application with a Ggoup object. Any users who are members of this group will automatically see the object. Using groups in this way can decrease performance, so use the function sparingly, or better yet, not at all. If you don't plan the use group association, switch off this functionality, which is set to yes by default.

Set application inheritance level

The Application Launcher's scan up through the tree for associated applications can be a slow business. If you can improve performance in this regard, you may as well. When the Application Launcher scans from the leaf object it is authenticated to, it reads this value and uses it to determine how far up the tree it has to search to find associated applications.

The tree shown in Figure 6-38 shows users in the Paris Sales Department. If you associate applications with the container Paris, then you should also set the application inheritance level to 2 or the users in Sales will not see them. If you set the inheritance level to 3, the Application Launcher will search unnecessarily high in the tree. In London, the structure is slightly different—users in Sales are one level deeper in the tree for some reason. You will need to proceed more carefully if the applications are associated to the London container. If all users in London are in a similar structure to New York and Paris, set the inheritance level to 2. This will be an appropriate setting for all users except Sales. Change the setting in `Users.Sales.London` to `3` to ensure that those users are catered for by allowing them to inherit the modified setting. The default setting is `1`.

Set refresh frequency

This setting is related to the automatic refresh setting discussed earlier. If you do not have Times Refresh enabled, this will be ignored. The default value on this setting is 3,600 seconds.

Specify email attribute

The application object contains a Contacts page that allows the user to contact the appropriate support person if they have trouble with the application. If you wish the support person's email address to appear for the user, set this option to the field in the user object that contains their email address. The default value here is Mailbox ID.

Enable users to view folders

If you wish users to see all the application icons in a single window and hide the folders from them, set this to no. The default setting here is yes.

Launcher Settings

Display start menu

If you are using the NAL window interface and you wish users to see the contents of the Start menu in that window along with the application objects, set this to either: Never show, Show always, Show when authenticated (only when authenticated), or Show when not authenticated (only when not authenticated). The default setting is Show when not authenticated.

Enable folder view

If you do not wish users to see folders in the Launcher Window, then set this value to no. The value is set to yes by default.

Enable log in

If you are using the NAL window interface and you do not wish the users to be able to have the Login option under the File menu, set this to no. The default value is yes.

Expand folder view on startup

The folders in the NAL window are normally visible and are normally unexpanded. If you wish them to be expanded by default, set this value to yes. The value is set to no by default.

Save window size and position

If you are using the NAL window frontend, you can cause any position or size changes to the window to be remembered by default so that the user can retain a favorite size and position between login sessions. If you wish the windows to have a standard size and position, change this setting to no.

Application Explorer Settings

Display icon on desktop

The Application Explorer can present a window on the desktop to allow users to view the applications in a similar way to the NAL window. If you do not want the window to be present, set this option to no.

Display system tray icon

When the Application Explorer is running it can display an icon in the system tray. This icon can be used to perform a manual refresh or to exit the Application Explorer. You can set this option to no to remove the Application Explorer icon from the system tray.

Name icon on desktop

If you have chosen to have the Application Explorer icon on the desktop, you may wish to give it a name to which users can relate. Define a name for the desktop object here. If you do not set a name, the folder will be called Application Explorer.

Workstation Settings

Enable Helper

This option allows you to have the Workstation Helper DLL installed and run by the Workstation Management Scheduler. The value is set to yes by default.

Enable timed refresh

This setting has the same functionality as "Enable timed refresh" described previously. It is set to no by default.

Read group objects for applications

This setting has the same functionality as the Read Group objects for applications described previously. It is set to no by default.

Set application inheritance level

This setting has the same functionality as "Set application inheritance level" described previously. It is set to 1 by default.

Set Refresh frequency

This setting has the same functionality as the "Set refresh frequency" described previously. It is set to 3,600 by default.

Application Folders

One of the essential components of Windows is that the application icons can be organized into groups. In the case of Windows 3.x, they were called Program groups, which have a single level. Under Windows NT/2000 and Windows 95/98, the Start menu has a folder structure that is virtually limitless. These groups are essential because icons can be surprisingly difficult to see and distinguish. It is amazing how hard it is to find an icon in a window with as few as 10 objects visible. The icon may be right in front of you and you may not see it. The Windows NT/2000 and Windows 95/98 Start menu has advantages in this sense because it forces the user to traverse down a list in a single direction rather than scan a windows in two directions. If you have a lot of applications installed in your tree, placing them all in a single window is messy and confusing for the users. It is much better to organize them in a useful way whether you use the Start menu or a set of subjective windows.

A very simple way of organizing applications is to use an Application Folder object. This object allows you to create a hierarchical structure and to place application objects in it, as shown in Figure 6-39. The folder is read when the Application Launcher runs on the workstation and dynamically builds the folder structure in both the Launcher window and in the Start menu. This gives you a very flexible and dynamic system for displaying the applications in a suitable way.

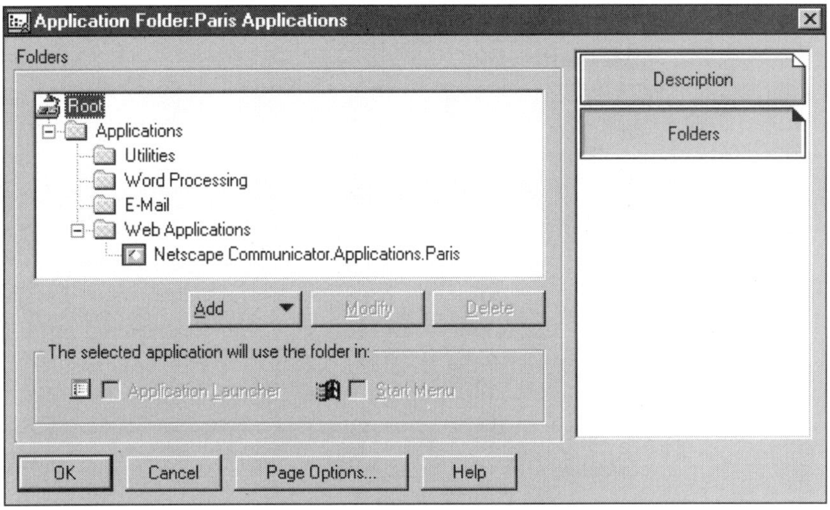

Figure 6-39. Application Folder object contents

Application objects can be placed just about anywhere in the tree, which is convenient for you. The user does not touch this object at all because the folder information is actually stored in the application object rather than the folder object. The Application folder is really a convenience for you so that you can easily visualize and manage the structure you have created. If you create a folder in a folder object with no application objects in it, the user will not see the folder. If the folder has applications in it that are not associated with the user or not visible to them for some reason, then they will also not see the object. This arrangement gives you a very flexible system for displaying all your applications to the user without having to visit the workstation to create a folder manually in the Start menu or Program Manager. A new folder will appear with the application icons when the Launcher is refreshed or when the user next logs in.

A Final Word

Whichever frontend interface you decide to use you will have a tool that will allow you to deliver applications to the users in a highly controlled way. The Application Launcher is one of the strongest features of ZENworks and is able to give you control over complex applications in a way that is unequaled by any other desktop management system. A note of caution: if you make a change to an application or install a new application, you have the power to accidentally wreck every machine on your network. You should perform as much testing as possible to ensure that a tool that should empower you to perform great things for the user will actually have the reverse affect.

There may be a host of settings which need to be carefully tailored. It is not always easy to discover how to make the installation look in the correct place for the settings. Suppose you decide to store all the user's personal files and settings in their home directory, which happens to be mounted as drive *F:* on all workstations via the login script. If you decide to store user-specific settings on that volume, you will have to tell the application where to look for them. For instance, in the case of Microsoft Word, the default template for the user is a file called *Normal.dot.* This file can be copied into place by modifying the target location of the file and tracking the distribution per user. To make Word look for the file in that location, you will need to modify a registry key in the user's own profile that will probably be stored on the network as well as either a roaming profile or a mandatory profile. The key HKEY_CURRENT_USER\Software\Microsoft\Office\8.0\Common\File New\Local Template\Default should be changed to *F:*. There are a lot of issues surrounding each application and how to configure it. The whole process of discovering and making the correct changes is essentially a black art. In most cases it is possible to find a way of configuring the application to a desirable state and you'll find you will get better at it. It is also a good idea to make a note of what changes you have made so that if you have to reinstall a new version, you have some idea of how you did it last time.

Another area to watch out for is UNC pathnames. If you have decided to use UNC paths as your mechanism for finding files, then that will be okay when you only have one application server. If you have several such servers, you may need to use an environment variable and a macro to ensure that an application running in London isn't actually looking and referencing files in New York. This is particularly the case when you are duplicating objects for each geographical location. The best way of ensuring that this is under control is to search for the server name in the registry section of the application object using the Find and Find Next functions. The Find feature is also available on the INI file page for 16-bit Windows applications. Even if you have decided not to use UNC pathnames, you will still find them lurking about in the registry. Microsoft Office has a particular tendency for this and even if you change them to hard-coded drive letters, they will be changed back to UNC pathnames after the distribution has occurred and the application is run for the first time. The good news is that it will at least resolve to the server from which it is being run.

The Application Launcher can be used for major or minor applications and also to make urgent changes to the workstations using the Force Run option. An important point to remember is that the Application Launcher will perform whatever you want on the remote workstation, but can be destructive if you have not tested it sufficiently.

7

Application Metering

I have discussed applications in great detail during the course of this book, covering both management and technical aspects. The one remaining issue that has not been covered is that of *metering*. Application metering is really another management function, similar to software inventory but more strictly about enforcement. In some cases, you may elect to purchase software on a per-workstation basis and indeed the license may dictate that you do this. In other cases, when you are permitted to share software licenses on the network, you will need to know that you are not exceeding the number of concurrent licenses that you have purchased.

Purchasing shared software is a bit of a lottery. If you have 500 workstations on the network and you wish to release a network version of Filemaker Pro, how many copies should you buy? You don't want to buy too few and yet you don't want to buy too many. This is a serious problem for network administrators working within the budget restraints that IT departments are so frequently exposed to. A system for managing concurrent licenses is required so that you are able to ensure that a service is being offered and that your organization is within the law.

> Software licenses vary enormously in their allowances and restrictions. If you plan to share licenses on your network, make sure the license allows it or you may be acting illegally!

Even if you decide to install some of your software on the workstation because the license terms are per-workstation, you may wish to ensure that these terms are being met. This can be done by metering the application and restricting the access to a particular server or user.

Preparing the Server

In the world of software metering, there are two types of metering systems available: the workstation-centric variety, which has an agent running on the workstation, and the server-centric variety, which monitors and manages from the server. The ZENworks application metering management is performed by the Novell Licensing Services (NLS), which runs on the server, but actually the prevention is performed by the NLS-aware Novell Application Launcher client running on the workstation.

To use ZENworks metering, you have to launch the application through the Application Launcher. You must also have the NLS component running on the server. These two components form a partnership, with the Application Launcher sending requests and the NLS server component performing authorizations. If the users are able to launch software without going through NAL, the launch will not be metered. The software metering component of ZENworks is a separate installation to the server and this must obviously be carried out before you can make use of any of it. The software metering installation is discussed in Chapter 2, *The ZENworks Installation.* Before you can even take this step, you must prepare the server or the metering component installation will not work.

Novell Licensing Services

NLS has been around for some time; it is used to ensure license compliance for the number of clients allowed to attach to the server. This is achieved by using a license certificate that may contain concurrent access for 100 workstations, for instance. The License Certificates used in this case are specific and require a special file containing a digital signature. These certificates can also be used by software vendors as a licensing mechanism. When you purchase software that is NLS-compliant, it will come with a disk containing a digital signature from which a license certificate can be created. The disk is used to create the NDS Certificate object that is queried by the NLS server when the software requests authorization. The NLS server can manage and monitor the number of client connections to the server. When a workstation starts up and a user logs in, the client will search for an NLS server. When the server has been contacted the client will attempt to be granted authorization for a connection to the server. The NLS process will check the certificate for availability and grant access if licenses are available.

If you are running NetWare 4.11, you will need to ensure that Support Pack 6 or greater is installed on the server or the ZENworks Software Metering will not work. NetWare 5 does not need any additional support packs for Software Metering.

ZENworks Software Metering uses another special certificate called a Metering Certificate. This is also termed an insecure license because the certificate is configurable by you and not by the software vendor. In order for the Software Metering to work, the NDS schema must be modified to accommodate the new object types. This step is performed by entering `LOAD SETUPNLS.NLM` at the server console prompt, which will modify and update the schema to accommodate License Certificate and Metering Certificates. When this process is finished you can enter the command `LOAD NLS.NLM` at the server console to start the NLS service. You should also enter this command in your *AUTOEXEC.NCF* startup file so that it will automatically start when the server starts.

Installing Software Metering

The next step is to install Software Metering to the NLS server. From the CD-ROM containing the ZENworks Full Pack, select Install ZENworks → Install Software Metering. Select the NDS tree you wish to install into and the server to which the files will be copied. The install process takes a few minutes and when all the components are in place you are ready to begin the metering process.

Creating a Metered Certificate

To meter a piece of software, a software license certificate is required. You will need a separate certificate installed for each application being restricted. This certificate is called a *Metered Certificate* and is created from the NWADMIN program by selecting the Tools → Install License → Create Metered Certificate. This will display a screen similar to that shown in Figure 7-1.

Enter the name of the software vendor or manufacturer such as Microsoft or Claris and the product name that you need to meter. In the example shown in Figure 7-1, the product name is entered as Office and not Word, because it is the Office product being licensed and not Word, which is only part of the product. The version number of the product can be entered, but if you use a version number with a decimal point it will be preceded with a backslash character as seen in the Filemaker Pro Certificate Container shown Figure 7-2. You will also need to indicate where the Certificate is to be located by indicating the context. If you selected the Parent container when you created the Certificate, this will be indicated already.

When you purchase the product, you will have purchased a certain number of licenses which, in the case of Microsoft Office shown in Figure 7-1, is two. If you wish to allow the license count to exceed this value on the understanding that you intend to purchase more licenses, then you are given the opportunity to enter that value here. This is quite useful for performing a function known as high-water

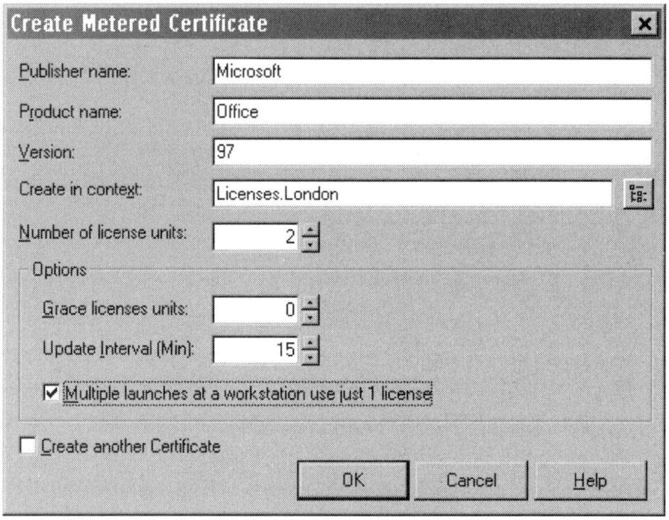

Figure 7-1. Creating a Metered Certificate

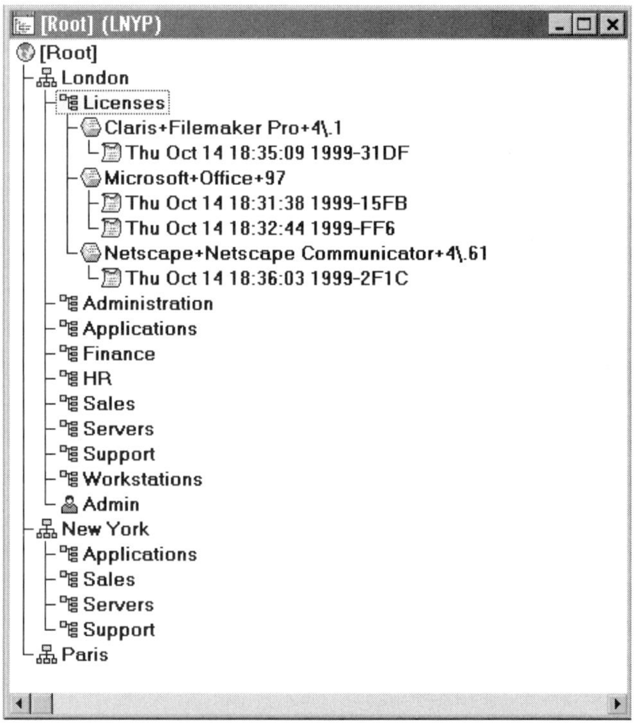

Figure 7-2. License Containers and Certificates

marking. This essentially means that you do not wish to stop your users from using the software when the licenses have been exceeded, you just want to be notified, so that you can buy more licenses. The update interval is the timed interval which the License Server will use to poll the certificate to see if any licenses have been consumed or released. The default value of 15 minutes is usually adequate here, but if your users tend to go in or out of the application quickly then you may wish to decrease the time interval.

When a user launches an application from the workstation that is licensed for multiple launches, it is possible to accommodate this as well. The checkbox labeled "Multiple launches at a workstation use just 1 license" is there for just this case. This function is useful either for launching the same application several times or when you wish to launch Microsoft Word and Excel at the same time, but consuming just one license. This option is also useful when an application is associated with a user and a workstation. If the user launches an application and then launches the same application through the workstation association, the number of consumed licenses will be two, rather than the allowed one unless the labeled "Multiple launches at a workstation use just 1 license" box is checked.

Make sure you get the details correct when creating a certificate, as you will not be able to change them later. The only way to correct a mistake is to delete the object and create it again.

When you have finished entering the details, click OK, but make sure they are correct, because you will not be able to change them later. If you subsequently wish to add more licenses, you will need to create a new certificate with exactly the same Publisher, Product name, Version, and context. Enter the number of licenses you have just purchased and a second certificate will be shown under the License Container similar to that shown with Microsoft Office 97 in Figure 7-2. This will increment the license count in the License Container. It is possible to remove the old certificate and create a new Container and Certificate, but this is disruptive and may not reflect the paperwork that may be in your possession.

License Containers

When the License Container and Certificate have been created you are able to view the details of the object. The details of the License Container are shown in Figure 7-3 and are as follows:

General

From this page you are able to see details regarding the number of licenses, which is a total of the licenses contained in the enclosed Certificates. You are also able to view other details such as the Highest number used, which is the high-water mark discussed earlier.

Users

From this page you are able to view the users who are currently consuming licenses from the container.

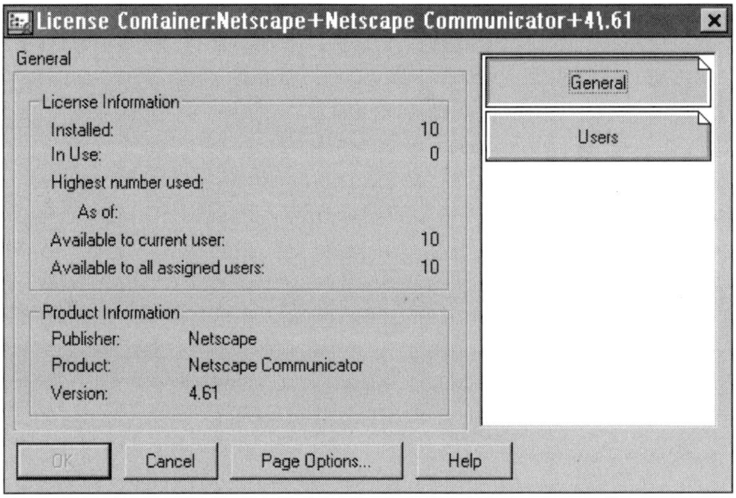

Figure 7-3. License Container details

License Certificates

License Certificates represent the pieces of paper you keep in your filing cabinet, which you have received from the software supplier. These pieces of paper keep you legal so long as you do not exceed the number of concurrent licenses. It is the task of the NDS Certificate objects to keep the number of licenses within these legal limits. The License Certificate contains several pages of information, as shown in Figure 7-4.

General

The General page does not contain any fields that are configurable by you. The page contains information only, such as the number of installed licenses, which is the total of all the certificates within the Container; the number in use, which includes the total number of available grace connections, and the number available, which does not include any grace licenses.

Users

This page is similar to the page available in the License Container; you are able to view the users who are currently consuming licenses, but in this case it relates to the number of users consuming licenses in the specific Certificate.

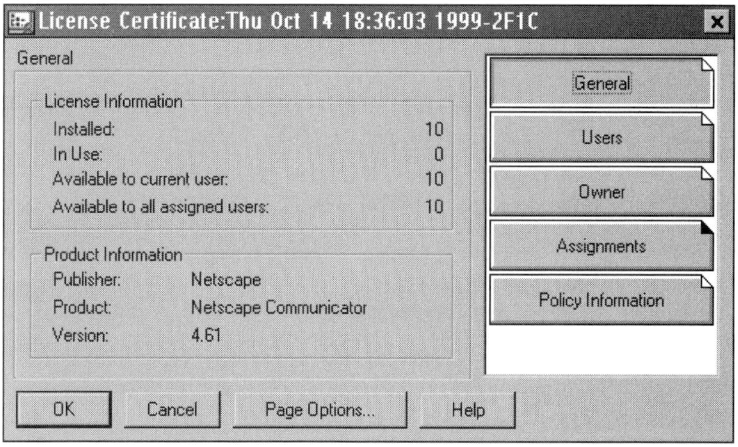

Figure 7-4. License Certificate details

Owner

Each License Certificate must have an owner and only the owner of the Certificate may reassign ownership. The default owner placed in the field is the creator of the Certificate.

Assignments

If you wish to make the License Certificate available only to a particular server or user, you are able to make that assignment in this page. To assign a particular server, use the NDS Browse button to navigate to the Server object. This server will then own the Certificate so that only users connected to that server will be allowed to use the application licenses assigned to the Certificate. Once a file server has been assigned to a Certificate, it is not possible to delete the assignment completely, although it is possible to assign the Certificate to another server. To assign the Certificate to a particular user, navigate to the user object and select the user who owns the certificate. Several users can be added to this list if need be.

Policy Information

The Policy Information page provides information that you entered when you created the License Certificate. It will also display current information such as how many users are using the Certificate.

Linking the Certificate with an Application

The License Certificate must be linked to an application if you want it to actually do something. This linkage is performed through the Software Metering page in the application object, which appears after you have installed the Software Metering component and is shown in Figure 7-5.

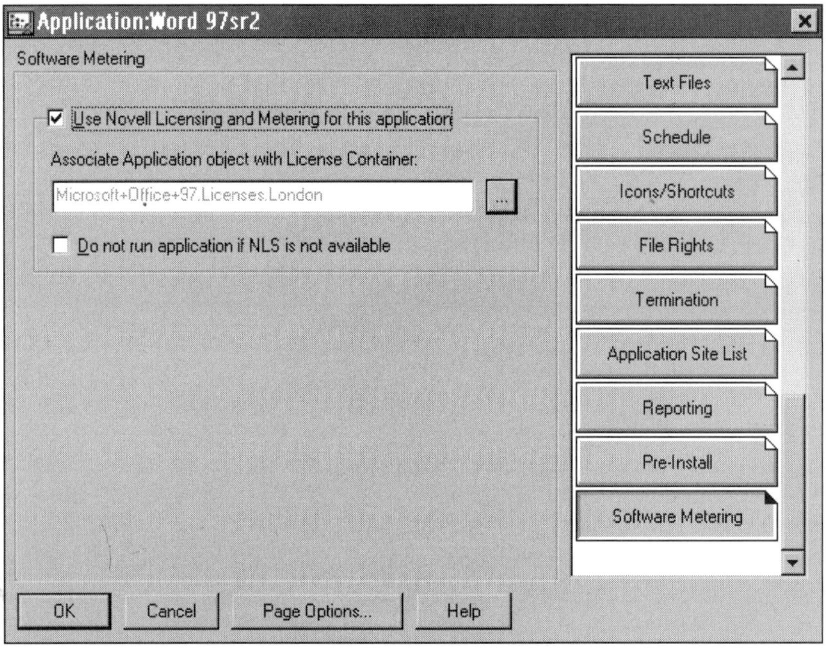

Figure 7-5. Associating the Application with the Certificate

The Software Metering page allows you to select which License Container is to be associated with the application. First, you will need to enable Metering for the application by checking the "Use Novell Licensing and Metering for this application" box. From the "Associate Application object with License Container" field, use the Browse button to browse the NDS and select the license container which you have created to restrict the application.

If for some reason the NLS server is unavailable, you may choose to run the application anyway. If you really wish the application to run only when metered, check the "Do not run application if NLS is not available" box. If your NLS server and your application server are running on the same server, you may not be able to run the software anyway, but if they are separate servers, then enabling this feature is a very strict practice, but also probably a legal necessity.

The License Meter is now in place and should work with the selected application. When all the licenses have been consumed, the user unlucky enough to subsequently run the application will be disallowed with an error message similar to that shown in Figure 7-6.

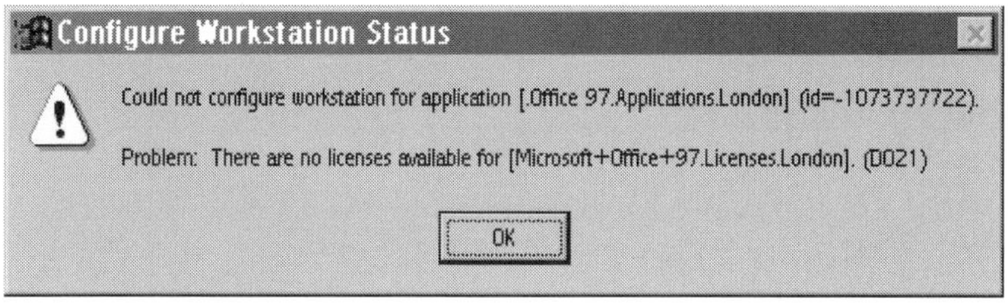

Figure 7-6. Software Metering prevention message

A Final Word

The software metering function in ZENworks is quite straightforward to install and run. None of this functionality will work unless you use the Novell Application Launcher (NAL) because it is the NLS-aware component that does the metering. This means that you may need to take steps to prevent users from easily selecting the executables and running them directly.

8

Remote Management

One of the strongest features of ZENworks desktop management is the Remote Management suite of utilities. This facility allows the Helpdesk operators to assist users without leaving their offices. The Remote Management utilities allow the operator to connect to the remote workstation and assist the user in a variety of ways. This can be a simple chat using a chat window, or the ability to completely take control of the workstation with the screen, keyboard, and mouse shared with the user. These functions allow sophisticated assistance without having to visit the workstation, even if the workstation is miles away.

> Make sure you have agreements in place before offering this service. There are some users who you may wish to be excluded from this service because of the nature of the files on their system. Be careful: there may be laws governing how privacy is guaranteed in your country!

There are clear security problems associated with using Remote Management on workstations. If anyone could gain access to a workstation on the network and take control, they would have access to all of the information on the PC. This is clearly a problem when the workstation is used for processing private or confidential information such as human resources personal data or patient records in a doctor's office.

Remote Management Prerequisites

The Remote Control facility is not a system that can be implemented straight away. You will need to get other components in place and working before you can consider using it. The following steps must be taken before any attempt to use Remote Management can be considered:

The Remote Management Agent must be installed
: Each workstation that you require to be controlled must have the Remote Management Agent installed. There is an agent for Windows 3.x, Windows 95/98, and Windows NT/2000. For more information about the installing the Remote Management Agent, see Chapter 2, *The ZENworks Installation.*

TCP/IP must be installed on the workstation
: Most of the Remote Management functions use the TCP/IP protocol rather than IPX. You will need to ensure that TCP/IP is installed on the workstation and that valid address details are entered. You will also need to ensure that the same provision is made for the Remote Management operators.

A Remote Management policy must be present for the user or workstation
: Each workstation or user must have a Remote Management policy associated with them for the Remote Management Agent to be configured correctly. More details about policy packages are available in Chapter 4, *ZENworks Policy Packages.*

The Workstation Manager must be installed
: In order for the Remote Management policy to be enforced, the Workstation Manager must be installed and running on the workstation. For more information about the installing the Workstation Manager Agent, see Chapter 2.

The workstation object must be imported and created in the NDS
: The mechanism for connection to the workstation is through the *NWADMIN* program using the workstation object as a reference. The workstation object must exist in the NDS for this to work. For more information about the registration and creation of workstation objects see Chapter 5, *Workstation Objects and Inventory.*

The Remote Control Operator must be authorized
: Each workstation object has to have a remote operator assigned. This is a security measure to ensure that Remote Management can only be performed by authorized personnel. For more information about the Remote Operators of workstation objects, see Chapter 5.

How Remote Management Works

In order for any Remote Management to be carried out on a remote workstation, the Remote Management Operator must have certain NDS rights. These rights allow a user object to perform Remote Management without granting them full administrator privileges. The rights are assigned to every workstation object that needs to be managed by a particular user. This means that if you wish only certain users in London to remotely manage all the workstations in London and none in New York and Paris, the user must be added to each workstation object in London. This is obviously a tedious job, but one which you are fortunately saved from by the Manage Remote Operators Wizard. To use this utility, select the workstation object or an OU containing workstation objects in the *NWADMIN* Browser window and select Tools → Workstation Remote Management → Manage Remote Operators. This will reveal a window which will allow you to select individual workstation objects, workstation groups, or Containers through the usual NDS Browser window. When you have selected the target workstations, click the Next button, which will reveal a window similar to Figure 8-1.

Figure 8-1. Manage Remote Operators Wizard

This window allows you to specify which Remote Management utilities will be permitted on the workstation for the set of users. Each of the four Remote Management utilities shown is covered later in this chapter. After specifying which are to be used, click Next and select which user object, group object, or Container is to be granted these rights.

Most of the Remote Management functions require a simple TCP/IP socket connection between the remote operator console and the remote workstation. The remote workstation's address information is read from the workstation object and a connection is established. The exception to this is the all powerful Remote Control

Utility. When the Remote Management Operator establishes a connection to a remote workstation, a token is written to the workstation object to ensure that subsequent Remote Control Operations are not attempted. The remote workstation checks the token as authorization to complete the connection. Because the workstation object may be replicated to other servers, only the Master Replica can be used for this purpose. This may cause a delay in establishing the initial connection and during disconnection, but will not affect the transmission speed between the Remote Management Operator and the remote workstation.

Remote Ping

The Remote Ping facility is used for testing the availability and functionality of the workstation's Remote Management Agent. If you are trying to connect to the workstation and it refuses to connect by either giving an error message or, more likely, just waiting forever to connect, it may be because the Remote Management Agent is not running for some reason. The Ping function may be the best way of determining whether the Remote Management Agent is actually running on the end workstation.

To use ping, select the workstation object in the *NWADMIN* Browser window and select Tools → Workstation Remote Management → Ping Remote Management Agent. The utility will take a few moments to connect and if the agent is not responding a message "Remote Management Agent is not Running" will appear. If the connection is successful, a screen will appear similar to that shown in Figure 8-2.

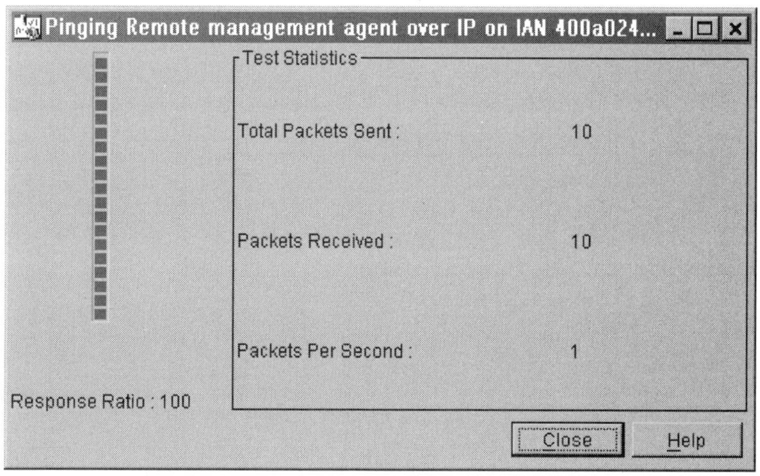

Figure 8-2. Remote ping

The ping will respond to either a TCP/IP or an IPX connection and should return a response ratio of 100. A ratio of less than 100 may be caused by network failure, overload, or simply failure of the Remote Management Agent.

Remote Control

The most popular and useful feature of Remote Management is the Remote Control. This utility will allow you to share the remote workstation's video, keyboard, and mouse. To use Remote Control, select the workstation object in the *NWADMIN* Browser window and select Tools → Workstation Remote Management → Remote Control. The remote workstation screen will appear in a window on your workstation similar to that shown in Figure 8-3. You will also be able to use the keyboard or mouse on your workstation in the window, which is the remote workstation. The screen, keyboard, and mouse will still be operational for the remote user. You are also able to issue special keyboard commands that will normally be locally mapped. These keys are shown in the top right corner of the remote-control window. The buttons perform special functions on the remote workstation as detailed in Table 8-1.

Table 8-1. Remote Control Buttons

Icon	Title	Description
	Start	Equivalent to the Start key on the keyboard
	Task Switcher	Equivalent to Alt-Tab on the keyboard
	Reboot	Equivalent to Ctrl-Alt-Del on the keyboard
	System Key Pass Through	Enable the Windows Alt and Ctrl system keys on the remote workstation
	Navigate	If the remote screen is too large for the window, use this button to navigate the remote desktop

These keys allow the Remote Management Operator to have full control of the remote workstation, even forcing a reboot if necessary.

Remote View

A Remote View session is very similar to Remote Control, except you have no control over the workstation. This means you can see what the user is doing, but are unable to gain access to the remote machine with your keyboard and mouse. To use Remote View, select the workstation object in the *NWADMIN* Browser window and select Tools → Workstation Remote Management → Remote View. This

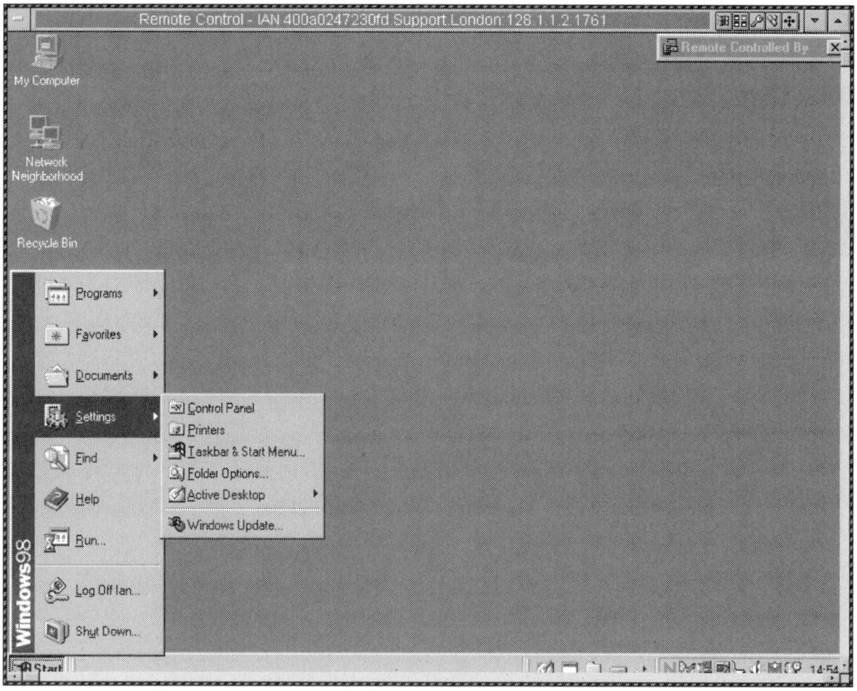

Figure 8-3. Remote Control

will bring up a screen similar to that shown in Figure 8-3 except it will be the user controlling the workstation rather that the Remote Management Operator.

Remote File Transfer

It is possible that during the process of diagnosing a fault on the remote workstation, you will need to transfer a file or a number of files to or from the system. This process can be carried out using the Remote File Transfer utility. To use Remote File Transfer, select the workstation object in the *NWADMIN* Browser window and select Tools → Workstation Remote Management → File Transfer. This will connect to the Remote Management Agent and bring up a window similar to that shown in Figure 8-4, allowing you to select the file to be transferred and the target destination. The utility will also allow you to delete or rename files on the remote workstation. You will only be able to copy files to or from disks that are physically present on the machine. No access to remote drives will be permitted.

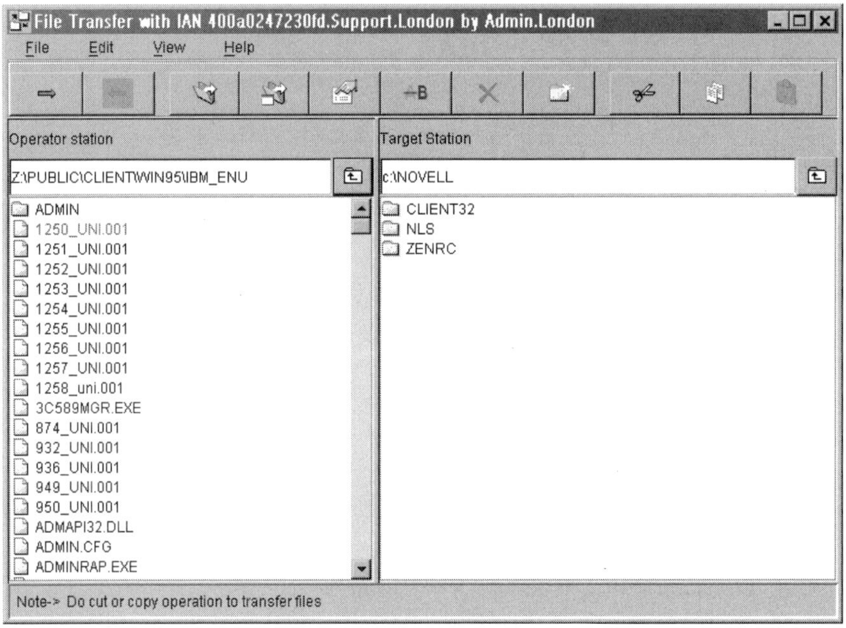

Figure 8-4. Remote File Transfer

Remote Execute

If you wish to run a program on the remote workstation, this can be easily done using the Remote Execute facility. To use Remote Execute, select the workstation object in the *NWADMIN* Browser window and select Tools → Workstation Remote Management → Remote Execute. This will bring up a window similar to that shown in Figure 8-5. Enter the name and full path if necessary in the dialog box; the command will be passed to the agent on the remotely managed workstation.

Remote Chat

One of the simplest utilities and the most useful is the Remote Chat program. To use Remote Chat, select the workstation object in the *NWADMIN* Browser window and select Tools → Workstation Remote Management → Chat. This will connect to the Remote Management Agent and bring up a window similar to that shown in Figure 8-6. The tool will allow you to have a real-time message conversation with a user at the remote workstation.

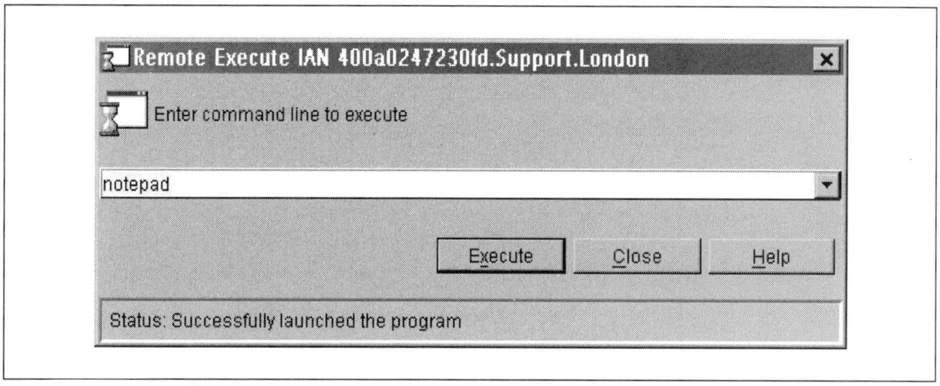

Figure 8-5. Remote Execute

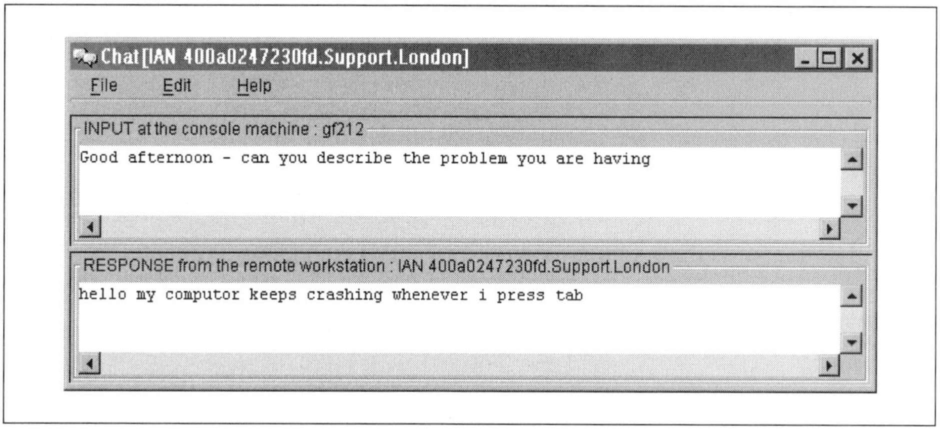

Figure 8-6. Remote Chat

Remote Diagnostics

To be able to connect to a remote workstation and perform diagnostics is very useful, particularly when a user is having a problem with the workstation at the time. If the user is having trouble with a certain application, it is also possible to remotely execute the program on the workstation, then run the diagnostics. To use Remote Diagnostics, select the workstation object in the *NWADMIN* Browser window and select Tools → Workstation Remote Management → Remote Diagnostics. This will connect to the Remote Management Agent and bring up a window similar to that shown in Figure 8-7.

The diagnostic screen will show the information listed in the sections that follow.

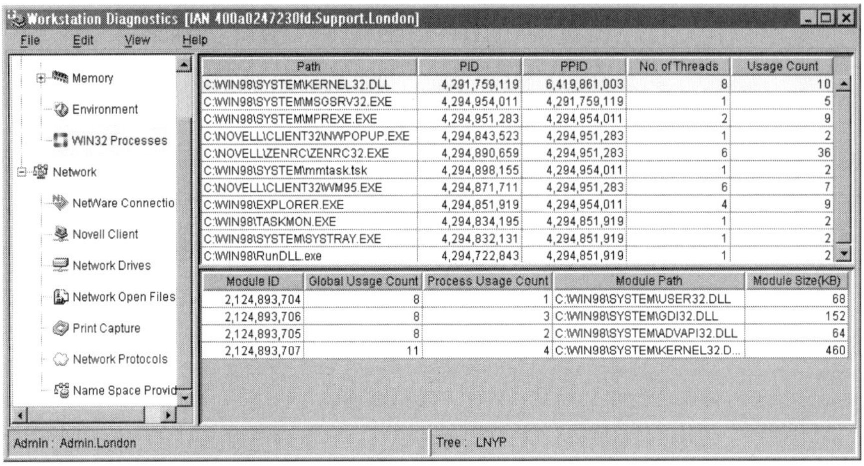

Figure 8-7. Remote Diagnostics

Operating System Information

Windows Memory

Selecting this item will display a table showing the physical memory on the workstation along with the amount in use, the amount free, and other information such as the page file size and usage.

Environment

This option will display all the environment variables defined on the system.

Event Log

Under Windows NT/2000, the event log contains valuable information about what is going on and going wrong on the system. This information can be displayed through the diagnostics tool, allowing you to view the System, Security, and Application components of the event log.

Device Drivers

This item will display a list of device drivers installed on an NT/2000 workstation and the state of the driver.

Services

The Windows NT/2000 services are displayed in a table showing the name of the service and the current state.

Win32 Processes

This item is relevant to Windows 95/98 where it shows all the processes running on the system, along with information such as its size and usage.

Network Information

NetWare Connections

This item displays information about connections to the server, such as the connection type (NDS or Bindery), NDS tree name, server name, and connection type.

Novell Client information

The configuration state of the client is displayed here, such as the preferred server user context and version of the client.

Network Drives

This section displays information about which drives are mapped, their size, filesystem type, and the rights the user has to the filesystem.

Network Open Files

When a user has files open on a network volume, they are listed here along with the server, where the user has the file open, and the volume name.

Print Capture

This section lists the networked printer connected and the port to which it is connected.

Network Protocols

This item contains information about any protocols installed on the workstation, the address information, socket type, and message size.

Name Space Providers

This area displays information about Winsock name resolution, including information about DNS, Service Advertising Protocol (SAP), Domain Name Resolution (DNS), and Service Location Protocol (SLP). Information about the providers and whether they are connected is also displayed.

A Final Word

If you wish to use Remote Management on your network, make sure that the issues of privacy are clear to you, your management, and your users. The tools listed here will be very useful to you and you will obviously have a clear picture of what you wish to use them for. However, your users and management may not. It is a very good idea to tell them about it or it could cause serious problems for you. The Remote Control utility may be an emotive issue for your users, so tell them first or they may think you have been spying on them!

Make sure that your regular users do not have DNS rights to remote control other workstations. It is easy enough to grant simple rights for users to do this. These utilities should be clearly under your management control, so don't let them escape.

If you plan yo use Remote Management over a WAN link, make sure you have enough network bandwisth. A 128-K link will run Remote Control, but *very* slowly. Even over a clean 10-MB Ethernet running half duplex, it is quite jerky. Test what the response will be before you off the service.

A

The Future of ZENworks

In the process of writing this book, ZENworks has gone through two version releases and the product is growing and improving all the time. ZENworks is very good for managing components of your network of which you have a lot. To date, this has been your Windows workstations, but now two new products have just become available to assist with managing your servers and network. ZENworks for Servers and ZENworks for Networks are likely to be purchasable products from Novell, but downloadable trial versions are available from *http://www.novell.com/download.* Console One is freely available for download and is being shipped with NetWare 5.1.

ZENworks for Servers

When you have a lot of servers, keeping them up to date can be a bind. Applying Service Packs to a lot of servers is a mundane task requiring individual attention to each server. ZENworks for Servers allows you to perform much of the same tasks for your servers as ZENworks for desktops does for your workstations. The work required to distribute software across the network to your servers is an operation that currently has to be performed manually and is therefore usually done during the daytime. This product allows you to perform distribution automatically overnight or at times when the network is not busy.

ZENworks for Servers allows you to distribute using what is called *Tiered Electronic Distribution.* The main distributing server can be configured to distribute to proxy servers that perform the distributions on its behalf. If you have several servers located across a WAN link, one of them can be configured as a proxy server so that the distribution is not performed multiple times across the network. Network bandwidth is conserved as much as possible by zipping the data to be transferred into compressed files. These files are transferred across the network to the receiving server, where they are unzipped and the files distributed.

ZENworks for Networks

The problem with networks is that they are a series of black boxes that connect a series of wires together and are great when they work, but a nightmare when the don't. Networks have emerged over the last few years to become much more complex than the 10-MB Ethernet networks which once ruled most organizations. The latest standards for 100-MB and 1000-MB Ethernet allow you to upgrade components of your network to reduce bottlenecks and improve throughput. But where are these bottlenecks? Which links require upgrading? Which segments of the network are error-prone?

ZENworks for Networks allows you to manage all those network hubs and routers in a simpler way than you have in the past. You no longer need to visit each device or remotely connect to it to reprogram it—even if you can remember how to do it. What happens if the network manager is away and a major device needs to be reprogrammed? This product allows you to save network device configurations in NDS objects so that a reconfiguration becomes a much more straightforward operation.

One of the most important aspects of network management is monitoring. A single piece of cable can carry a large amount of data providing for the complex communications required between devices. How do you know what is happening on that piece of cable? Are packets of data being corrupted, requiring constant retransmissions? The way to answer these questions is to use a network monitor. ZENworks for Networks assists you with monitoring your network components so that when an error occurs you will know about it straight away, before the users start complaining to you.

Console One

Console One is Novell's replacement for the *NWADMIN* program. This new interface is a Java-based application that runs under Windows or on the NetWare 5 server. This program allows you to manage NDS objects and NetWare filesystems. It is intended to add a great deal more functionality to the management interface, but most importantly it allows objects to be managed from the server console—something that *NWADMIN* could never do.

B

Integrating Other Authentication Systems

NDS for Solaris and Linux

In the real world of IT there exists the need to use different operating systems to provide different services. One such system is Unix, which is often used to provide serious services and applications. Unix has an authentication system of its own which does not easily integrate into other systems. If you require Unix systems for the support of special services or a number of Unix workstations to support high-end applications, you may well have its authentication system alongside your existing NDS. This can be irritating for users who just wish to log in and get on with their work, but when connecting to a Unix system for, say, email, have to enter a different password.

It is clearly beneficial to consider how the authentication systems can be integrated in some way. If you have decided that NDS is the best way forward for your organization, then NDS for Solaris or NDS for Linux may be the answer for you.

These products allow you to integrate a Unix system into NDS by making the Unix system appear as an NDS-aware server. The NDS for Solaris/Linux products allow the authentication system on Unix to be routed through to the NDS using the Pluggable Authentication Module (PAM). This module intercepts requests for authentication from the Unix system and redirects them to the NetWare NDS. This greatly simplifies and integrates the authentication of a Unix server in your organization.

If you have a series of Unix workstations that need to be integrated, there are a couple of approaches that can be used:

NDS for Solaris/Linux on each workstation
: This is the obvious choice for those who have just a few workstations to integrate. Each workstation has NDS for Solaris/Linux installed and will authenticate to the NetWare NDS.

Network Information Service on the Unix workstations
: This is probably the best choice if you have a lot of workstations that are not Solaris or Linux. In this case, you can use the Network Information Service (NIS) to allow the Unix workstations to authenticate to the NIS server, which should also be running NDS for Solaris/Linux.

NDS for NT

In most cases, the NetWare client can be used to integrate Windows NT systems into your NDS. This client will also work for Windows NT servers including Windows Terminal server. In some cases you may need to integrate a Windows NT domain into your NDS. This may be required if you are using Microsoft Exchange or Microsoft SQL Server, which are configured to use Windows NT domains for authentication and rights. If this is the case, you may need to use NDS for NT to integrate the domain into the NDS.

NDS for NT creates special groups within NDS allowing you to associate your users with standard domain groups. The contents of these groups are then replicated to the Windows NT Domain Controller and made available. Whenever a new user is associated with one of the domain groups, the account is automatically included on the Domain Controller. This allows Windows domain-centric applications to seamlessly integrate in the NDS authentication system.

C

Other Sources of Information

This book covers the product in some detail and outlines how it could or should be done. It gives advice about what can go wrong, what to do if it does, and how to avoid problems. There are always problems with implementing such systems and particularly with installing applications and making them work. The following list of information sources may also be of use to you.

ZENworks Help

If you need further information about ZENworks from me, you can go to my ZENworks help web site at:

http://www.zenhelp.com

This site provides useful "how to" detail about ZENworks. It also provides an email link to me, giving you the opportunity to pose questions to me directly.

ZENworks Cool Solutions

This is a site run by Novell that has a large archive of information. This is a really useful site; put it in your bookmark list:

http://www.novell.com/coolsolutions/zenworks/index.html

App Notes and Developer Notes

App Notes and *Developer Notes* are monthly magazines produced by Novell. They frequently contain extremely useful information about NetWare products and are frequently written by the engineers who actually wrote the code. These magazines are also online at:

http://developer.novell.com/research/

Zen Networks

The Zen Networks web site is a commercial site where you can buy consulting or even buy application object templates. The guys who run this site are really knowledgeable. Contact them at:

http://www.zennetworks.com

Trevor's Unofficial NetWare Group

Trevor Davies is a Senior Consultant, working for Novell Consulting Europe. His web site has lots of useful information:

http://www.tung.nu

The Distributed Management Task Force

If you want more information about the Common Information Model discussed in Chapter 5, *Workstation Objects and Inventory,* there is lots online at:

http://www.dmtf.org

Bibliography

Garrett, B. and K. Wilson. *Overview of Novell's IntranetWare Client for Windows NT.* Novell Application Notes May 1997: pp 3-18.

Hendrick, B. *Overview of NetWare Client 32 for Windows 95.* Novell Application Notes November 1996: pp 3-27.

Novell Inc. *ZEN 2 Inventory Database Schema.* ZENworks Cool Solutions 1999.

Novell Inc. *ZENworks 2 Online Documentation.* 1999

Lewis, M. *A Secure Remote Control Is a Good Remote Control.* ZENworks Cool Solutions 1999.

Liebing, E. *Installing NetWare Client 32 for DOS/Windows.* Novell Application Notes May 1996: pp 21-46.

Liebing, E. *NetWare Client 32 for DOS/Windows: Overview of Architecture and Features.* Novell Application Notes May 1996: pp 5-20.

Liebing, E. and K. Rhodes. *Accessing IntranetWare Resources with the NWGINA Logon Interface and the NetWare Provider.* Novell Application Notes May 1997: pp 73-106.

Maggitt, A. and T. Ritchey, *Windows NT User Administration.* O'Reilly & Associates, Inc. 1999

Prior, K. *Implementing Novell's NT Workstation Manager*. Novell Application Notes June 1997: pp 33-48.

Rhoades, S. and E. Leibing. *Understanding the Advanced Settings in the Novell Client for Windows 95/98*. Novell Application Notes April 1999: pp 24-52.

Wilson, K. and B. Anderson. *Using the Client 32 GUI Login Utility and the NetWare Application Manager*. Novell Application Notes May 1996: pp 61-86.

Wilson, K. and J. Hudler. *Accessing Network Resources with the GUI Login Utility and the Network Provider*. Novell Application Notes November 1996: pp 96-128.

Wilson, K. and B. Hegerhorst. *Setting Up Network Printing with Client 32 for Windows 95*. Novell Application Notes November 1996): pp 151-171.

Wootton, S. *Application Launcher Software Metering*. ZENworks Cool Solutions 1999.

Zacker, C. *Zero Administration for Windows*, O'Reilly & Associates, Inc. 1999.

Index

Numbers

16-bit applications, configuring WOW for, 181

A

ACK (acknowledgement), 47
actions, 78
.adm files, 123
Administration Menu setting, 49
Administrator Notes, 195
Administrator program, installing, 30
ADSI (Novell Active Directory Service Interface), 25
Advanced button, disallowing users access to, 39, 70
Advanced Login tab, 39
Advanced Settings button (Scheduler), 80
Advanced Settings tab (NetWare client configuration), 40–50
after snapshot, 172
alert beep setting, 41
.aot files, 172
  creating application objects with, 173
application dependencies, 178
application distribution reports, 152
Application Explorer, 163–166
  settings for, 225
application files, 207–209
application folder objects, 15, 226
  where to put them, 20
application launch reports, 152
Application Launcher NT Service
  Windows NT/2000, 23
  workstation software, installing, 21
Application Launcher Window, 163–166
application management, 8, 159–228
application metering (see Software Metering)
application object macros, 196
application objects, 15, 136, 172–218
  creating, 173
  grayed, displaying, 179
  GUID and, 185
  installing, 30
  linking, 216
  making them work, 219–221
  NAL and, 160–162
  template file, 172
  where to put them, 20
    importance of, 162
    options for, 193
  ZENworks reporting tool, 148
Application Site List, 216
  configuring for mobile users, 219
application support
  Windows 95/98 client, 65
  Windows NT/2000 client, 55
applications
  adding to base desktop operating system, 6
  conflicts between, managing, 178
  displaying with application folder objects, 226

applications (*continued*)
  distributing, 182–186
    always, 184
    prompting before, 183
    showing progress, 183
  forcing termination, 213–215
  installation consistency, 163
  linked to License Certificates, 236
  load balancing, 191
  managing (see application management)
  placing near associated objects, 162
  pre-installing, 217
  run options, 181
  running as secure/unsecure system, 181
  running on remote workstation, 244
  scheduling, 211
  snAppShot tool and, 166–172
Appstation, 85, 97
architecture
  Windows 3.x client, 68
  Windows 95/98, 61
  Windows NT/2000 client, 53–54
ASCII files, managing, 116
asset management report, 152
association tables, 155–157
associations, 77
Associations button (policy package Wizard), 77
Associations page, 192–194
authentication, 71, 106
  Dynamic Local User policy package, 80
  forcing via computer system policies, 104
  mechanism for provided by NetWare, 11
  systems, integrating other, 251
auto reconnect feature, 41
autoexec.bat, Windows NT logon policies and, 99
.axt files, 172
  creating application objects with, 173

B

backgrounds, display policies for, 89
Backspace key (NWADMIN program), 32
backups, NDS, 29
base desktop operating system, image of, 6
.bat files, managing, 116
beep setting, 41
before snapshot, 169
binary files, managing, 116
bindery services, replication for, 18
BIOS revision date, 150
broadcast messages
  setting for receipt by workstations, 47
  timeout setting, 45
broadcast messenger, setting for, 47
burst mode setting, 41

C

cache
  Cache NetWare Password setting, 41
  File Cache Level setting, 43
  File Write Through option, 43
  Max Cache Size setting, 44
cacls program, 181
Cancel Desktop Login setting, 41
checksum setting, 41
CIM (Common Information Model), 153
Client Configuration policy (NetWare), 116
client login box, Advanced Login tab, 39
Client tab, 36–38
Close Behind Ticks setting, 42
color scheme policy, 93
colors, display policies for, 89
command line, placing extra parameters on, 180
Common Information Model (CIM), 153
common.adm files, 123
components, 7–8, 11–13
  association tables, 155–157
computer extensible policies, 123
computer printer, installing workstation software for, 21
Computer Printer policy, 117
computer system policies, 85–88
  Windows 3.x, 116
  Windows 95/98, 103–115
  Windows NT, 103–115
config.pol, 123
configuring
  Application Site List for mobile users, 219
  desktop operating system, 4–6
  Helpdesk program, 72
  NAL, 221–226
  NetWare clients, 35–52
  Workstation Manager, 70

workstation objects, 135–139
WOW for 16-bit applications, 181
consistency of desktop operating system across workstations, 5
Console One, 250
Contacts page, 192
container policy objects, 15
container policy package, 74, 75
container search policy, 121
containers (container objects), 14
Contextless Login tab, 39
Control Panel (Desktop Preferences policy), 83
Control Panel policies, 89–93
cost of hardware/software, choosing network operating system and, 3
Country (C=) container, 15
crashes, housekeeping after, 81
create object dialog box, 76
creating
application objects, 173
policy packages, 76–78
workstation objects, 132, 134
Custom button (Dynamic Local User policy package), 81
custom folders policy, 97
custom user interface policy, 97

D

data integrity, setting for, 50
database, querying, 154–157
database server, 139–141
date of files, test for, 178
DDE (Dynamic Data Exchange), 181
Default Capture tab, 50
default profile, 84
default user interface, 97
Delay Writes setting, 42
Delete key (NWADMIN program), caution with, 32
Description page, 186
desktop configuration/customization, 89
desktop maintenance, 8
desktop management, 7
choosing network operating system and, 3
software for, installing, 30
desktop operating system
base, 6
booting, 71
choosing, 4
configuring, 4–6
consistency, 5
roll out, 6
searching for on workstation, 150
system policy, 95
desktop policies, 93
Desktop Preferences policy, 83–85
Details button (policy package Wizard), 78
Details page (Dynamic Local User policy package), 81
dialup networking policy, 107
directory service, 13
disable SAP advertising policy, 108
disabling (see enabling/disabling)
disk space, checking for sufficient, 178
display policies, 89
Distributed Management Task Force, 153
Distribution page, 182–186
Distribution Scripts, 187
.dll files, 78
DOS
applications, choosing desktop operating system and, 4
long filenames and, 42
NetWare client for, 7
options policies, 97
ZENworks components and, 7
DOS Long Name option, 42
DOS Name setting, 42
drive mappings
for CD-ROMs, 186
disconnecting, 182
planning, 37
drivers, searching for on Windows 95/98 workstations, 151
drives, restrictions, policies for, 102
Dynamic Data Exchange (DDE), 181
Dynamic Local User policy, 57
Dynamic Local User policy package, 80

E

Edit button (Policy Scheduler), 79
email sent by Help Requester, 13, 82

Enable Software Inventory box, 145
enabling/disabling
  Help Requester, 82
  policies, checkboxes for, 87
  scanner program, 142
  software inventory, 145
  workstation inventory, 141
  Workstation Manager, 70
End Of Job function, 42
Enter key (policy package Wizard), 77
Environment Pad setting, 42
environment variables, 178, 202
  configuring via Environment page, 180–182
events, 79
.exe files, 78
Explorer Shell, 94
explorer.exe, 97
extensible policies, 123

F

failure report, application distributions and, 152
fault tolerance, 17
  replicas for, 18
Fault Tolerance option, 191
Fault Tolerance page, 189–191
.fil files, 172
File Cache Level setting, 43
file entries, snAppShot tool options for, 169
File Handles, setting for, 50
file management, Windows 3.x computer system policy, 116
file server, choosing network operating system for, 2–4
file sharing policies, 107
File Write Through option, 43
filedef.txt file, 172
files
  remote transfer, 243
  tests for, 178
filesystem drivers, 62
  Windows NT/2000 client, 53
filesystem rights, 213
first network drive
  defining, 36
  setting for, 43
folder entries, snAppShot tool options for, 169
folder objects, 186
folders, 186
Force First Network Drive setting, 43
force-run applications, 176
Full Pack, 12

G

Gatherer process, 139
general workstation report, 151
geographical diversity
  application objects and, 216
  choosing network operating system and, 3
ghost program, 220
GINA (Graphical Identification and Authentication), 57
Global Unique IDentifier (GUID), 185
graphical user interface (GUI), 35
grayed application objects, displaying, 179
grouping workstation objects, 133
groups (group objects), 14
groups, tree design and, 16
GUI (graphical user interface), 35
GUID (Global Unique IDentifier), 185
guidelines for replicas, 18

H

Handle Network Errors setting, 43, 46
hardware
  changes, tracking on workstations, 8
  report, 152
hardware inventory, 12
  (see also workstation inventory)
Help Requester, 72
  configured/enabled by Helpdesk policy, 82
  email sent by, 13
Helpdesk policy, 82
Helpdesk program, 13
  configuring, 72
  (see also Remote Management)
Hidden option for running applications, 181
Hide Start menu subfolders option, 98
HKEY_CURRENT_USER key, 83
  settings for, 203–205
HKEY_LOCAL_MACHINE key settings, 203–205

Hold Files setting, 43
housekeeping after crashes, 81

I

icons, 211
  order of for running applications, 176
  titles, 175
Icons/Shortcuts page, 211
idappl.ini, 146
Identification page, 174–176, 220
IEEE (Institute of Electrical and Electronic Engineers), 13
ignore settings, 87
images, 5
  replication software for, 6
impersonation option, 80
Info button (Helpdesk program), 73
infrastructure upgrade, choosing network operating system and, 2
.ini files
  entries, options for, 170
  managing, 116
  settings, 205–207
INS key (NWADMIN program), 76
insecure system, 80
Install Only button (Identification page), 174
Install ZENworks option, 29
installing
  Administrator program, 30
  application objects, 30
  applications, Pre-Install page, 217
  desktop management, software for, 30
  NetWare Licensing Service, 31
  NWADMIN program, 30
  server software, 28–31
  Software Metering, 31, 231
  unattended installations, 27
  workstation software, 21–27
  ZENworks, 21–31
Institute of Electrical and Electronic Engineers (IEEE), 13
integer values for icons, 176
Internet Explorer, policies for security/security levels, 101
inventory, 8, 141–157
  enabling for workstation objects, 139
  extracting data from (see reporting/reports)
  hardware, 12
  lists, 149–151
  reports (see reporting/reports)
  software, 12, 145–147
  workstation, 141–144
  workstation inventory policy, 125–127
inventory database, 153
inventory server, 139–141
IP Gateway (see Novell IP Gateway)
IPX transport protocol, 50

L

language, setting for, 46
Large Internet Packet Start Size setting, 43
Large Internet Packets setting, 43
Launch Scripts, 187
leaf objects, 14
legacy applications, choosing desktop operating system and, 4
License Certificates, 31, 230, 234
  linking to applications, 236
License Containers, 233
licenses (see software licenses)
life expectancy of vendors, choosing network operating system and, 3
Limit SAP Broadcast Queries setting, 44
Link Support Layer Max Buffer Size setting, 44
Link Support Layer (see LSL)
List Editor, 147
load balancing, 191
Locality (L=) container, 15
location
  scanner program, 142
  workstation objects, 131
  (see also placement; geographical diversity)
Location Profiles tab, 38
Lock Delay setting, 44
Lock Retries setting, 44
Log File setting, 44
Log File Size setting, 44
Login Dialog Box, 38
  Advanced button and, 39, 70
login, policy for restricting, 121
login process
  Windows 95/98 client, 65
  Windows NT/2000 client, 57
  Workstation Manager, 69–72

login script variables, 200–202
logon policies
Windows 95/98, 105
Windows NT, 99, 113–115
long filenames visible to DOS, setting for, 42
Long Machine Type setting, 44
lookup time, 17
LSL (Link Support Layer), 64, 68

M

MACHINE environment variable. setting for, 44
Macintosh, 7
macros, 171, 195–202
application object, 196
maintenance
desktop, 8
install-only objects for, 175
Manage Remote Operators Wizard, 240
Management Information Base (see MIB)
Mandatory Profile (Desktop Preferences policy), 85
Master Replica, 18
Max Cache Size setting, 44
Max Cur Dir Length setting, 45
Max Read Burst Size setting, 45
Max Write Burst Size setting, 45
memory, 179
memory size, searching for, 151
Message Timeout setting, 45
messages
broadcast, 45, 47
sent by workstation, setting for, 49
Metering Certificates, creating, 231–235
MIB (Management Information Base), 25
Windows 3.x, 27
Windows 95/98, 25
Microsoft GINA (MSGINA), 53
Microsoft Internet Explorer, 101
Microsoft Office, duplicating application objects and, 173
Minimum Time to Net setting, 45
mobile users, configuring Application Site List page for, 219
modifying contents of policy packages, 77
MPR (Multiple Provider Router), 58, 61
MS-DOS
options policies, 97
(see also DOS)
MSGINA (Microsoft GINA), 53
MSGINA.DLL, 57
Multiple Provider Router (see MPR)
MUP (Multiple Universal Naming Convention Provider), 54

N

NAL Explorer, 163–166
NAL (Novell Application Launcher), 8, 11, 159–228
components, 160
configuring, 221–226
how it works, 160–162
shell restrictions policies and, 94
software for, installing, 30
Software Metering and, 230
testing, importance of, 227
user interface, 163–166
workstation objects and, 136–138
NAL service, 164
NAL shortcuts, 136
NAL Window, 163–166
Nalexpld.exe program, 164
Name Cache Level setting, 45
name resolution
connection setting for, 48
Name Resolution Timeout setting for, 45
naming
policy packages, 76
workstation objects, 132
workstations, 125
NCIMAN.EXE, 27
configuring NetWare clients, 35
NCP Max Timeout setting, 45
NDPS (Novell Distributed Print Services)
Windows 3.x, 27
Windows 95/98, 25
Windows NT/2000, agent for, 22
NDS Certificate object, 230
NDS database, 13
NDS for Linux, 251
NDS for NT, 252
NDS for Solaris, 251
NDS Manager program, 16, 19

NDS (Novell Directory Services), 1, 13–21
  authenticated access to Windows NT/2000, 22, 77
  backing up, 29
  NAL and, 162
  object types, 14
  policy packages, 11, 75
  Unix, integrating into, 251
  workstation objects, 129–131
NDS tree
  design of, 15
  partitioning, 16
  testing, 34
  workstation objects and, 130
NDSMGR32.EXE, 19
Net Status Busy Timeout setting, 46
  Handle Network Errors setting and, 43
Net Status Timeout setting, 46
  Handle Network Errors setting and, 43
NetWare
  clients, 7, 11, 35–68
    client for Windows 3.x (see Windows 3.x client)
    client for Windows 95/98 (see Windows 95/98 client)
    client for Windows NT/2000 (see Windows NT/2000 client)
    configuring, 35–52, 116
    workstation software, installing, 21
  filesystem integration
    Windows 95/98 client, 62–64
    Windows NT/2000 client, 54
  filesystem rights, granting to workstations, 143
  network infrastructure upgrade, choosing network operating system and, 2
  password, cache setting for, 41
  policy packages, 7
  Release 4.11, Software Metering and, 230
  services (see NetWare services)
  user capacity, choosing network operating system and, 3
NetWare Client Configuration policy, 116
  configuring NetWare clients, 35
NetWare Graphical Identification and Authentication Module (see NWGINA)
NetWare I/O Subsystem (see NIOS)
NetWare IP, 51
NetWare Licensing Service, 12
  installing/loading automatically, 31
NetWare Loadable Modules (NLMs), 68
NetWare Protocol setting, 46
NetWare services
  Windows 95/98 client, 62
  Windows NT/2000 client, 53
network adapters, searching for, 151
network address, 138
Network Associates, 13
Network Control Panel, configuring NetWare clients, 35
network drive, first, 36, 43
network information report, 152
Network Management Responder (NMR), 25
Network Neighborhood, servers listed in, 28
network operating system, choosing, 2–4
network path, 110
network policies, 91, 94, 104–108
Network Printers setting, 46
Network Provider
  Windows 95/98 client, 66
  Windows NT/2000 client, 57–59
network resources, 182
network service providers, 57
network sharing (Windows NT), policies for, 111
network timeout, setting for, 46
NIOS (NetWare I/O Subsystem), 61
  Windows 3.x, 68
  Windows 95/98 client, 64
NIS (Network Information Service), 252
NLMs (NetWare Loadable Modules), 68
NLS (Novell Licensing Services), 28
  Software Metering and, 230
NMR (Network Management Responder), 25
Novell
  guidelines for replicas, 18
  recommendations
    for NDS tree design, 16
    about partitioning, 17
Novell Active Directory Service Interface (ADSI), 25
Novell Application Launcher (see NAL)

Novell Client Installation Manager, 27
configuring NetWare clients, 35
Novell Dial-in Services, Windows 3.x and, 26
Novell Directory Services (see NDS)
Novell Distributed Print Services (see NDPS)
Novell IP Gateway
Windows 3.x, service for, 27
Windows 95/98, 25
Windows NT/2000, service for, 23
Novell Licensing Services (see NLS)
Novell NDS Provider ADSI, Windows 95/98 and, 25
Novell Network Provider for NT, 58
Novell Remote Access Dialer, Windows 95/98 and, 25
Novell Remote Management (see Remote Management)
Novell System Tray, setting for, 49
Novell Target Service Agent
Windows 3.x, 27
Windows 95/98, 25
Windows NT/2000, 23
Novell Workstation Manager (see Workstation Manager)
Novell ZENworks (see ZENworks)
NT user printer policy, 85
NTFS filesystem, policies for, 114
NTLM, 57
NTSCAN32.EXE, 142
ntuser.dat, 83
NWADMIN program, 31–33
Backspace key, 32
creating policy packages, 76–78
Delete key, caution with, 32
installing, 30
Metered Certificates, creating, 231
registry entries, 30
reports, running, 148
Supervisor rights, setting, 59
workstation objects, creating, 134
(see also Console One)
NWGINA, 53
Workstation Manager, 69
NWLanguage setting, 46

O

Object Linking and Embedding (OLE), 181
objects, 13
number of per partition, recommended maximum, 17
where to put them, 19–21
importance of, 13, 15
(see also application objects; workstation objects)
ODI (Open Datalink Interface)
Windows 95/98 client, 64
Windows NT/2000 client, 55
OLE (Object Linking and Embedding), 181
operating system
replicating, 220
specifying, 179
(see also desktop operating system; network operating system)
Opportunistic Locking setting, 46
Organization (O=) container, 16
Organizational Unit (OU=) container, 16

P

Packet Burst Read Window Size setting, 47
Packet Burst setting, 46
Packet Burst Write Window Size setting, 47
packet delivery settings, caution with, 40
packets, settings for, 43
PAM (Pluggable Authentication Module), 251
partitions, 14
creating, 16
replicating, 17–19
workstation objects and repartitioning, 130
password policies, 92, 106
patches, testing, 33
PATH environment variable, 203
path to executable/application icon, 176
peer-to-peer networking
file and print sharing, policies for, 107
network policy for preventing, 94
performance
application objects and, 216
importance of tree design, 15
partitioning and, 17

personnel (see users)
ping, 242
placement
  objects, 19–21
    importance of, 13, 15
  policy packages, 19
    importance of, 76
planning
  drive mappings, 37
  importance of, 9, 157
  inventory function, 139
  policy packages, importance of, 75
  sample for workstation development, 5
Pluggable Authentication Module (PAM), 251
poledit program, 86
  .adm files and, 123
policy check, 71
Policy Editor (see poledit program)
policy file, 123
policy package objects, where to put them, 19
policy package Wizard, 76
policy packages, 7, 11, 74–128
  creating, 76–78
  Dynamic Local User, 80
  modifying contents of, 77
  naming, 76
  NDS and, 75
  placement, importance of, 76
  planning, importance of, 75
  rules for, 75
  testing, importance of, 87
  WAN and, 75
  vs. Windows policies, 74
  workstation objects and, 136
Policy Scheduler, 79
Policy Viewer, 78
Polled Broadcast Message Buffers setting, 47
portable computers, Location Profiles tab and, 38
Pre-Install page, 217
Print Header setting, 47
print jobs, setting for, 47
Print Provider
  Windows 95/98 client, 67
  Windows NT/2000 client, 60
print sharing policies, 107
Print Tail setting, 47
printer drivers, Service Packs for, 118
printer mappings, 187
printer ports, setting for, 46
printers
  policies for, 92
    adding/configuring, 117
  Windows NT
    NT user printer policy for, 85
    policies for, 112
printers (printer objects), 14
privacy, Remote Management and, 238, 247
processors, 179
  family/speed, searching for, 150
Programs folder, 98
Protocol Preferences tab, 50–52
\public\zenworks\database\zeninv.db, 139
Pure IP, 51

R

RAM, 179
RAS Configuration policy, 118
RAS (Remote Access Service), 118
Read-Only Compatibility setting, 47
Read-Only Replicas, 18
Read-Write Replicas, 18
rebooting workstations, 103, 184
Receive Broadcast Messages setting, 47
recognition configuration for software inventory, 145
recommendations
  about partitioning, 17
  for replicas, 18
  for NDS tree design, 16
redirectors, Windows NT/2000 client, 53
.reg files, 95
Regedit/Regedt32, 95
registering workstation objects, 131–134
registry entries, options for, 171
registry keys, 88
  color scheme policy, 93
  custom folders policy, 98
  desktop policies, 93
  dialup networking policy, 107
  disable SAP advertising policy, 108
  display policies, 90
  drive restrictions policies, 102

registry keys (*continued*)
  file sharing policies, 108
  Internet Explorer security/security levels policies, 101
  MS-DOS options policies, 97
  network policies, 91, 94
  network sharing policies (Windows NT), 111
  NTFS filesystem, policies for, 114
  password policies, 92, 107
  print sharing policies, 108
  printer policies, 92
  printers (Windows NT), policies for, 112
  remote access (Windows NT), policies for, 112
  run only Windows applications policy, 96
  run policy, 110
  shell restrictions policies, 95
  SNMP
    configuration policies for, 109
    policies for, 108
  Start menu subfolders, policy for, 98
  system policies, 93
    operating system policy, 96
  system policies update policies, 104
  testing for, 179
  "Track distribution per user," applying, 221
  update policies, 104
  user level access control policies, 105
  user profiles policy, 110
  Windows 95/98 logon policies, 106
  Windows load policies, 103
  Windows NT
    logon policies, 100, 114
    user profiles, policies for, 115
  Windows NT Shell restrictions policies, 99
  Windows setup policies, 111
  Windows tour program policies, 111
  ZAK system policies, 101
registry settings, 203–205
Remote Access Service (RAS), 118
remote access (Windows NT), policies for, 112
Remote Chat, 244
Remote Control utility, 240, 242
Remote Diagnostics, 245–247
Remote Execute, 244
Remote File Transfer, 243
Remote Management, 8, 12, 238–248
  how it works, 239–241
  policies for, 119–121
  software for, installing, 30
  workstation objects and, 131, 138
Remote Management Agent
  testing functionality of, 241
  Windows 3.x, 27
  Windows 95/98, 25
  Windows NT/2000, 24
Remote Ping, 241
Remote View, 242
Remove Drive from Environment setting, 48
repartitioning, workstation objects and, 130
replicas, 18
replication, 17
  affect on network, 17
  partitions, 14, 17–19
reporting/reports, 148–157
  application distribution, 152
  application launch, 152
  application objects and, 216
  asset management, 152
  inventory, 151
  tool for, 148
requirements for operating systems, 2–4
resilience, 18
Resolve Name Using Primary Connection setting, 48
resources for further information
  Distributed Management Task Force, 153
  ZENworks, 253–255
restrict login policy, 121
restrictions, 86
  drives, policies for, 102
  shell, policies for, 95
  Windows NT Shell, policies for, 99
rights
  filesystem, 213
  workstation objects and, 136, 139
"ring fencing", 122
Roaming Profile (Desktop Preferences policy), 83
rollout, 6
root, 14

rules for policy packages, 75
Run Application Install button (snAppShot tool), 169
run only allowed Windows applications policy, 96
run options for applications, 181
run policy, 109
run-once applications, 176

S

SAP (Service Advertising Protocol), 44
scan time, report of, 149
scanner program, 142
  software for, 126
Schedule page, 211
Scheduler, 79
Scheduler Icons setting, 49
schema extensions, 30
screen resolution, display policies for, 89
screensavers, display policies for, 90
Search Dirs First setting, 48
search drives, setting for, 48
Search Mode setting, 48
search policy, 121
secure system, running applications as, 181
security
  Remote Management and, 238
  trusted tree and, 71
Security Identifier (SID), 81
Send Message setting, 49
Server Message Block (see SMB)
server names, cache setting for, 45
server software, installing, 28–31
server timeout, setting for, 46
servers
  authenticating to, 28
  load balancing, 191
  replicating partitions from one to another, 14
  Software Metering, preparing for, 230
servers (server objects), 14
Service Advertising Protocol (SAP), 44
Service Location Protocol (SLP), 52
Service Pack for printer drivers, 118
Set Station Time setting, 49
settings tab, 89
shell restrictions policies, 94
  (see also entries at Windows NT Shell; Windows 95 Shell)
Short Machine Type setting, 49
shortcuts, 211
Show Edit Login Script Item setting, 49
Show Novell System Tray setting, 49
Shrink Path To Dot setting, 49
SID (Security Identifier), 81
Signature Level setting, 49
Simple Network Management Protocol (see SNMP)
SLP (Service Location Protocol), 52
SMACHINE environment variable, setting for, 49
SMB (Server Message Block), 58, 64
SMS (Storage Management Service), 27
snAppShot tool, 160, 166–172
snapshotting a PC
  after snapshot, 172
  before snapshot, 169
  quick method for, 167
  uses for, 172
SNMP (Simple Network Management Protocol), 25
  policies for, 108, 109
  Windows 3.x, 27
  Windows 95/98, agent for, 25
software
  changes, tracking on workstations, 8
  desktop operating system tracking, 5
  image replication, 6
  searching for on workstations, 151
  server, installing, 28–31
  special run on server, choosing network operating system and, 2
  workstation, installing, 21–27
software inventory, 12, 145–147
  (see also workstation inventory)
software licenses, 8, 145, 229
Software List Editor, 147
Software Metering, 8, 12, 229–237
  installing, 31, 231
  option for, shell restrictions policies and, 94
Software Metering page, 218
software patches, testing, 33
software recognition program, 126
staff (see users)
Start menu
  placing restrictions on, 94
  policies for, 97

Starter Pack, 11
Storage Management Service (SMS), 27
Storer process, 139
sub-containers, creating, 15
Subordinate Replicas, 18
success/failure report, application distributions and, 152
Supervisor rights, 59
Sybase database, 29
Sybase ODBC driver, 148
Sybase process, 139
Sync Distribution GUIDs option, 186
sys volume
- installing client software to, 30
- \public\zenworks\database\zeninv.db, 139

system changes, finding, 166–172
system policies, 93, 108–111
- operating system policy, 95

system policies update policies, 104
System Requirements page, 177–179

T

Taskstation, 85, 97
TCO (Total Cost of Ownership), 1
TCP protocol, 52
TCP/IP protocol, 29, 50
- Remote Management and, 239

TCP/IP socket connection, Remote Management and, 240
TDI (Transport Driver Interface), 54
template file, 166, 172
Terminate and Stay Resident (TSR) program, 55
Termination page, 214
testing
- files, 178
- importance of, 157
- NAL, importance of, 227
- NDS tree, 34
- policy packages, importance of, 87
- registry keys, 179
- Remote Management Agent functionality, 241
- software patches, 33
- soliciting users' help for, 128
- workstation objects and, 131

Text File page, 210
Tiered Electronic Distribution, 249
timeout setting
- broadcast messages, 45
- network, 46
- server, 46

Total Cost of Ownership (TCO), 1
"Track distribution per user", 217
- applying to registry keys, 221

Transport Driver Interface (TDI), 54
transport protocols, 50–52
tree, NDS (see NDS tree)
trouble tickets, 13, 73
- sent via email, configuration for, 82

True Commit setting, 50
trusted tree, 70
TSA (see Novell Target Service Agent)
TSR (Terminate and Stay Resident) program, 55

U

UDP (User Datagram Protocol), 52
unattended installations, 27
unattend.txt, 27
UNC pathnames, 176, 228
UNC (Universal Naming Convention), 54
Unix, integrating into NDS, 251
unsecure system, running applications as, 182
update policies, 104
URLs
- Distributed Management Task Force, 153
- ZENworks, 253

Use Extended File Handles setting, 50
Use Video BIOS setting, 50
User Datagram Protocol (UDP), 52
user extensible policies (see extensible policies)
user history, 138
user level access control policies, 104
User Login, Policy Scheduler and, 79
user policies, 85–88
user policy package, 74, 75
user profiles policy, 110
User Remote Management policies, 119
user settings, NAL and, 222
user system policy packages, 88–103
user.dat, 84

users
  acquired expertise, choosing network operating system and, 2
  Advanced button, disallowing access to, 39, 70
  Advanced Login tab and, 39
  application distribution success/failure report, 152
  communicating with, 9
  desktop operating system, training program for, 6
  number of, choosing network operating system and, 3
  restricting Windows applications, 96
  Roaming Profile and, 83
  soliciting help for testing, 128
  workstation history, 138
  workstation objects, right to modify, 138
users (user objects), 14

V

verifying workstation objects, 133
version of files, test for, 178
version stamp, 186
video adapters, searching for, 151
virtual device drivers (VXD), 62
VLM (Virtual Load Modules), 55
Volatile User option, 81
volumes (volume objects), 14
VXD (virtual device drivers), 62

W

wait time, setting for, 45
wallpaper settings, desktop policy and, 93
WAN (Wide Area Network), 15
  policy packages and, 75
  tree design and, 16
Windows 3.x
  applications, choosing desktop operating system and, 4
  computer system policies, 116
  NetWare client for, 7, 67
  policy packages for, 7
  user policy objects, 15
  Windows 3.x client, 67
  workstation policy objects, 15
  workstation software, installing, 26
Windows 3.x client, 7, 67
Windows 95 Shell, 97–99
Windows 95/98
  computer system policies, 103–115
  desktop operating system, choosing as, 4
  NetWare client for (see Windows 95/98 client)
  policy packages for, 7
  scanner software, 142
  security and, 89
  user policy objects, 15
  user system policy packages, 88–103
  workstation policy objects, 15
  workstation software, installing, 24–25
Windows 95/98 client, 60–67
  application support, 65
  architecture, 61
  Client Configuration policy for, 116
  login process, 65
  NetWare filesystem integration, 62–64
  Network Provider, 66
  Open Datalink Interface, 64
  Print Provider, 67
Windows load policies, 103
Windows macros, 197
Windows Networking API (WNet), 58
Windows NT
  computer system policies, 103–115
  logon policies, 99, 114
  NDS for, 252
  user profiles, policies for, 115
  user system policy packages, 88–103
  (see also Windows NT/2000)
Windows NT I/O Manager, 53
Windows NT Shell, 97–99
  restrictions, policies for, 98
  Setup menu, configuration policies for, 113
Windows NT/2000
  16-bit applications, configuring WOW for, 181
  desktop operating system, choosing as, 4
  NetWare client for (see Windows NT/2000 client)
  policy packages for, 7
  scanner software, 142
  user policy objects, 15
  workstation policy objects, 15

Windows NT/2000 (*continued*)
  workstation software, installing, 22–24
  (see also Windows NT)
Windows NT/2000 client, 53–60
  application support, 55
  architecture, 53–54
  Client Configuration policy for, 116
  login process, 57
  NetWare filesystem integration, 54
  Network Provider, 57–59
  Open Datalink Interface, 55
  Print Provider, 60
Windows on Windows (see WOW), 99
Windows policies vs. ZENworks policy packages, 74
Windows Policy Editor (see poledit program)
Windows setup, policies for, 110
Windows tour program, policies for, 111
Windows.adm files, 123
winnt.adm files, 123
WINSCAN.EXE, 142
Winsetup program, 21, 29
wizards
  Manage Remote Operators, 240
  policy package, 76
WNet (Windows Networking API), 58
working directory, changing, 180
workstation group objects, where to put them, 21
workstation groups, 15
workstation import policy, 124, 131–134
workstation inventory, 141–144
workstation inventory policy, 125–127
Workstation Manager, 11, 57, 68–72
  configuring, 70
  enabling/disabling, 70
  login process, 69–72
  Scheduler, 79
  Windows 3.x, 27
  Windows 95/98, 25
  Windows NT/2000, 23
  workstation software, installing, 21
Workstation Manager dialog box, 70
workstation objects, 11, 15, 129–147
  configuring, 135–139
  creating, 132, 134
  grouping, 133
  inventory, enabling, 139
  naming, 132
  NDS and, 129–131
  placement, importance of, 129
  registering, 131–134
  Remote Management and, 131
  testing, importance of, 131
  verifying, 133
  where to put them, 20, 124, 130, 131
workstation operating system (see also desktop operating system)
workstation policy package, 74, 75
  enabling workstation inventory from, 141
workstation registration program, time last run, 139
Workstation Remote Management policy, 120
workstation scan time report, 149
workstation settings, NAL and, 226
workstation software, installing, 21–27
workstations
  application distribution success/failure report, 152
  desirable/undesirable characteristics, 5
  file listing files installed on/changes to, 172
  general report, 151
  granting NetWare filesystem rights, 143
  grouping, 136
  inventory lists, 149–151
  logon policies, 113–115
  naming, 125
  rebooting, 103, 184
  registering, 31
  requirements, choosing network operating system and, 3
  testing Remote Management Agent functionality, 241
WOW (Windows On Windows), 99
  configuring for 16-bit applications, 181
wowexec errors, 100
WSREG.EXE program, 31, 133

X

X.400 email service, 13
X.500 standard, 13

Z

ZAK (Zero Administration Kit), 85
  policies for, 100
zeninv.db, 139
ZENworks, 1, 10–13
  components, 7–8, 11–13
  Full Pack, 12
  future trends, 249
  installing, 21–31
  objects, where to put them, 19–21
  policy packages (see policy packages)
  reporting tool, 148
  resources for further information, 253–255
  Starter Pack, 11
ZENworks Application Launcher NT Service, 23
ZENworks for Networks, 250
ZENworks for Servers, 249
ZENworks Remote Management (see Remote Management)
Zero Administration Kit (see ZAK)
Zero Effort Networking (see ZENworks)

About the Author

Gerald Foster is a computer officer in the University of Cambridge Computing Service. He has an M.Sc. in computer science, specializing in computer networking. He has considerable experience with providing strategic solutions for IT departments and rolling out Windows NT Server and Workstation in the UK. He has spent the last year moving the University of Cambridge Public Workstation Service from Windows 3.1 to Windows NT Workstation using ZENworks to integrate into the large Novell NetWare service.

Colophon

Our look is the result of reader comments, our own experimentation, and feedback from distribution channels. Distinctive covers complement our distinctive approach to technical topics, breathing personality and life into potentially dry subjects.

The animal on the cover of *Desktop Management with Novell ZENworks* is a gelada. The gelada baboon is found primarily in highlands of Ethiopia and Eritrea. A majority of the gelada population lives in the Semeien Mountains National Park in Ethiopia.

Gelada baboons live in groups of one male with several females and their offspring. These groups are referred to as one male units, or OMUs. Grooming is exhibited by all members of an OMU between the females and their male leader; it is very important to the social stability of the group. When the male is unable to to provide grooming attention to all of the females (due to over-capacity), unity within the group is lost. The unattended females form new groups with roaming males.

The females within the OMUs are generally the true leaders of the group. If an outside male attempts to take over the group by challenging the current male, the females may choose to support or oppose their own leader. Regardless of who wins the physical fight, the females will chase the unwanted male from the group with their own show of physical force.

Maureen Dempsey was the production editor and copyeditor for *Desktop Management with Novell ZENworks*. Jane Ellin was the proofreader. Sarah Jane Shangraw and Mary Anne Weeks Mayo provided quality control. Brenda Miller wrote the index.

Hanna Dyer designed the cover of this book, based on a series design by Edie Freedman. The cover image is a 19th-century engraving from *The Illustrated*

Natural History: Mammalia, by Rev. J.G. Wood. Emma Colby produced the cover layout with QuarkXPress 3.32 using Adobe's ITC Garamond font.

Alicia Cech designed the interior layout based on a series design by Nancy Priest. Mike Sierra implemented the design in FrameMaker 5.5.6. The text and heading fonts are ITC Garamond Light and Garamond Book. The illustrations that appear in the book were produced by Robert Romano and Rhon Porter using Macromedia FreeHand 8 and Adobe Photoshop 5. This colophon was written by Maureen Dempsey.

Whenever possible, our books use RepKover™, a durable and flexible lay-flat binding. If the page count exceeds RepKover's limit, perfect binding is used.

How to stay in touch with O'Reilly

1. Visit Our Award-Winning Web Site

http://www.oreilly.com/

★"Top 100 Sites on the Web" —*PC Magazine*
★"Top 5% Web sites" —*Point Communications*
★"3-Star site" —*The McKinley Group*

Our web site contains a library of comprehensive product information (including book excerpts and tables of contents), downloadable software, background articles, interviews with technology leaders, links to relevant sites, book cover art, and more. File us in your Bookmarks or Hotlist!

2. Join Our Email Mailing Lists

New Product Releases

To receive automatic email with brief descriptions of all new O'Reilly products as they are released, send email to:
listproc@online.oreilly.com
Put the following information in the first line of your message (*not* in the Subject field):
subscribe oreilly-news

O'Reilly Events

If you'd also like us to send information about trade show events, special promotions, and other O'Reilly events, send email to:
listproc@online.oreilly.com
Put the following information in the first line of your message (*not* in the Subject field):
subscribe oreilly-events

3. Get Examples from Our Books via FTP

There are two ways to access an archive of example files from our books:

Regular FTP

- ftp to:
  ftp.oreilly.com
  (login: anonymous
  password: your email address)
- Point your web browser to:
  ftp://ftp.oreilly.com/

FTPMAIL

- Send an email message to:
  ftpmail@online.oreilly.com
  (Write "help" in the message body)

4. Contact Us via Email

order@oreilly.com
To place a book or software order online. Good for North American and international customers.

subscriptions@oreilly.com
To place an order for any of our newsletters or periodicals.

books@oreilly.com
General questions about any of our books.

software@oreilly.com
For general questions and product information about our software. Check out O'Reilly Software Online at **http://software.oreilly.com/** for software and technical support information. Registered O'Reilly software users send your questions to: **website-support@oreilly.com**

cs@oreilly.com
For answers to problems regarding your order or our products.

booktech@oreilly.com
For book content technical questions or corrections.

proposals@oreilly.com
To submit new book or software proposals to our editors and product managers.

international@oreilly.com
For information about our international distributors or translation queries. For a list of our distributors outside of North America check out:
http://www.oreilly.com/www/order/country.html

5. Work with Us

Check out our website for current employment opportunites:
www.jobs@oreilly.com
Click on "Work with Us"

O'Reilly & Associates, Inc.
101 Morris Street, Sebastopol, CA 95472 USA
TEL 707-829-0515 or 800-998-9938
(6am to 5pm PST)
FAX 707-829-0104

International Distributors

UK, Europe, Middle East and Africa (except France, Germany, Austria, Switzerland, Luxembourg, Liechtenstein, and Eastern Europe)

INQUIRIES
O'Reilly UK Limited
4 Castle Street
Farnham
Surrey, GU9 7HS
United Kingdom
Telephone: 44-1252-711776
Fax: 44-1252-734211
Email: information@oreilly.co.uk

ORDERS
Wiley Distribution Services Ltd.
1 Oldlands Way
Bognor Regis
West Sussex PO22 9SA
United Kingdom
Telephone: 44-1243-779777
Fax: 44-1243-820250
Email: cs-books@wiley.co.uk

France

INQUIRIES
Éditions O'Reilly
18 rue Séguier
75006 Paris, France
Tel: 33-1-40-51-52-30
Fax: 33-1-40-51-52-31
Email: france@editions-oreilly.fr

ORDERS
GEODIF
61, Bd Saint-Germain
75240 Paris Cedex 05, France
Tel: 33-1-44-41-46-16 (French books)
Tel: 33-1-44-41-11-87 (English books)
Fax: 33-1-44-41-11-44
Email: distribution@eyrolles.com

Germany, Switzerland, Austria, Eastern Europe, Luxembourg, and Liechtenstein

INQUIRIES & ORDERS
O'Reilly Verlag
Balthasarstr. 81
D-50670 Köln
Germany
Telephone: 49-221-973160-91
Fax: 49-221-973160-8
Email: anfragen@oreilly.de (inquiries)
Email: order@oreilly.de (orders)

Canada (French language books)

Les Éditions Flammarion ltée
375, Avenue Laurier Ouest
Montréal (Québec) H2V 2K3
Tel: 00-1-514-277-8807
Fax: 00-1-514-278-2085
Email: info@flammarion.qc.ca

Hong Kong

City Discount Subscription Service, Ltd.
Unit D, 3rd Floor, Yan's Tower
27 Wong Chuk Hang Road
Aberdeen, Hong Kong
Tel: 852-2580-3539
Fax: 852-2580-6463
Email: citydis@ppn.com.hk

Korea

Hanbit Media, Inc.
Chungmu Bldg. 201
Yonnam-dong 568-33
Mapo-gu
Seoul, Korea
Tel: 822-325-0397
Fax: 822-325-9697
Email: hant93@chollian.dacom.co.kr

Philippines

Global Publishing
G/F Benavides Garden
1186 Benavides Street
Manila, Philippines
Tel: 632-254-8949/637-252-2582
Fax: 632-734-5060/632-252-2733
Email: globalp@pacific.net.ph

Taiwan

O'Reilly Taiwan
No. 3, Lane 131
Hang-Chow South Road
Section 1, Taipei, Taiwan
Tel: 886-2-23968990
Fax: 886-2-23968916
Email: taiwan@oreilly.com

China

O'Reilly Beijing
Room 2410
160, FuXingMenNeiDaJie
XiCheng District
Beijing, China PR 100031
Tel: 86-10-66412305
Fax: 86-10-86631007
Email: beijing@oreilly.com

India

Computer Bookshop (India) Pvt. Ltd.
190 Dr. D.N. Road, Fort
Bombay 400 001 India
Tel: 91-22-207-0989
Fax: 91-22-262-3551
Email: cbsbom@giasbm01.vsnl.net.in

Japan

O'Reilly Japan, Inc.
Yotsuya Y's Building
7 Banch 6, Honshio-cho
Shinjuku-ku
Tokyo 160-0003 Japan
Tel: 81-3-3356-5227
Fax: 81-3-3356-5261
Email: japan@oreilly.com

All Other Asian Countries

O'Reilly & Associates, Inc.
101 Morris Street
Sebastopol, CA 95472 USA
Tel: 707-829-0515
Fax: 707-829-0104
Email: order@oreilly.com

Australia

Woodslane Pty., Ltd.
7/5 Vuko Place
Warriewood NSW 2102
Australia
Tel: 61-2-9970-5111
Fax: 61-2-9970-5002
Email: info@woodslane.com.au

New Zealand

Woodslane New Zealand, Ltd.
21 Cooks Street (P.O. Box 575)
Waganui, New Zealand
Tel: 64-6-347-6543
Fax: 64-6-345-4840
Email: info@woodslane.com.au

Latin America

McGraw-Hill Interamericana
Editores, S.A. de C.V.
Cedro No. 512
Col. Atlampa
06450, Mexico, D.F.
Tel: 52-5-547-6777
Fax: 52-5-547-3336
Email: mcgraw-hill@infosel.net.mx